The Aging Experience

Studies in Society

A series edited by Ronald Wild which sets out to cover the major topics in Australasian sociology. The books will not be 'readers', but original works — some will cover new ground and present original research, some will provide an overview and synthesis of source materials and existing research. All will be important reading for students of sociology.

Titles include:

Cities Unlimited Kilmartin and Thorns
The Migrant Presence Martin
Social Stratification in Australia Wild
Race, Class and Rebellion in the South Pacific Mamak and Ali
Children and Families in Australia Burns and Goodnow
Johnsonville Pearson
Australian Community Studies and Beyond Wild
Open Cut Williams
The Ethnic Dimension Martin/Encel

Studies in Society: 10
Series editor: Ronald Wild

The Aging Experience

CHERRY RUSSELL

Lecturer in Sociology, Cumberland College of Health Sciences

Sydney
George Allen & Unwin
London Boston

First published in 1981 by
George Allen & Unwin Australia Pty. Ltd.,
8 Napier Street
North Sydney, N.S.W. 2060

National Library of Australia
Cataloguing-in-Publication entry:

Russell, Cherry
    The aging experience

    Includes index.
    ISBN 0 86861 267 7.
    ISBN 0 86861 275 8(pbk.).
    1. Aged-Australia- Social
    Conditions. 2. Aging. I. Title.
305. 2'6'0994

Library of Congress Catalog Card Number: 81-68331
Set in 10 on 11pt Times by
Syarikat Seng Teik Sdn Bhd, Kuala Lumpur

Printed in Singapore by
Singapore National Printers (Pte) Ltd.

Contents

1 Introduction

Most old people don't describe themselves that way. Given a question-naire which asks them if they think of themselves as young, middle aged, or old, the majority of people over 60 opt for 'middle aged'. Quite a few of the rest, including those in their 80s and beyond, select 'young'.

What does this tell us about the subjective experience of aging? Does it mean that old people fail to see their wrinkles and grey hair? That seems unlikely. Does it mean, as a few researchers have sug-gested, that old people avoid the *label* 'old' as a means of distancing themselves from a social category encrusted with negative stereotypes of uselessness, decrepitude, and dependence? This is closer to the mark. I believe, however, that there is more to it; that the term 'old' simply does not mean the same thing to older people as it does to the rest of us.

In recent years a new industry has sprung up to study the 'problem of old age' in modern society. It is called gerontology, and its adherents have produced a mass of data in a relatively brief period. Most of the questions gerontologists ask are not about the subjective experience of aging. They are, rather, questions about the objective difficulties which older people face: failing health and mobility, inade-quate resources, and reduced social contact.

Mapping the distribution of these objective characteristics is cer-tainly an important task if society is ever to bring its aged members in from the cold. But it is not the only valuable enterprise toward which social theorists need to direct their attention. As an anthropologist, my principal interest is in the way people perceive their world, in the meanings which they impute to their experience of it. Without such understanding, anthropologists (and others) maintain, we have only a hollow and imperfect understanding of social processes and problems.

The extent to which old age in modern society carries a cultural load of negative stereotypes or stigma has been well documented. Rather less attention has been paid to the effects of this stigmatization on those who have entered the status of 'old person', on the ways in which they attempt to cope with their negative evaluation.

This book is about coping strategies. It is not a study in the sociology of old age, for there is no such thing. It is a sociological study of some people who live in an Australian urban municipality who happen to be old; it focuses not on the distribution of attributes or patterns of behaviour among a population, but on relationships, interactions, and meanings. It does not focus on old age as a social problem, but on old age as a socio-cultural phenomenon. My principal descriptive concern is with the lived experience of aging, with the effects of 'being old' on the self-conceptions and interpersonal relations of individuals who live in a society which stigmatizes that status.

I found the experience of 'getting inside the heads' of these people a profoundly depressing one. This reaction is not typical among gerontologists who analyse quantitative data. In objective terms, they point out, the aged in modern society are more often 'integrated' than not. Deprived they may be of productive roles and social power, but they have, it is claimed, strongly supportive primary networks of family and friends. Increasingly, too, the aged are being provided with special facilities — retirement housing, clubs, and so forth — and there is growing awareness among professionals of all kinds that they need to know and do more about elderly people.

My pessimism does not spring from the objective situation of the aged. Certainly most old people need more money. Some need adequate housing and better care facilities. But these are problems with which our society is already equipped to deal, given a will to do so. The sadness I feel when I reflect on the elderly people who told me about their lives and whom I observed in their day-to-day activities results from what I came to understand of their personal and interpersonal experiences as people with 'spoiled identities', of their constant struggle to cope with society's denial of them as normal, competent, adult human beings. Public institutions, personal networks, or individual wealth ensure their survival, the perpetuation of their bodies. But the experience of being old is often a lonely and relentless struggle for meaning.

During the early period of fieldwork I hesitated to ask the elderly people I met the question which personally most intrigued me: What is it really *like* to be old? It seemed somehow a rude question, almost as if one were asking someone how it felt to be disfigured or mentally retarded. At that stage, the sociological significance of old age as stigma had not occurred to me.

One day I was chatting with a 90 year-old widow. She had had two major operations in the past 18 months and was totally blind. Suddenly she chuckled and said, 'You know, my dear, you look at me and see an old lady. But in my head I'm the person I was at your age'. I was then 28.

In the introduction to a classic sociological treatise, Dennis Wrong (1961) relates the apocryphal story of Gertrude Stein's last moments on earth. Bedridden with a fatal illness, she is reported to have suddenly muttered, 'What, then, is the answer?' Pausing, she raised her head, murmured, 'But what is the question?' and died. According to Wrong, all sociological questions are ultimately existential as well as intellectual questions. Yet old people themselves rarely speak to us of their experience from the pages of contemporary research literature. One gets the impression that old age simply 'happens' to the individual, that his or her response to the ravages of biology and time is that of a passive victim. I now challenge this. Old people, I believe, are active participants in the aging process. As objective indicators of 'oldness' and changes in their social environment make their external impress, elderly people constantly define and redefine themselves and their situations.

This does not mean that I believe all or most old people are 'well adjusted' in terms of some normatively determined yardstick by means of which non-aged persons measure 'the good life' and, by implication, 'the good old person'. I am not concerned with whether or not old people are cheerful, busy, and interested in the world around them. There are in fact many excellent and rational reasons why they should *not* be. The merry widow and the crabby recluse share a fundamental characteristic: they are fighting. It is not an irrational struggle against the 'reality' of growing old. It is the same struggle that we all engage in throughout out lives, the struggle to realise a conception of ourselves and our meaningful place in the world. Old people simply have to fight harder than most of us.

Throughout this book I present an implicit and occasionally explicit argument against a particularly influential sociological paradigm, that of role theory. I find it an insidious yet powerful form of sociological determinism, as well as an obfuscatory approach to the understanding of social reality. It is worse than meaningless to analyse old people in terms of the roles they occupy or have lost *unless we know what those roles mean to the people themselves*. When a blind and crippled widow in a nursing home describes herself as 'young' the questions we need to ask do not concern her objective situation alone. We also need to know what her subjective definitions are. Why she feels this way is the subject of this book.

In this study I have not aimed to add to the body of statistical information about Australia's aged population. Australia is not particularly well endowed with such information in comparison with other highly industrialised nations. But what we do know suggests, in general, the demographic and behavioural patterns observed in those societies apply here.

Certainly the task of collecting more detailed and comprehensive statistical data on the aged Australian population is an important and necessary one for social planners and sociologists alike. But statistics are only as valuable as the framework of meaning within which they are interpreted. As yet, satisfactory explanations of the various patterns and trends have not been forthcoming, even from overseas researchers. Beth Hess (1976b: 450), writing of her experience in assessing the state of knowledge regarding aging and old people for the first volume of *Aging and Society* (Riley and Foner, 1968), states: 'Having thus worked our way through thousands of pages of research, and having produced a volume of almost 600 pages of carefully weighed and interpreted "findings", we were nonetheless distressed at how very little one could say for certain about any aspect of aging or the lives of old people today.'

One reason for this uncertainty, I suggest, lies in the failure of researchers and research procedures to assign due weight to the perceptions and experience of elderly people themselves. The voices of the aged are seldom heard in gerontological accounts. Thomas Cole, in an essay on old age in twentieth-century America (cited in Fischer, 1978: 268–69), writes:

> it was certainly a source of frustration to me, as I realised that my research was not about old people themselves. Rather it concerned other people's ideas about old age and the social forces and interests which affected the emerging public policy with regard to the aged. Perhaps the lesson I learned was the extent to which older people have generally been treated as passive objects, recipients of their fate, rather than as active subjects.

Accordingly, our understanding of the *meaning* of everyday experience and behaviour in later life is seriously limited.

This premise underlies the present study. It is an examination of two main kinds of data: 45 elderly people's accounts of their lives, the significant experiences in them, their relationships with family, friends, and their attitudes and beliefs; and the results of participant observation of specific groups of old people. These basic data are supplemented by interviews with family members and welfare personnel and by some descriptive statistics.

There is no claim that the experiences of this small sample are representative of the aged Australian population. In important ways they are not, in part deliberately so. The area in which they live is affluent and well serviced. Many (though by no means all) live in enviable material circumstances. I attempted to minimize the potentially confounding effects of poverty on the experience of aging by selecting as the research site an exclusive residential area. I did not, however, eliminate poverty from the sample.

Both the collection of detailed life history materials and the technique of participant observation are time consuming, and the scope of the study has inevitably been limited. I did not attempt to compensate by restricting the heterogeneity of the sample. It includes men and women, the 'young aged' (under 70 years) and the 'old aged'; married, widowed, and single persons; wealthy and poor; healthy and infirm.

The aim throughout was not to specify rates, patterns, or correlations that can be generalised, but simply to locate and describe the patterns that were there (c.f. Richards, 1978). These patterns are, of course, suggestive of wider level processes and of formal structural explanations.

The organisation of this book reflects the fact that social gerontology is not and cannot be a unitary discipline. Behavioural outcomes in old age are the product of an interplay between socio-economic, cultural, psychological and biological factors.

For heuristic purposes, I have grounded my analysis in the major social networks to which my elderly subjects belong: formal organisations, and informal clusterings of friends and family. This framework has the advantage of subsuming the dominant interactional foci of gerontological research. At the same time, more specialised bodies of theory have grown up around each of these substantive domains. As a result, each empirical chapter can be read as a more or less independent sub-unit of the broader framework.

The overall aim of this book is not to argue the superiority of a particular 'theory of old age' — for none exists — but to illustrate the interpretive value of a certain, general sociological perspective for the study of old people. This perspective — the symbolic interactionist tradition of George Herbert Mead, Herbert Blumer, and others — stands in contrast to the sociology of social systems proposed by Talcott Parsons and his followers. Parsons' perspective, through the language of role theory, and through survey techniques dominates empirical research on old people. I argue that this perspective is not sufficiently sensitive to the experience of being an old person in a youth oriented society.

The cultural constant in my exposition is the symbolic loading of old age in this society with undesirable traits or stigma. The fact that old age is glossed with infirmity and dependence has important effects on the ways in which old people interact with the non-aged, with their families, and with each other.

A psychological constant is subsumed under the notion of exchange. I conceptualise motivation for interaction in terms of cost benefit considerations, and processes of interaction and withdrawal as part of the mechanism whereby individuals seek to achieve and maintain a favourable balance of resources and control. In old age, I argue, autonomy assumes paramount importance as a psychological need and a motivating factor in behaviour.

The Problematic Status of the Aged

Most gerontologists identify the central problem in old age as a problem of 'integration'. Increasingly, they argue, the aged are becoming segregated from the major structures and processes of modern society. Thus, a major goal of public policy towards the aged should be to 're-integrate' them.

One of the most fundamental constraints on the perspective from which we view the contemporary situation of older people is the set of beliefs we hold about their situation in the past. As Peter Laslett has pointed out, a body of popular, quasi-theoretical dogma informs our ideas about societal development and aging. Its central feature is a tendency to refer 'the deficiencies of the present . . . to the destruction of an idealised society at some point in the past' (Laslett, 1976:91). Our beliefs about the history of aging provide an *a priori* framework for identification of, and solutions to, old age as a social problem, and suggest which sociological variables will receive most research attention. Old age in relation to social change has been — and still is — incompletely understood. And the interaction between cultural tradition and the process of industrialisation is too complex and subtle for easy generalisation. The past is often characterised as a period of old age integration, in contrast to the contemporary segregation of elderly people. Although the thrust of this debate falls outside the scope of my central argument, some of its themes are briefly mentioned in Chapter 2. Before a more encompassing theory can be developed (and I am not here concerned with such a task), we need to have in much sharper focus the relationship between *contemporary* cultural values, structural arrangements and individual patterns of action and interacton in old age. Then we must search for those cultural factors in *this* 'period of history that sustain traits present in previous epochs . . .' (Henry, 1963:16).

Relationships between generations are inherently asymmetrical. They are associated with differential access to resources — material and non-material — and hence with differential potential for control over one's own life circumstances, as well as those of others. In some societies, or segments of society, the balance is culturally defined in favour of the older generation. They may even, through their control over land, property, or women, come to represent a 'privileged class' (Clark, 1972:264) vis-a-vis younger members. The power of the aged is greatest when they themselves are the articulators between major social institutions (economic, political, religious) and sub-systems, notably the family.

If a definition of integration were to rest on such instrumental factors alone, then one could characterise this position as the cultural ideal for elderly people. But, I argue, such a definition is inadequate. After all, in these terms, Howard Hughes would have been one of the most 'integrated' men of his time. Nor would Lear have had any understandable motive for relinquishing his power to the vagaries of filial piety. Perhaps no society has successfully codified the satisfaction of *emotional* needs in its formal structural arrangements (c.f. Henry, 1963: 20). The articulation of social and familial power may maximise the authority of an aged parent and assure the deferential behaviour of children, but it cannot guarantee their affection.

In any case, this 'ideal' situation has little applicability to the contemporary situation of elderly Australians. As a group, they are neither socially dominant, nor do they hold the reins of domestic power into the adulthood of their children. This does not mean that the concept of power is not an analytic tool of more general applicability in conceptualising the relationship between age and social structure. On the contrary, I suggest, it is a central consideration to which I turn in Chapter 2.

Organisation of Material

The development of modern social gerontology is inextricably linked with the awareness of old age as a social problem. This link is intrinsic to the nature of the gerontological task. As Fischer (1978: 194-195) remarks:

> Social gerontology has not succeeded in creating a body of theory... Probably, gerontology will never be a theoretical discipline in its own right, but rather a consumer of theory from other sciences. Its major function seems to be that of an applied social science... Its major role, perhaps, has been to destroy the myths which so thickly encrust the subject of aging, to oppose the age prejudice which has grown so strong... and to sharpen our sense of old age as a social problem.

Arguably, the role of the sociologist studying the substantive field of old age is constituted less in the application of solutions than in the understanding of the problem (c.f. Berger, 1963). She must ensure that the formal sociological tools and concepts brought to bear in this enquiry are appropriate to the task, that the sociological questions asked are indeed relevant to the understanding of everyday life as it affects aged persons today.

A necessary first step in this process is to locate the lived experience of elderly Australians within its structural context. This is attempted in Chapter 2. Here I construct a broad picture of the social conditions, which are directly reflected in the everyday experience of older people. Specifically, I show how the objective life chances of those who belong to the category of 'old people' are circumscribed by the prevailing system of economic, political and social relations. Of particular importance is the set of socially constructed meanings which attach to the category of 'old' — meanings which define its members as people of reduced capacity and social value and which confront the elderly as inescapable objective conditions of their existence.

I refer to this set of meanings as age stigma. How stigma is experienced by individual aged persons and how the system of relations it encompasses becomes objectified in their patterns of action and interaction is the empirical focus of this book. In other words, the study as a whole represents an attempt in Bourdieu's (1965: 22) words, to 'abandon . . . the fictitious alternative between a subjectivism bent on researching the place of the pure outpourings of a creative action that cannot be reduced to structural determinants and an objectivist pan-structuralism which claims to directly generate structures from structures by a type of theoretical parthenogenesis . . .'. Where this aim stands in relation to the dominant empirical tradition in social gerontology is the issue taken up in Chapter 3.

The conceptual focus in this tradition is the nebulous notion of integration. This term is one of the spongiest in the literature of sociology generally and of social gerontology in particular. Generally, various objective, quantifiable dimensions of behaviour are held to be 'integrative' of old people. Problems arise with this formulation, however, because there appears to be no simple correlation between these dimensions and the subjective experience of aging. Various studies show, for example, that feelings of loneliness are not related to actually being alone; that some aged couples who see their children *least* frequently have the highest morale; that negative feelings about being old *increase* with higher socio-economic status, and so on.

Briefly, I argue that integration has both an objective and a subjective dimension and that it has meaning only in the interrelationship between the two. It is meaningfully conceptualised only as a property of the individual social actor and not of the social system. Its locus is the conjunction of his or her personal biography with a particular historico-social structure, and not the articulation of normatively defined and sanctioned social roles.

The men and women I studied manifest different patterns of action and interaction in old age as the product of such conjunction. Each person brings to the experience of aging a unique set of material, social and psychological resources, needs, and desires. At the same time, the meaning of old age is culturally defined in negative terms, while the life options of those classified as old are circumscribed by economic and political processes. The aging individual redefines his or her identity and re-negotiates relationships with others in a process of interaction between self and this social environment. The interaction may usefully be interpreted as a process of social exchange, and its outcome will reflect balances and imbalances in the resources available to the aged actor in various contexts.

Chapter 4 introduces the research setting and elderly subjects, and outlines the process of data collection. Chapter 5 explores the expression of age stigma in welfare services for the elderly. The next two chapters focus on the immediate social environment of the aged in terms of the two social groups considered to be most relevant to personality, age peers and family. The continuing effects of age stigma are traced through the dynamics of peer network formation and dissolution. The contribution of family relationships to the construction of a life meaning and the conception of self is examined from an exchange perspective, and the significance of the marital tie is highlighted. In Chapter 8 I analyse the interrelation of these networks from a situational perspective and offer an empirically grounded typology of aging outcomes.

The lived experiences of old people are not, of course, unrelated to issues of national economic and social policy. Although a detailed analysis of such programmes is clearly beyond the scope of this enquiry, the concluding section does include some analysis of the limitations and counter-productivity inherent in much of the current aged welfare system.

2   The Aged in Australian Society

> The way a society defines its social problems and discusses their solutions, reflects, at least implicitly, a perspective; the perceived nature of a problem affects both the solutions one can imagine to be relevant and the solutions one is likely to pursue. (Maddox and Wiley, 1976: 5)

Old age emerged as a concern common to industrialised political systems in the late nineteenth and early twentieth centuries. In recent years, recognition of old age as a social problem has become institutionalised in what Estes (1979: 2) refers to as an aging enterprise, a 'congeries of programmes, organisations, bureaucracies, interest groups, trade associations, providers, industries, and professionals that serve the aged in one capacity or another.' Far from providing solutions, Estes argues, these developments have become part of the problem.

Dominant Perspectives on the Aged Crisis

A combination of biological, demographic and historical factors is usually put forward as explanation for the aged problem. Decline is seen as the inevitable fate of the organism. Old people have become a modern problem of crisis proportions, the argument goes, because they have become vastly more numerous and because their traditional source of support, the extended family, has broken down in the wake of industrialisation.

The biological decline model of aging
The popular conception of aging is infused with the notion of biological decline. Old age is characterised, on biological grounds, as a time of decreasing efficiency, and old people are viewed as being inevitably 'slower, less energetic, having a fading memory, declining intelligence, reduced learning ability, being socially isolated and

16

withdrawn, sexually uninterested and incapable of sexual activity (Bennett and Ahammer, 1977: 3).

The association of aging with frailty and disability permeates governmental pronouncements on aging. In 1976, for example, a committee was formed under the chairmanship of A.S. Holmes to enquire into federal programmes for the aged and infirm. The report of this committee (Holmes, 1977: 14) specifically notes 'that there are many other people with chronic disabilities who have needs similar to many of the aged and who can appropriately be assisted by the same policies and programmes'. The aged, it seems are *ipso facto* dependent, and this situation has reached crisis proportions because of the growth in their numbers.

Demographic changes
At the end of 1977, some 1 300 000 Australians were 65 years of age or more. This was more than double the number in 1947. As a proportion of total population, however, the increase in the number of aged persons since World War II has been quite small: from 8 per cent of the population in 1947 to about 9 per cent in 1977.[1] It was before 1947 that the aged proportion of the population increased significantly (see Table 1).

Table 1 *Proportion of Australian Population 65+*

Census of:	1921	1933	1947	1954	1966	1976
	4.4	6.5	8.0	8.3	8.5	8.9

Source: Borrie (1978: 6).

This 'age revolution', a result primarily of dramatically lowered infant mortality rates at the end of the nineteenth century, has meant that an increasing proportion of people now live long enough to develop chronic, degenerative diseases which necessitate reliance on others for sheer survival (c.f. von Mering and Weniger, 1959). This problem has been compounded because the traditional 'others' are no longer organised as they once were.

Family breakdown
One of the most fundamental influences on the perspective from which policymakers view the contemporary situation of older people is the set of beliefs popularly held about their situation in the past. In particular, assumptions about the historical role of the family as the principal source of support for the aged have been used to explain the contemporary problems of the aged and to justify a range of policies and programmes. Until recently, it was generally accepted that three

generation households had typified living arrangements prior to industrialisation of the modern world. In line with this view, contemporary isolation of the aged has been attributed to the breakdown of
these arrangements in the wake of mechanisation and urbanisation. A
common theme in Australian discussions is the need to restore and
strengthen these ties in modified form. Emphasis on the role of the
family tallies with the decremental model of aging. Dependence is implicitly conceptualised as the 'natural' condition of older people, and
dependence on relatives is the most appropriate and acceptable form.

Current dimensions of the aged problem: definitions and solutions.

According to the authors of *Old Age in Three Industrial Societies*, a
major cross-national survey of old people:

> The basic preoccupation of social gerontology as it has emerged
> within the last two decades may be categorized as being concerned
> with integration versus segregation. Are old people integrated into
> society or are they separated from it? This is perhaps not only the
> most important theoretical question in social gerontology today but
> also the key question affecting all social policies concerning the
> aged. (Shanas *et al.*, 1968: 3)

That old age is characterized by a generalized decrease in social participation, in both collective and individual terms, has become a
sociological 'given'. The position of old people as a group, it is
argued, has shifted over time in relation to the formal institutions of
society from a situation of integration to one of increasing segregation. Declining social involvement is also seen to constitute a central
problem for the aging individual. The reasons for aging segregation
and isolation are held to be self evident: older persons as a statistical
aggregate suffer from low income, poor health, and multiple role loss
— all factors which reduce opportunities for social interaction, and
which are taken as the defining criteria in discussions of integra-
tion/segregation.

Shanas and her associates assert (1968: 426) that the contemporary
situation of old people can be categorised as that of segregation from
the formal economic, political, and social structures of industrial
society but of integration through informal, primary structures,
especially the family. Others agree that primary integration in old age
is problematic only for a minority (Maddox and Wiley,1976).

The concept of integration itself, however, is vaguely defined.
Shanas and her associates suggest that integration is related to four
variables: health (or functional capacity); family relationships; work;

and income. Health is related to the individual's 'ability to participate in social life' (1968: 8). The elderly are seen to be 'knitted into the social structure through the relationships they have with their relatives, friends, and acquaintances, and through the roles they perform in these relationships' (1968: 8-9). Men in particular are also 'knitted into the social structure through their participation in the workforce' (1968: 9). Finally, differentials of income affect the extent to which people can participate in social life.

Others apply this concept in essentially similar terms. Rosow (1976: 47) sees the 'factors that integrate' old people into society as the holding of property and power; group memberships (social networks); and the performance of major social roles. In particular, 'older people are relatively well off and socially integrated if they are (a) married and living with spouse; (b) still at work; (c) have no major loss of income; and (d) are in good health' (1976: 49).

Income

For the majority of aged Australians, the age pension is their sole or major source of income. Table 2 documents the increase in numbers of age pensioners over the past two decades, and Table 3 shows the low level of pensions in relation to average weekly earnings.

These and overseas figures indicate that relative poverty is a major disadvantage associated with aging in modern society. In Australia, the question of aged poverty has received considerable attention in recent years. Debate has centred around the findings of the Commission of Inquiry into Poverty chaired by Professor R.F. Henderson (1975) Using an avowedly austere poverty line based on the basic wage, the Commission found that aged pensioners constituted the largest single group in poverty, or 47 per cent of all poor income units. Some 24 per

Table 2 *Age Pensioners — percentage of relevant age group 1957-76*

At 30 June	Pensioners as a Percentage of the Relevant Age Group (a)
1957	45.8
1962	52.9
1967	53.2
1972	62.0
1973	67.8
1974	·72.9
1975	76.1
1976	75.4

(a) Age pensioners as a percentage of all females 60 years and over, and all males 65 years and over.
Source: Social Indicators, No. 2, 1978, p.119; and Jones (1979: 83).

Table 3 *Age and Invalid Pension Rates, compared with Consumer Price Index and weekly earnings 1967-77*

June	Consumer Price Index (six capitals)	Weekly Pension Rate as a Percentage of Average Weekly Earnings	
		Standard Rate	Married Rate
	1966-67 — 100	Per cent	
1967	101.3	20.5	37.1
1968	104.2	19.4	35.1
1969	107.2	19.3	34.5
1970	111.2	19.0	33.5
1971	117.2	18.0	32.1
1972	124.5	19.1	33.5
1973	134.7	20.2	35.2
1974	154.1	20.5	35.8
1975	180.2	23.3	38.8
1976	202.4	23.1	38.3
1977	229.6	23.3	34.6

Source: Social Indicators, No. 2, 1978, p. 121; and Jones (1979: 84).

cent of aged income units were classified as 'very poor' and a further 22 percent as 'rather poor', before housing costs (Henderson, 1975: 235).

Work

Low income in old age is primarily a reflection of the low level of pension benefits. Dependence on social security payments is in turn a product of non-participation in the workforce.

Figures on labourforce participation rates by age show the 'continuation of a slow trend to lower participation rates for males above about the age of 55 years' (Borrie, 1978: 82).

Only a small proportion of aged persons have access to paid employment, a situation which is seen as the product of three main factors: technological obsolescence, the increasing bureaucratisation of conditions of employment (notably the institutionalisation of fixed retirement ages), and patterns in the aggregate demand for labour which, in Australia, lags increasingly behind its supply.

Health

In Australia, as elsewhere, demands on the health care system increase with age. American estimates suggest that 8 to 15 per cent of non-institutionalised persons over 65 are either bedfast or housebound, and a further 6 to 16 per cent are able to go outdoors only with difficulty. Australian data on the subject are sketchy, but reveal something of the extent of disability among the aged population.

A Victorian survey (Hutchinson, 1954: 104) found 3 per cent bedridden, but only one-third were permanently so confined. A higher proportion were not bed-bound but were confined to their homes: 2 per cent of the men and 4 per cent of the women. In Marrickville, Sydney, 10.2 per cent were found to be restricted in this way (Robb and Rivett, 1964: 15).

A Sydney survey of elderly people seeking accommodation through voluntary agencies (Sorrell, 1972) found that almost half the sample had some defect of sight or hearing ranging from severe to slight, 38 per cent had some restriction in use of limbs, and 46 per cent had some other significant physical disorder. Other studies report from 30 per cent (Hutchinson, 1954: 104) to more than half (Robb and Rivett, 1964: 13) with one or more disabilities, the incidence increasing with age. In Mount Gambier, South Australia, 55.1 per cent of elderly respondents claimed to have more than one handicap (sight, hearing, mobility or mental health) (Radford and Peever, 1976: 73).

The elderly utilise hospital beds more intensively than any other age group (Hammerman, 1978: 465). It has in fact been argued (Jones, 1979: 165) that Australian health services, particularly institutional facilities, 'concentrate on the aged'. At the same time, the aged are vastly over-represented as clients of various community welfare services. Individual studies of community aid centres, home nursing and other welfare services suggest that the aged account for up to three-quarters of their clients (Horowitz, 1975; Duigan, 1975; Harper and Morey, 1977; Douglas, 1977). The aged are also disproportionately heavy users of physician services. Ryan (1979: 60) advises that 'no doctor should embark on . . . a [general practice] career unless he enjoys treating old people'. A recent discussion of the aged in relation to the Australian health delivery system is found in Ford (1979).

Not surprisingly, a large amount of current health care expenditure is absorbed by the aged. The greatest proportion of these costs, as of health care expenses generally, originate in hospitals, nursing homes, and other institutions (Jones, 1979: 61). In fact, the recent emphasis on domiciliary services for the elderly can be traced directly to a concern for the escalating costs of institutionalisation.

Family relationships
The one bright spot perceived in an otherwise gloomy picture is the relationship maintained by the elderly with their family. Australian sociological research has established the existence of modified extended kinship networks characterised by routine visiting and the exchange

of services (Oeser and Emery, 1957: 135; Fallding, 1957; Martin, 1967, 1970; Bryson and Thompson, 1972). For the majority of aged Australians, it seems, contact with non-resident family members is a regular occurrence: at least three-quarters are in touch on a weekly basis.[2] This kinship network functions as a source of financial assistance, especially from the older generation to the younger, and as the principal form of help in emergencies (Oeser and Emery, 1954: 135; Fallding, 1957: 59; Martin, 1970: 313). Some families routinely exchange household services; perhaps one-quarter of aged persons living alone depend for some aspects of household management on help from outside relatives.[3]

Further support for the integrative role of the family is derived from documentation of the over-representation of those without family ties among the institutionalised aged population. The 'preventive effects' of family relationships are widely argued, along with pleas for government action to strengthen family ties (see e.g. Lefroy, 1977; Bower, 1974; Howe, 1979).

Clearly, prevailing conceptions of the reasons for old age segregation locate the source of the problem in what are seen as the unique disadvantages and disabilities of aging and old people *per se*: they are unemployable and sick, because they are old. Accordingly, institutional responses to the aged problem have approached the elderly as a special 'disability group' with a definable set of special needs. An array of public policies and formal services has been implemented to cater for these needs.

The most important single item in welfare expenditure on the aged are cash payments in the form of old age pensions. Those in receipt of a pension are also entitled, subject to a means test, to various allowances on medical costs, transport, municipal rates, telephone rental, and so on. More than three-quarters (77.2 per cent) of age pensioners were eligible for these pensioner fringe benefits at 30 June 1978 (Department of Social Security, *Annual Report*, 1977–78: 6–7).

The government also provides assistance to aged people through payments to various organisations. In June 1978, for example, there were 29 884 persons accommodated in self-contained flats and 20 108 in hostels provided under the Aged or Disabled Persons Homes Act and Aged Persons Hostels Act. A further 10 935 people were in nursing homes which had received government grants. Subsidies are also paid for the establishment of Senior Citizens Centres, the delivery of Meals on Wheels, the operation of home care services, and other community welfare activities. At 30 June 1978, there were also 2 186 people in receipt of a special benefit paid by the Department of Social Security to those caring for sick or invalid relatives at home (Department of Social Security, *Annual Report* 1977–78).

A number of recent governmental enquiries contain recommendations for the direction of aged welfare policies. Two of the most important were the Commission of Inquiry into Poverty (Henderson, 1975), and the Committee on Care of the Aged and Infirm, chaired by A.S. Holmes (1977).

Income
Surprisingly, in view of the low level of pension benefits, there is no suggestion from government policy makers or their advisors that the monetary value of the pension be increased. It is not considered necessary since, according to the Poverty Report, the majority of aged are redeemed from poverty by low accommodation costs. Just over 60 per cent of Australian aged, the Report notes, are home owners. After housing costs, the proportion of poor aged income units drops from nearly half to just 7.6 per cent (Henderson, 1975: 235).

Other factors are also seen to alleviate the elderly's financial situation. In a subsequent article, Henderson (1977: 104) argues that the age pension is really only a 'supplementary measure' for home owners and for those aged boarding with relatives. Overall, he concludes that the old are not really all that badly off since: (1) the majority own their own homes; (2) many receive various forms of help from their children; and (3) some disadvantaged groups are worse off (*sic*). Thus he proposes that improved welfare measures for other 'disability groups' such as the unemployed should take priority over raising the old age pension: 'The more that is given to the aged, the less is available for others' (1977: 104). He advocates instead the expansion of domiciliary and other services which focus on the minority of single aged private renters as the group most in need.

Work
The Poverty Report recommends, but does not specify, provisions to enable aged persons to continue in employment if they so desire. It stresses, however, that 'there is a consensus that the aged should not have to work for a living' (Henderson, 1975: 236); as a group, they inherently 'suffer disadvantages on the labour market' because of poor health and obsolescence of skills. Accordingly, the provision of 'non-onerous and part-time jobs' is to be encouraged, as well as the use of the elderly as volunteers in community services projects. The Holmes Report (1977: 33) reiterates this theme, noting in particular that 'those assisting the frail aged should be encouraged to use the paid or unpaid services (often part-time) of the fit aged'.

Health
The Committee on Care of the Aged and Infirm expresses most con-

cern about the high costs involved in aged health care and identifies three main contributing factors: the expense of institutionalisation, the growth of user demand resulting in part from lack of financial barriers to health services and facilities, and the wasteful absence of coordination and rationalisation among existing services. Ameliorative measures proposed include a shift in emphasis away from institutional care towards domiciliary services, a consolidation of domiciliary programmes into a single community care programme, and an expansion of private health insurance, especially to cover nursing home fees.

Social relationships

In general, the special needs of the elderly are considered to be most appropriately served by supporting the individual's personal networks, especially family members. According to Henderson (1977: 100), for example, 'our welfare throughout our lives depends mainly on our families, our friends, our neighbours, and on our network of private contacts in the community. Action by government, public provision, is supplementary'.

Government action, it is argued, should be directed to the expansion and coordination of domiciliary and other services. The social (as well as health and economic) functions of community services, such as delivered meals, are stressed, and the possibility of using Senior Citizens Centres as bases for a coordinated welfare system has been raised (Holmes, 1977: 60).

As I have already suggested, dependence on one's family is seen as appropriate and acceptable. The Domiciliary Nursing Care Benefit was explicitly introduced (in 1973) 'to encourage people to look after their aged relatives in their own homes' (Holmes, 1977: 45-46). Dependence on government, on the other hand, is not acceptable. It 'encourages' idleness and individual irresponsibility. The only acceptable form of old age insurance is through the self-reliance inherent in a system of private enterprise. Thus the Holmes Report recommends the expansion of private health insurance 'to encourage self-reliance and to reduce dependence on governments' (Holmes, 1977: 102).

Such, briefly, are the dominant perspectives on the nature of the aged problem and on appropriate institutional solutions to it. The assumptions underlying this perspective can be summarised as follows:

1. The aged constitute a special and more or less homogeneous 'disability group'.

2. The special problems and needs of the aged derive primarily from the inevitable biological decline of the aging process itself. In modern society these problems have been exacerbated by technological, demographic, and family changes.

3. The 'differentness' of the aged warrants special treatment for them.

4. The problems of the aged can be broken down into clearly defined categories, each of which demands the operation of an appropriate service together with a coordinating infrastructure.

5. The natural responsibility for primary care of the aged rests with family members, whose efforts should be encouraged and supported by appropriate services and facilities.

Critique of the Dominant Perspective

Critical analysis reveals fundamental inadequacies in the way in which the old age problem has been conceived and explained. In the first place, biological decline, the age revolution, and family breakdown do not account for the disadvantaged status of elderly Australians. These notions not only obscure the real dimensions of the problem and their aetiology, but help to perpetuate it by legitimating inappropriate solutions.

The biological decline model encourages a negative image of all older people. Yet the empirical evidence suggests that this view of aging is to a large extent untrue and 'is inappropriate for the description of psychological and behavioural aging' (Bennett and Ahammer, 1977: 3). Findings of regressive changes in the latter part of the lifespan, far from reflecting intrinsic aging phenomena, are often artifacts of inappropriate methodology or of social deficits associated with old age. The prevailing view depicts the aged as a homogeneous 'disability group' and justifies universalist policies which ignore significant differences within the aged category.

The role of demographic change is similarly inadequate as an explanation for the mid-twentieth century aged problem. Although there has been an increase in absolute and relative numbers of aged persons in all industrialised political systems, this does not of itself constitute a social problem.

In Australia particularly, the notion of an 'age revolution' and its consequences has been greatly exaggerated. Compared with other Western nations, the percentage of aged in the Australian population is small (Table 4) and will show only a modest increase by the end of the century. The social and economic impact of these demographic trends has been widely misinterpreted. As Borrie's (1978) analysis shows, higher proportions in the dependent aged group are offset by lower proportions in the juvenile group; the proportion of working age population will not decrease (Table 5).

Table 4 *Population Age Structure in Selected Countries*

Country	Date	Percentage in age groups				65 and over as percentage of 20–64
		0–19	20–64	65 +	Total	
Australia	1971	37.5	54.2	8.3	100	15.4
Japan	1970	32.6	60.3	7.1	100	11.7
Canada	1971	39.4	52.5	8.1	100	15.4
New Zealand	1971	40.9	50.6	8.5	100	16.8
Italy	1971	31.6	57.7	10.7	100	18.5
U.S.A	1970	37.9	52.2	9.9	100	18.9
Netherlands	1971	35.5	54.2	10.3	100	18.9
Denmark	1969	31.2	56.7	12.1	100	21.3
U.K.	1971	30.8	56.1	13.1	100	23.4
Germany*	1971	29.7	56.9	13.4	100	23.6
Sweden	1971	27.6	58.5	13.9	100	23.8
France	1968	32.2	54.4	13.4	100	24.7

*Federal Republic.
Source: National Superannuation in Australia: Interim Report of the Committee of Enquiry, (AGPS, Canberra, 1974) p. 109; and Jones (1979: 83).

Table 5 *Age Distribution by 'Working' and 'Dependent' Groups, 1976, in the Transition to a Stationary Population*

Age Group	Distribution per cent	Distribution per cent in transition to stationary situation	stationary (c. 2031)
0–14	27	23	21
15–64	64	67	65
65+	9	10	14
All ages	100	100	100

Source: N.P.I. (1975: 285); and Borrie (1978: 105).

In any case, the fundamental issue is that the aged are not *inherently* dependent. The fact that an increase in their numbers is seen to constitute a problem reflects *socially* constructed conditions.

Finally, the belief in extended family breakdown does not fit empirical reality. Recent research has demonstrated that the constellation of high status and extended family care popularly believed to characterise the position of old people in pre-modern Western society is a greatly romanticised reading of the past. Three-generation households were not a common feature of social organisation in England, Western Europe, the United States or Australia prior to industrialisation, nor was old age a uniformly valued period of life. The problematic situation of aged people in Western society today cannot be adequately explained as a product of industrialisation and the supposed breakdown of the extended family (Laslett, 1976; Stone, 1977; Swain, 1979).

Clearly a major re-examination of the nature and causes of the aged problem is in order. In this book I offer a sociological interpretation of aging in Australian society which challenges taken-for-granted assumptions about old people and their social problems. My analysis is framed in the theoretical tradition known as the 'social construction of reality'. Socially constructed meanings about aging and old people influence the experience and life chances of individuals who enter that status, and at the same time, function to legitimise specific institutions of power and interest. Overwhelmingly, these meanings and their institutional ramifications have negative consequences for the elderly. But as the case studies I present later illustrate, the aged are not simply passive objects of discrimination. They actively resist the affronts which society mounts against their autonomy and dignity, and participate — albeit often with limited resources — in constructing their personal worlds.

The standard of living of elderly Australians is not determined by degeneration inherent in the biological process of aging but by socially created conditions. These conditions consist of ideologies and structural interests. The most important ideological constraints on the situation of the aged are of two principal kinds. First is the specific construction of reality about the nature of old people and their problems. The definition of old age as a period of biological decline which produces certain special needs legitimates the creation of segregative policies and programmes and thereby obscures the structural aetiology of old age deprivation. This ideology has negative social and emotional consequences for all elderly people. Second is the more general set of beliefs which underpin the operation of the capitalist state, namely the Protestant ethic of work and profit and its attendant emphasis on individualism (see e.g. Wild, 1978: 166–67). In these terms, minimal state intervention in welfare is justified, and the individual can be blamed for his or her lack of foresight in planning for the retirement years. This set of beliefs does not affect all aged persons in an equally negative fashion.

Ideologies do not function in a political or economic vacuum. They are intimately related to the distribution of resources and power in Australian society. In the process of institutionalising a negative and segregative view of the elderly, social policies for the aged bolster the interests of governments, professional and business groups, and a wide spectrum of public and private welfare bureaucracies. In this process, social constructions become objective reality.

The Social Construction of Reality

Negative stereotypes and prejudices about the aged are embedded in the dominant Australian culture. Along with sexism and racism, 'agism' has been rationalised on the grounds of old people's biological deficiencies, a situation which prevails independently of the current state of scientific knowledge about biologically based deficiencies (c.f. Rogers, 1975).

Beliefs, attitudes and values about aging, in other words, are socially constructed. This sociological truism is a commonplace in the gerontological literature. But few attempts have been made either to analyse its relationship to dominant economic and political institutions or to document the effects of age stigma on the personal experience and interpersonal relations of elderly people.

Illustration of the general devaluation of old age and of particular cultural stereotypes about old people can be drawn from a variety of sources. I have already shown how they emerge in official thinking on the issue.

Expressed motivations for the establishment of specific welfare programmes further reflect this view of the aged as simply one more 'disabled' group. A community health programme introduced in 1973 had as one of its tasks to provide 'rehabilitation services for the aged, the handicapped, alcoholics and any other dependent persons' (Holmes, 1977: 50). Emphasis is on the infirmity of old age, even in the provision of ostensibly social amenities. In extending commonwealth assistance to Senior Citizens Centres, for example, it 'was envisaged that the centres would become bases for the development of welfare services which would be coordinated with other services for the aged' (Holmes, 1977: 60), in particular with domiciliary care.

Our public media also disseminate a negative view. Old age in general is not a popular media topic. Old people are generally not programmed for or about: they are 'poor consumers' and 'poor copy' (Hess, 1976).

When old age does receive attention in our newspapers, it is usually in connection with a limited number of negative themes: poverty, infirmity, accommodation needs, loneliness, hospitals and nursing homes, death, scientific research into slowing the onset of old age, and the problems faced by families with aged relatives.[4] Positive images of old age appear to apply only to atypical old people, especially those outstandingly successful in life.[5]

In general, though, media references to old age are conspicuous by their absence. Martel's (1968: 57) study of American magazine fiction between 1890 and 1955 refers to the 'symbolic abandonment' of the aged:

> In 1890, the aged characters have a fair number of close associations with younger adults. In 1955, not a single character over age 60 is described as having a close reciprocal attachment with a middle-aged or young adult. Their only significant associations are with peers or children. Their destiny seems to be one of banishment — to the 'senior citizen' magazines.

Special magazines for the aged have recently appeared in Australia, and the public radio network has a weekly programme for 'seniors'. Overall, the situation may be described in a paraphrase of Summers' (1975: 81) statements about the treatment of women in the media: 'Old people's doings are relegated to the far corner of the national consciousness, their separatism confirmed by the special magazines and sections of (media) which are devoted to them, and their objectification completed by their being treated as special categories of description and anaylsis.'

Unfortunately, negative images of the aged also permeate Australian welfare-oriented research. Though obviously well intentioned, much of the applied research on the aged in Australia is coloured by elements of agism. A close examination of this literature reveals the extent to which popular stereotypes and 'conventional wisdom' about old people inform the methodology and interpretation of survey research.

One such study (Sach, 1975) was commissioned by the Australian government's Poverty Inquiry to investigate the supply and demand for different kinds of aged persons' accommodation in Melbourne. An important clue to the underlying value orientations of the researcher, who was working on behalf of the Victorian Council on the Aging, is found in the ideas expressed as to what constitutes the 'ideal' living arrangements for older people and more importantly, what kind of older person is in turn 'ideal' for these arrangements.

An independent lifestyle, involving maintenance with community support in the person's own home, is described as appropriate for those old people who have a 'cheerfully oriented mental state'. Institutionalisation, on the other hand, is the preferred solution for those with 'mental disturbance'. Presumably, an old person is only capable of independent living if he or she is 'cheerful'. The phraseology also seems to suggest that the non-cheerful are, *ipso facto*, 'mentally disturbed'.

Similar ideas about appropriate lifestyles for older people inform the working definitions of a Sydney survey, which was conducted for the NSW Council on the Aging (Sorrell, 1972). In the study, an assessment of 'mental state' was made on a four-point scale. Note 'was made of a number of "negative" intellectual and emotional attitudes comprising anxiety, confusion, loss of memory, lack of interest, loneliness, sense of rejection, suspicion, hostility and unusual behaviour' (Sorrell, 1972: 15). This assessment was made by the interviewers.

Quite apart from the questionable methodology involved in assessing such complex psychological phenomena on the basis of an interview about accommodation needs,[6] the clustering of traits is itself truly remarkable. Taken at face value, it is difficult to find any common element on which the characteristics are classified as 'negative attitudes'. In no objective terms could 'loneliness' and 'suspicion' for example, be taken as comparable phenomena. And even if an aged person *were* 'hostile' and 'suspicious' perhaps he or she had good reason to be. I found considerable evidence of well-intentioned domiciliary workers exerting pressure on frail old people to enter a nursing home. The 'hostility' and 'suspicion' that sometimes greeted me in my imperfectly understood role as 'researcher' were therefore eminently realistic and justified. Similar considerations undoubtedly apply to feelings of 'rejection'. The elderly in out society *are* frequently rejected.

This evaluation was put to other use within the survey. A close association was reported between 'mental state' and 'isolation', the latter being interpreted as 'a personal inability to form social relationships' (1972: 19). 'Isolation' was assessed on a scale of four categories:

1. Had some close relationship to one or more persons daily or weekly.

2. Saw one or more persons regularly but not as frequently as in 1.

3. Not isolated from social contacts but not in Class 1 or 2.

4. Casual social contacts only or suffering from desolation due to separation or loss (1972: 19).

The implicit assumption is clear: an old person who has infrequent social contacts must be suffering from a *personal* inadequacy; the correlation between having few contacts and also having 'negative attitudes' (already partly *defined* in terms of having inadequate social relations through the inclusion of 'loneliness') offers further proof of the stereotype that the only 'good old person' is a sociable and cheerful old person.

Overall, the Report is infused with a sense that old people are simply not competent, even to assess their own needs. In the conclusion, it is strongly recommended that housing officials obtain 'an independent assessment rather than accepting the applicants' own views' (Sorrell, 1972: 30).

This tendency to denigrate the significance of old people's assessments of themselves appears in other research. Robb and Rivett (1964: 36), for example, asked their informants if they found their incomes adequate, and then they comment: 'Obviously, too much weight should not be attached to the answers . . . '. Since their entire body of data consists of old people's answers to such questions, this caveat is remarkable.

Clearly, old people are conceptualised as somehow 'different' from other adults. Whereas a voluminous feminist literature locates a fundamental problem for many women in the fact that they are defined by, and their interaction is limited to, the narrow world of the family, it seems that old people have — and should have — their emotional and instrumental needs satisfied within this microcosm. In this context Jennie-Keith Ross (1977: 193) remarks: 'It would seem bizarre to suggest that any other age group, except perhaps extremely young children, should find all of its social participation within the immediate family, and yet this formula is frequently applied to older people'.

It is also informative to note the press treatment accorded a recent manifestation of Grey Pantherism in Australian politics. A front-page article in the *Sydney Morning Herald* (May 25 1979) on 'Australia's first Grey Panther', a candidate in a forthcoming by-election, described him as '60 and grey-haired if not very pantherish. He ... has twinkly blue eyes, a pink complexion and is rather chubby'. One wonders how a 'normal' candidate would react to such a description of his political qualifications.

The fact that caring for the aged in any capacity is a low status occupation provides further indication of the devaluation of old age and old people in modern society. Doctors derive little professional prestige from association with the elderly as patients (Kane and Kane, 1978: 915). Nursing home personnel are less well paid, have lower levels of training, and are less satisfied in their work than are their counterparts in other areas of the health care system. Nurses relate that they work with the aged only as a last resort.[7] Ambulance drivers sound their sirens less urgently and drive more slowly when the patient is an older person (Sudnow, 1971).

Evasion of old age in modern society is partly an existential phenomenon. Society avoids reference to aging because, in de Beauvoir's (1970: 10) words, 'in the old person that we must become, we refuse to recognize ourselves....'. As Berger and Berger (1976: 355) suggest, being '... youthful is widely looked upon not simply as the happy condition of those favoured by nature ... but as, in some way, a moral duty for *everyone*. Consequently, to be old ... appears not only as misfortune but in some fashion as moral failure'. By constructing a social category of old age peopled by beings whose moral, as well as physical and social, characteristics are unlike our own, we eschew identification with the category and therefore with our own tenuous mortality: 'Until the moment it is upon us old age is something that only affects other people. So it is understandable that society should manage to prevent us from seeing our own kind, our fellowmen, when we look at the old' (de Beauvoir, 1970: 12).

Another reason for the negative objectification of old people lies in the failure of researchers to let the elderly themselves speak of their experience. This methodological issue is taken up in Chapter 3 where I examine the ways in which the aged themselves conceptualise the experience of growing old.

A more fundamental factor to be considered here is the reciprocal linkage between socially constructed 'reality' about old age and the dominant institutional order of Australian society. The following discussion focuses on economic and political linkages.

The Political Economy of Aging

As Estes (1979: 4) has pointed out, 'certain ways of thinking about the aged as a social problem (and the logical extension of these views into social policies) are rooted in the structure of social and power relations and...they reflect and bolster the social location of their adherents and proponents'. The dominant cultural system, I have suggested, defines old people as dependent and in some fundamental way 'different' from other adults. These beliefs have shaped conceptions of the aged problem and hence of appropriate solutions for it. Basically, they function to rationalise and legitimate an array of services designed to cater for the needs of the aged as a separate and unique 'disability group'. This approach, which Estes (1979) has dubbed the 'services strategy', is analysed in Chapter 5. Here I will consider the economic and political situation of Australian aged and examine their participation in the welfare state.

From its inception, the Australian welfare state has included the aged as a special category of persons in need. Indeed, the aged were the first disadvantaged group to benefit from changing attitudes towards the role of the state at the end of the nineteenth century.

There was never an Australian version of the English poor law requiring government responsibility for the destitute. As in America (c.f. Zimmerman, 1976), voluntary charitable associations played the central role in systems of social welfare in nineteenth century Australia. The oldest of these organisations in Australia, the Benevolent Society of New South Wales, began operating an outdoor relief scheme in 1818. In 1821 it initiated indoor relief in the form of the Sydney Benevolent Asylum: 'a refuge for the distressed, an hospital for the diseased, an asylum for the aged poor, and a home for the wretched wanderer' (*Annual Reports*, 1820, quoted in Kewley, 1965: 8).

Direct government intervention on behalf of the aged can be traced to 1862, when the Benevolent Society's indoor relief activities were limited and the colonial government was made directly responsible for caring for the destitute aged and infirm. A number of other voluntary organisations in existence at this time also operated asylums for the aged and infirm. All such facilities came under government control. By the end of the century, government expenditure on the maintenance of the aged and infirm in asylums constituted over 42 per cent of total expenditure on charities under its direct control, an amount only fractionally less than that devoted to the care of destitute children. Friendly Societies, based on their English counterparts, proliferated during the latter part of the nineteenth century, but neither they nor trade unions made provision for their members in old age (Kewley, 1965: 13).

Table 6 indicates that the aged were over – represented among inmates of New South Wales insane asylums in the latter part of the nineteenth century. Almost 13 per cent of inmates were aged 60 years or more, whereas only 2.5 per cent of the total state population was aged 65 or over (Dixon, 1977: 2). Undoubtedly then, as now (c.f. Bennett and Ahammer, 1977), psychogeriatric admissions often reflected underlying *social* deficits.

Table 6 *'Insane' Population Under Care in New South Wales, 1883*

Age	Number	Per Cent
Under 20 years	199	6.64
Between 20 and 30	471	15.72
Between 30 and 40	688	22.96
Between 40 and 50	766	25.56
Between 50 and 60	488	16.28
Between 60 and 70	268	8.94
Between 70 and 90	117	3.90
Total	2997	100.00

Source: The Australasian Medical Gazette, III, July 1884; p.233.

It would appear from the scant data readily available that for a substantial proportion of the aged population the onset of physical decline necessitated seeking public relief. Writing in the late nineteenth century, Trollope (1967: 711) commented that Australian swagmen 'rarely trouble the benevolent asylums of the colonies until they have become objects of charity from physical infirmities'. And again: 'The defence to be made for such a benevolent asylum as that at Melbourne is to be found in the fact that its comforts, comfortable as they are, attract at present only the old and the sick' (1967; 710 – 11).

The latter comment reflects the prevailing nineteenth century belief that such institutions were social evils which supported the feckless and lazy. The following citation upholds this view, and also reveals the inevitable gloss between old age, decay, and uselessness. Discussing 'The Scarcity of Subjects for Dissection', the *Australian Medical Gazette* (1869) remarked on the decision not to permit the bodies of deceased inmates of the Melbourne Benevolent Asylum to be given to the anatomical school:

The vast majority of inmates who die in the Asylum are worn out by chronic disease and old age; their bodies would not be very valuable for anatomical purposes; nevertheless, we think that the committee did not act wisely in throwing unnecessary obstacles in the way. There can be no valid reason why the bodies of persons maintained for years, in comfort and idleness, in this institution at the public expense, should not be available for so necessary and useful a purpose as the teaching of anatomy. (*The Australian Medical Gazette*, Sept. 15, 1869; 191)

By the 1890s, however, a complex of new social, political and economic circumstances dramatised the need for a different approach to the problem of aged infirmity and destitution. According to Dixon (1977), three major factors combined to usher in a new era in Australian welfare policies: First, the 'noticeable aging of the Australian population during the 1890s caused by the rapid influx of immigrants 40 years earlier, increased the incidence of aged destitution' (Dixon, 1977: 1). From 2.9 per cent of the population in 1891, those aged 65 years or over accounted for 4.0 per cent by 1901. Second, economic depression caused a dramatic leap in unemployment and a consequent influx of elderly people into the existing public relief institutions. These indoor relief facilities, barely adequate before, became overloaded. In Victoria, severe overcrowding resulted in the imprisonment of numbers of aged poor. A public outcry ensued. Finally charges of corruption and maladministration within the Benevolent Society of New South Wales led to 'a demand for more efficient use of public funds...' (Ford, 1979: 76). The overwhelming sentiment was for an extension of government support in all areas of charitable relief, and the aged were the first group to benefit from this trend in public opinion. A system of old-age pensions was instituted as a more 'enlightened' method of dealing with the problem of the destitute aged.

From the point of view of the dominant political interests of the day, a more apt description of this development would be 'enlightened self interest'. The evolution of policies for the aged cannot be divorced from their politico-economic context, nor can their benefit be interpreted as conferring unmixed blessings. Their present form has been, and continues to be, shaped by conflict between sectarian interests, and their implementation has proved in important ways to the detriment of many of the aged themselves.

Although the introduction of aged pensions was partly due, as we have seen, to demographic changes, the aged were still a relatively small segment of the population. Economic recession had highlighted the inadequacy of charitable institutions as instruments for the alleviation of poverty, and the publicity surrounding evidence of waste and incompetence in their management of substantial public funds compelled governments to act (c.f. Jones, 1979: 12-13).

At the same time, the prolonged depression had lent credence to the developing political arm of the labour movement, which challenged the work ethic and argued for a structural rather than an individual explanation of poverty. A variety of policy options was mooted, but economic and political considerations favoured a non-contributory pensions scheme.[8]

In any case, it was not envisaged that the costs of an aged pensions scheme would be excessive. When the commonwealth old-age pensions scheme was introduced in 1908, the expectation of life from birth was only around 55 years for men and 59 years for women (Borrie, 1977: 13). As Jones (1979: 15) points out, the 'question was treated as yet another relatively minor problem to be solved in a pragmatic way'. But the scheme quickly proved far more expensive than had been anticipated and, Jones (1979: 16) suggests, 'may never have been introduced if the later costs had been known'. By then it was too late; the old-age pension became the first welfare 'sacred cow'.

Another major source of apprehension about the scheme was that it would discourage thrift and work effort. The work ethic, values of self-help, and disinctions between 'deserving' and 'undeserving' poor have been influential throughout the history of Australian welfare development. Recipients of the old-age pension had not only to be destitute, but to be morally worthy. Under the early Victorian and New South Wales administration, applicants were subjected to undignified and often harsh probings of their character by local boards (Jones, 1979: 15).

Policy makers were in fact much more favourably inclined towards a contributory scheme of some kind. Reluctantly, they were forced to recognise the financial and administrative impracticality of such a plan. But the concept was not forgotten. As Dixon's (1977) analysis shows, discussions of social welfare policy during the first half of the century were dominated by the social insurance issue. Successive non-Labor governments attempted to introduce a compulsory contribution aged pension scheme. These efforts were frustrated by opposition from sectarian interests, especially the medical profession, employer groups, the Labor Party, and the Country Party. The latter feared that the scheme would adversely affect small farmers.

By the 1950s, slightly less than half of Australia's aged were receiving a pension. The federal Liberal government, balking at increased state participation in welfare, shifted its focus back to the voluntary sector. Under the Aged Persons Homes Act, initiated in 1954, the commonwealth provided generous subsidies to non-profit organisations which established accommodation for the elderly. Similar provisions were extended to cover aged persons hostels in 1972.

The 1960s saw this trend towards specialisation of services and reliance on the voluntary sector continue. The domiciliary care system, run by non-profit agencies with handsome commonwealth support, was expanded. This development was justified on the humanitarian grounds of allowing the elderly to remain in their familiar environment. A more basic motivation was the escalating cost of institutionalisation.

According to Jones (1979: 42), the late 1960s marked a turning point in Australian welfare policy. Universalism became the dominant trend, with aged pensions in the vanguard of the development. In 1969, under mounting pressure from aged pensioners, the means test was substantially liberalised (c.f. Ellis, 1981). Abolition of the means test became an electoral carrot offered by both major parties. Labor's victory in 1972 accelerated the universalist trend, and also 'shifted the emphasis to government as a supplier of services' (Jones, 1979: 48) rather than of cash benefits.

Despite the Poverty Report's recommendation that Australian policy should focus on the needy group among the aged, the direction in welfare programmes during the 1970s has been towards universalism (c.f. Jones, 1979: 82–86). In 1975 the means test on the age pension was abolished for those over 70. It was reimposed in 1978, though at a more generous rate than applies to most other social service benefits. Other universalist policies include the progressive removal of death- duties, and the subsidisation of various social and welfare services from which all aged persons benefit, such as retirement housing, Senior Citizens Clubs and Meals on Wheels services.

In order to understand this contradiction and, concomitantly, to gain a fuller picture of needs and problems among the aged, it is necessary to move beyond the dominant classless view of aging. The situation of Australia's aged in the later part of the twentieth century is obscured rather than clarified by the conception of old people as a more or less homogeneous 'disability group'. In her application of a Marxist perspective to the study of old age, de Beauvoir (1970: 16–17) argues that

> the class struggle governs the manner in which old age takes hold of a man: there is a great gulf between the aged slave and the aged patrician, between the wretchedly pensioned ex-worker and an Onassis ... (W)e have two classes of old people, the one extremely numerous, the other reduced to a small minority; and these two classes are brought into conflict between the exploitees and the exploited. Any statement that claims to deal with old age as a whole must be challenged, for it tends to hide this chasm.

Ward (1978) has elaborated this view in relation to Australian society. He contends 'that aging is a markedly different experience for members of different classes under any social formation, and that under capitalism it is a disagreeable experience for the major part of the population, i.e the working class' (1978: 49). Property rights are seen as the major factor which differentiates the situation of the aged bourgeoisie from that of the proletariat: 'The individual's experience of aging is fundamentally affected by where he/she stands in relation to the property dividing line' (Ward, 1978: 49).

There can be no argument with the Marxist assertion that the aged do not constitute a homogeneous group. On the other hand, a simple dichotomy between working class aged and ruling class aged does not allow us to account fully for differential experiences in later life.

In the first place, there are finer degrees of gradation in the material circumstances of older workers than a two-fold scheme would suggest. There are major lines of division within the group of employed workers: compare, say, the income and security of home owning, superannuated white collar elderly with the situation of propertyless pensioners (c.f. Wild, 1978: 161–68).

Second, it is quite misleading to imply as Ward (1978) appears to do that old age is a disagreeable experience *only* for the working class. As de Beauvoir (1970) demonstrates, wealth and property are not unassailable barriers to the physical and socio-cultural stigmata of aging. In reconsidering the way in which the problems of the aged have been defined, then, it is necessary both to take into account the fact that the aged are internally stratified and to incorporate the ways in which they themselves perceive the situation.

Income

A fundamental criticism of the Poverty Report has been raised by Collins and Boughton (1977:4):

> While an extremely valuable documentation of the *extent* of poverty, it fails to analyse the basic *causes* of poverty... As a result, the policy prescriptions it offers are poorly founded. This fault is not accidental, nor by way of oversight. Rather, it stems from the basic assumptions implicit in the Report. These assumptions determine the questions to be posed about poverty and the range of solutions to the problem which are considered to be feasible.

By focusing on the manifestation of poverty in various 'disability groups' the Report implies that poverty results from the specific disadvantages of each of these categories, rather than from the political economy of Australian society itself. As far as the aged are concerned, this is a familiar argument. The aged are 'different', with 'special' problems: if they are poor, it is because they are old.

In effect, the Report presents a classless view of old-age poverty. It treats the aged as a more or less homogeneous category. The exceptional aged who are not poor include 'those who have speculated sucessfully in real estate...' (Henderson, 1975: 235). Inflation however is seen as a threat to 'those who have prudently put their cents aside...' (ibid.). In other words, it would appear that the non-poor aged are astute *individuals*, rather than members of a category of persons similarly located in the stratification system. Such an orientation obscures the fact that the poor aged are those dependent on pensions, and that such dependence is largely determined by past participation in the workforce.

In a similar vein, the Report's stress on home ownership as an alleviating factor in old age ignores class differentials. Eighty per cent of high-income earners but only 55 per cent of low-income earners are home owners (Kemeny, 1977: 50). As Kemeny (1977: 51) points out, home ownership in Australia acts:

> as something of a substitute for low old-age pensions...the principle involved [is] of minimising welfare provision and encouraging individuals to cope with old-age poverty with minimal assistance from the state. As with all such policies, however, it is those in the higher socio-economic groups who are best able to cope and who benefit most.

In line with the ideology espoused in the Report of the Committee on Care of the Aged and Infirm (Holmes, 1977), Henderson affirms the undesirability óf dependence on government and the 'natural' responsibility of the primary group. Thus the 'special' needs of the elderly are deemed to be most appropriately served by supporting their personal networks. This is to be achieved by the expansion and coordination of domiciliary and other services.

Apart from the obvious fact that the resources of an individual's personal network reflect class differences, there are socio-emotional factors to be considered in the dependence of an aged person on his or her family and friends. In general, actual income has been found to be a poor predictor of either social involvement or life satisfaction.[9] Nor is an objectively low income necessarily felt to be inadequate by the individual.[10]

There does appear, however, to be a strong association between finding income inadequate and living with relatives, especially for the non-married (Robb and Rivett, 1964: 37; Hutchinson, 1954: 71). Hutchinson in fact suggests from his data that 'some pensioners who find their income too small are forced to live, if they can, with married children. The pension, in fact, is thought inadequate because it is insufficient for them to live on alone.'

Work

Bureaucratization of employment conditions, technological obsolescence, and declining aggregate labour demand do not affect all older workers equally. The self employed are not subjected to bureaucratic regulation of retirement ages, thus middle and upper middle class businessmen and professionals are free to remain in the workforce on their own terms. Similarly, aggregate employment has fallen most sharply in manufacturing and other industries where unskilled and semi-skilled jobs have traditionally clustered. White collar occupations, by contrast, have increased and these workers are supported in their retirement by income from superannuation.

Work, as an objective criterion of integration, is believed to have a positive association with other integrative factors, notably income and social contact, and with life satisfaction — in so far as the aged person who works 'is rendering a service to which the community attaches a value... [and] is "making a contribution"' (Robb and Rivett, 1964: 23). There is a close association between paid employment and income, but the association between employment and other criteria of integration is less clear cut. Among the significant findings:

1. The meaning/value component in work is slight for the majority of aged persons. Working through preference rather than from economic necessity is associated with type of employment namely, with autonomous work.[11]

2. Compulsory retirement is a factor in only a minority of decisions to stop work. Many leave before the 'official' retiring ages, primarily as a result of illness and accidents or simply because they wanted to.[12]

3. Even among those who feel their income to be inadequate, few are actively seeking work or would take it up if they had the opportunity.[13] It may be, Hutchinson (1954: 73) concludes, 'that the large reservoir of potential workers in this age group is to some extent imaginary. The fixed retirement age was definitely welcome to more than half of the minority who worked on this understanding.'

4. Dissatisfaction with retirement is the exception rather than the rule.[14]

These findings reflect more widespread class differentials. Job satisfaction has been shown to be highest for men in professional and managerial jobs, and lowest among the unskilled (Health Commission of NSW 1979: 5).

Health

As with the issue of aged poverty, the health problems of the elderly are perceived as deriving from their unique and biologically inherent disadvantages. Since health care for aged pensioners is 'free', there is little attention to internal differentiation among the elderly population in terms of access to or quality of care in health services and facilities. Instead, policy emphasis is placed on reducing the cost to the community of maintaining the burden of aged sickness and disability.

In line with the prevailing construction of reality about the inherent degeneration of aging, discussions of the health status of the aged focus on the high incidence of chronic diseases among them. The implication is that old age is equivalent to infirmity and dependence.

Yet the majority of aged persons report their own health as good to excellent, often despite the presence of a chronic disorder. Although older people see physicians more often and use hospitals more frequently than other age groups, American data (Estes, 1979: 100-101) indicate that:

1. Over 80 per cent do *not* use hospitals in a given year.

2. Thirteen per cent report no physician consultations in the same period.

3. The presence of a chronic disease does not always lead to medical care utilization. For example, only 43 per cent of arthritis sufferers report a medical consultation during the year.

In other words, equating old age with illness or infirmity obscures the considerable variability within the aged population and suggests the existence of a widespread and 'special' problem. Yet, as Jones (1979: 163) points out, a high proportion of the Australian population uses medical services: 'The ill cover a wide range of age groups and are not the young and the old exclusively'.

There is also evidence of considerable social class differences in mortality and morbidity among Australian adults, with lower status groups faring less favourably (Taylor, 1979). American data suggest that the experience of ill health in old age is not distributed randomly across the social strata: the poor aged have 46.6 days of limited activity per year, compared to 31.2 days for the non-poor aged (Estes, 1979: 100). In America, Hammerman (1978) has demonstrated that the elderly poor make less use of health services than the non-poor.

In determing integration through quantifiable criteria a strong relationship between 'objective' physical disabilities on the one hand and actual behaviour and life attitudes on the other is predicted. Most studies find fairly similar distributions of physical disabilities among aged Australians. Certain types of disability — those which restrict mobility — affect some kinds of social activity.[15] It seems, however, that the elderly may often be quite sucessful in compensating for such physical disabilities, and that actual behaviour may not always correlate closely with 'objective' assessments.[16]

Considerable overseas evidence attests to the absence of close correlation between aged people's attitudes to their health status and their actual physical disabilities. Their principal consideration is the ability to function more or less autonomously; it is only when independence of action is grossly impaired by illness that elderly people will report themselves as seriously limited in this respect (Rosow, 1967).

When autonomy is restricted, subjective well being is negatively affected. Hutchinson found:

> that elderly people who were unwell during the four weeks preceding the day of their being interviewed were three times as likely to complain of loneliness as those who were in good health during the same period. Similarly,people who are (on self report) physically restricted in their movements, through arthritis or some similar disorder, are more liable to loneliness. (1954: 77–78)

In other words, subjective life satisfaction is more closely related to *autonomy* than to 'objective' health status.

Family Relationships

Important class-based differences in patterns of family contact have been reported. Upper middle status families studied by Martin (1967, 1970) appear to be least involved and working class families most involved in kin ties. In addition, the latter have more kin living in close proximity, often within walking distance, while the middle class families in Martin's study tended to rely for contact on the telephone and the car rather than on 'dropping in'. There is also evidence that upward mobility reduces the amount and intensity of kinship contact (Encel, 1970: 273–4).

The subjective dimension of family activity has been minimally explored in the Australian literature. Some indirect evidence suggests that aged people may perceive their situation quite differently from other family members. A study of requests made to the NSW Council on the Aging found that the majority of calls (58 per cent) came from a relative of the aged person. The elderly people themselves presented 23 per cent of the cases.[17] Aged persons were more than twice as likely as were relatives to seek help about changing their present accommodation. Relatives on the other hand were almost three times as likely to seek domiciliary assistance and four times as likely to perceive a medical problem, compared to the aged themselves.

Other sketchy findings support more extensive overseas documentation of the absence of a close association between frequency of contact with kin and subjective well being. In Australia, as elsewhere, expressed life satisfaction is most strongly correlated with marital status: bereavement, rather than simply being alone, is the principal factor associated with feelings of loneliness (Townsend, 1968).[18]

Most researchers report that a strongly held norm of autonomy characterizes relationships between separate households. Martin's respondents 'were adamant that relatives must not be allowed to run one's life' (1970: 313). Fallding in fact suggests that the provision of various services to aged relatives reinforces the underlying norm of generational independence:

> It was generally considered better for relatives not to become over-dependent on one another for material support, and better to help maintain aged parents in their own separate dwellings, if they needed such help, than to take them into their own home ... Thus efforts were made to keep the immediate family group as free as possible from the interfering control of relatives. On the other hand, as relatives' willingness to help largely depended on a family's having their favourable opinion, a degree of control was inescapable (1957: 59).

Another recurring theme is the voluntary character of kin ties. Martin notes that people were 'highly selective in their interaction with kindred, near and remote' (1970: 313). Oeser and Hammond reiterate this view, pointing out that 'the close blood relations form the central core of [the] friendship group, but even among them one chooses "close" relations' (1954: 23). Little is known, however, of the dynamics of family caring relationships or the variables involved in decisions to undertake home support or seek alternatives such as institutionalisation.

However, a Sydney survey found that the necessity for sharing facilities provided a strong incentive to move, on the part of an old person, particularly when a kitchen had to be shared.[19] This incentive existed even when sharing was with relatives.[20] Contrary to conventional expectations, cohabitation with or proximity to children and/or grandchildren was not defined by many as a desirable arrangement.[21]

Summary

Aged Australians do not constitute a homogeneous socio-economic group. Unfortuntely, detailed information on the major socio-economic divisions is not available. However, Wydell (1975) has roughly delineated three major income strata among the half million aged persons in New South Wales in 1971.

1. A lower stratum of approximately 100 000 persons having no property and relying solely on a pension for income.

2. A middle stratum of approximately 300 000 persons who have some capital assets and a pension and/or earned income.

3. An upper stratum of approximately 100 000 persons of considerable private means.

Wild (1977, 1978: 161–2) suggests that these income strata have the following social characteristics:

1. The lower stratum, of whom at least half can be classified as very poor and most of the remainder as rather poor, have a common background of unskilled occupations and low levels of education. They 'are not poor just because they are old', Wild (1978: 161) writes, 'rather their social situation, which was probably precarious in the first place, is made worse because they are old, cannot work, are infirm, or lack resources'.

2. The middle stratum 'have skilled manual or non-manual occupational backgrounds and actively participate in such voluntary associations as Senior Citizens Centres, bowling clubs and the churches' (1978: 162).

3. The upper stratum come from professional or business backgrounds. They do not participate in age-graded organizations, but in age-heterogeneous clubs to which they have always belonged and which tend to segregrate on the basis of income and status characteristics.

This typification of the socio-economic divisions among the aged Australian population is an important corrective to the classless view, though it is somewhat misleading. In the first place, the distribution of voluntary association memberships is erroneous, a point I take up in a later chapter. Second, although the majority of lower income aged come from lower stratum occupational backgrounds, other forms of structural inequality such as gender also influence the longitudinal pattern. Many of the elderly unmarried and widowed upper status females in my sample had suffered severely reduced circumstances in their old age, and in terms of income alone, would belong to the lower stratum.[22]

Depicting the aged as a homogeneous 'disability group' lends support to uniform policies which ignore significant differences within the aged category. Partly as a result, all older people are coloured with the same stigmatized brush as being dependent, frail and in need of special help and services. Overall, as I show in Chapter 5, institutional arrangements based on this premise act less to benefit the aged than to maintain and expand the interests of certain dominant groups.

Inadequacy of 'Objective' Criteria

In summarizing these data, emphasis also needs to be placed on the extent to which an operational definition of integration in 'objective' terms — health, income, work and social contacts — helps us to make sense of empirical reality. Of particular importance is the extent to which these criteria subsume the subjective dimension of life satisfaction. Without such a correlation, we have a hollow representation of reality.

The association between conventional indicators of integration and subjective well being is difficult to specify. The paucity of data presents an immediate problem. Further, the data we do have may not be comparable. Hutchinson, for example, asked his informants if they were lonely; Robb and Rivett enquired of the old people in Marrickville if they were satisfied with life. Thus they may not be measuring the same phenomenon. Four times as many Victorian women as men complained of loneliness (Hutchinson, 1954: 77). By contrast, Robb and Rivett (1964: 11) found no difference between the sexes in numbers who were satisfied with life. Hutchinson (1954: 77) reports that 'the poorest people are the most, and the richest the least, frequently without companionship' and that old age pensioners are more liable to complain of loneliness than are others of the same age. Robb and Rivett (1964: 85) report that 'old people receiving only the pension are more likely than others to declare themselves dissatisfied with life, the correlation being significant'. However, there are no significant differences between the proportions of 'satisfied' persons among pensioners who get only the pension, those who get other income also, and non-pensioners.

Any relationship which may exist between 'objective' indicators (such as health, socio-economic status and social contacts) and subjective experience is at best an extremely complex one which simple correlational analysis cannot measure in any meaningful way. There seems to be a cluster of interrelated subjective factors which is more closely associated with feelings of well being than is the cluster of objective dimensions: it is not so much the 'objective' factors which seem to be important, but rather the individual's *perception* of these factors as being satisfactory or unsatisfactory. Moreover, the degree of satisfaction appears to be particularly defined by older persons in terms of autonomy. Thus it is not only people's definitions of their situations which constitute meaningful components of integration, but also the extent to which they feel they are in *control* of these definitions. This issue is taken up in more detail in Chapter 3.

What this chapter seeks to demonstrate is that biological factors do not explain the problematic status of the aged. The focus has been on the ways in which beliefs, attitudes and values about aging are socially constructed. I have attempted to document the 'social distribution of knowledge' about old people and its manifestation in patterns of social stratification. In the following chapter I begin to consider how this social knowledge influences elderly people's behaviour.

Notes

1. By comparison, the aged in England and Wales had already reached 14.2 per cent of the population by the mid-1970s; in Sweden 15.1 per cent and in East Germany 16.3 per cent (Borrie, 1978: 7).
2. Hutchinson's figures on informal social contact do not differentiate between contact with kin and with non-relatives. Just under three-quarters of his informants had received 'a friendly visit' during the seven days preceding the interview (1954: 79). This figure applies to both casual and regular visitors. Only half had paid a visit in the preceding seven days (1954: 80). Similar proportions are reported for Marrickville (Robb and Rivett, 1964: 9). Almost 80 per cent of subjects in a Mount Gambier, S.A., survey had one or more living children. Of those, three-quarters had at least one of these children living within five miles. Of these, 81.3 per cent (63.8 per cent of all) were 'in touch' at least once a week and a further 6.6 per cent (5 per cent of all) at least once a month. Of the total sample, 38.4 per cent had a close relative 'less than 10 miles away and available if necessary', and 10.1 per cent had a close relative 'less than 10 miles away and helps me' (Radford and Peever, 1976: 77). Unfortunately in other data on visiting and help patterns, no distinction was made between family and friends. Only 65.5 per cent claimed to visit 'friends and relatives' at least once a week, and 62.9 per cent are visited at least once a week (Radford and Peever, 1976: 82). About 3 people in 10 received assistance with various household tasks from 'family and friends' (Radford and Peever, 1976: 83). In the Sydney accommodation survey (Sorrell, 1972), 37 per cent of the group interviewed had no living children nearby. The remainder were 'reasonably accessible' to their children: 71 per cent had other relatives living nearby and 80 per cent had friends within visiting

distance. About three-quarters of the group exchanged visits with relatives; 1 in 10 reported no visiting with relatives. More than one-quarter (28 per cent) of the households were described as 'extended families'. Of these, about 4 in 10 lived with children; 3 in 10 had grandchildren in the home.

3. Fallding (1957: 59) reports from a study of 38 urban families: 'A number of parents gave a considerable amount of time to household cleaning or household repairs for their aged parents, to securing medical attention for them, conducting their business affairs, or providing them with opportunities for recreation, or means of transport....' In Kew, Victoria, 22.9 per cent of aged persons living alone obtained help with household management from a family member or relative. A slightly higher proportion in this upper middle class area (25.7 per cent), however, obtained paid help (cited in Robb and Rivett, 1964). Sorrell's (1972) study found that in 29 per cent of households no outside help with daily duties was received but in 33 per cent assistance came from relatives, in 11 per cent from friends and neighbours, and in 38 per cent from paid help. A proportion of widows in Marrickville report that they receive gifts of money (6.7 per cent), of clothes (7.4 per cent), or of food (4.4 per cent) from relatives (Robb and Rivett, 1964: 31).

4. See for example Barker (1971), Bolder (1971), Cove (1973), de Brito (1971), Frizell (1969; 1971), Forbes (1973), Hailstone and Guerin (1973), Horin (1975), McIlwraith (1972), Martin (1971), Moffit (1970), Richardson (1971), Samuel (1974), Silcock (1971), Smith, M. (1975), Smith, V. (1971), Summers (1976), Yeomans (1976), *Canberra Times* (Jan 8 1972; p.2).

5. One popular book dealing with the misconceptions in attitudes toward old age is Alex Comfort's *A Good Age* (1977). It was prominently reviewed in the *Sun-Herald Magazine* (July 31 1977), alongside photographs of Charles de Gaulle, Helena Rubinstein, and George Bernard Shaw in their later years.

6. The qualifications (if any) of the interviewers to make such assessments are not specified.

7. See discussion in Swain and Harrison (1979).

8. For a full discussion of this issue see Dixon (1977).

9. Hutchinson, for example, found that the lower the actual income, the less likely were people tó *receive* visits, but that 'the well-to -do *pay* visits only slightly more often than the very poor' (1954: 80).

10. Attitudes of the elderly towards their income suggest that about one in five find it inadequate (Robb and Rivett, 1964: 36), a figure which may rise to one in three among pensioners (Hutchinson, 1954: 70). In Mount Gambier, only five per cent claimed they were 'unable to manage' on present income (Radford and Peever, 1976: 69).

11. Very few of the aged in the Victorian survey who were in the workforce had taken or remained in employment 'because they prefer to work than be idle' (Hutchinson, 1954: 67). Nine out of 10 worked solely or primarily because of economic necessity. Hutchinson (1954: 67) found: 'Roughly half the people who said that they "just preferred" to continue working

came from among company directors, owners of businesses, and the higher managerial grades, and, on a lower economic level, the small shop-keepers. In addition, the farmers and the agricultural workers showed a greater tendency to stay on at work merely because of personal preference.'

12. Hutchinson (1954: 65), Robb and Rivett (1964: 22). As causes of retire-ment, illness and accidents were found in Marrickville to be more impor-tant than all other causes put together (Robb and Rivett, 1964: 28); one in eight simply wanted to stop (1964: 22).

13. Hutchinson found that of those who expressed a desire for employment the vast majority did so through economic incentive: 'those who would take a job for the pleasure of being occupied and taking a part in the work of the community are in a minority' (1954: 72). Even among those who found their income inadequate, about 80 per cent would not take up full or part-time work if they had the opportunity. Similarly, in Robb and Rivett's survey, only one man was seeking full-time work and two part-time work; no woman sought paid employment of any kind (1964: 28). Further, Hutchinson points out 'that the proportion of the unemployed people who had actually sought other work since retirement was very small — by no means all of those who expressed a desire for employment had taken any steps to find it for themselves' (1954: 73).

14. Robb and Rivett also asked their respondents for their attitudes toward retirement. Fully three-quarters of the retired said they were satisfied with retirement (1964: 28). Of those who were dissatisfied, nine said they miss-ed work, three mentioned loss of income, and one missed friends at work. In a Western Australian survey cited by Robb and Rivett the majority of urban pensioners (85 per cent of men and 82 per cent of women) said they were 'happy in their retirement'. Among all non-pensioners, 95 per cent of the men who were not working full or part-time and 68 per cent of the women stated that they were happy in their retirement.

15. Restrictions on movement and impairment of vision in particular have been found to affect rates of visiting, the receipt of visits and incidental conversations (Robb and Rivett, 1964: 65–66).

16. For example, in Sorrell's study, fully 87 per cent of the old people rated 'completely independent' on a scale of 'ability to manage', despite the prevalence of physical handicaps in the sample. The researchers also found that 'the old person's own assessment of his or her health proved a better indicator than the interviewer's assessment' (1972: 16).

17. Other referred sources included friends (7 per cent), doctors (0.7 per cent), social workers (8 per cent), and others (2.8 per cent).

18. One in 4 of the divorced, nearly 1 in 5 of the widowed, but only 1 in 16 of married elderly Victorians said they were lonely (Hutchinson, 1954: 77). Robb and Rivett correlated expressed satisfaction with household com-position, and analyse the results as follows: 'There is a highly significant correlation between living alone or with non-relatives, on one hand, and alleging dissatisfaction on the other. The link is so strong as to suggest a casual connection, even though being dissatisfied and living alone or with non-relatives are both correlated with other conditions besides isolation'

(1964: 11-12). However the existence of statistically significant differences needs to be interpreted with caution. Robb and Rivett's data show that of all persons living alone almost five times as many are satisfied as are dissatisfied. In fact, the proportion living alone and dissatisfied almost exactly equals the proportion living with spouse and a child and dissatisfied. This simply highlights the inadequacy of survey data for the interpretation of meaning.

19. None of the 11 people who shared accommodation in private houses, lived in tenements, or in a caravan or a tent was opposed to moving. Similarly, 27 per cent of those who had sole use or minimal sharing were opposed to moving as against 9 per cent of those who shared with two or more persons (Sorrell, 1972: 27).

20. Twenty-nine per cent of the sample lived with their families. Of these, only 10 per cent were opposed to moving, as against 27 per cent of those who had no family. 'This inclination to move on the part of those living with their families', the study notes, 'appeared to be related to personality conflicts or conditions of living such as overcrowding' (Sorrell, 1972: 28).

21. The researcher finds it 'worth recording that all of those living with their families who were actively and without qualification looking forward to moving were living in homes where there were children' (Sorrell, 1972: 28). Proximity of friends and positive attitudes towards neighbours were associated with reluctance to move, though proximity of children and relatives was not.

22. In sociological terms, the distinction between deprivation relative to one's earlier circumstances and a lifelong history of poverty is significant (Runciman, 1971), not least in terms of the effects on subjective attitudes and outlook.

3 Old Age as a Sociological Problem

The previous chapter outlines the ways in which the dominant Australian culture sees old age as a social problem. In line with this view, Australian gerontological surveys have focused on a predictable inventory of old age problems: health, income, employment, housing and other measures of standard of living, and social contact, particularly with family members.

Most of the data in gerontology have in fact been collected through welfare oriented social surveys. For all practical purposes, Bromley (1974: 65) has suggested, the history of social gerontology *is* the history of social welfare: it was 'merely one facet of the wider concern that social scientists and political reformers had for disadvantaged sections of the community, particularly the very poor'.[1] Johnson (1978) has delineated five general categories of data-based studies within this dominant empirical tradition.

Studies of social and physical morbidity

These epidemiological studies seek to determine the extent of social and physical disabilities among the aged population. They classify, according to pre-set standards, those in need of various forms of assistance. In Australia, the most comprehensive survey of this kind has been made in connection with poverty (Henderson, 1975).

Quality of life studies

These are concerned with various material aspects of old people's environment, including income, access to public facilities, ownership of major home appliances, and the like. In this context, by far the greatest amount of attention has been directed towards accommodation. In Australia, the bulk of these kinds of data have been collected through small-scale localised surveys (see e.g. Robb and Rivett, 1964; Dewdney and Collings, 1965; Stephenson, 1971; Radford and Peever, 1976). There is in addition a relatively voluminous literature on special accommodation for the aged: sheltered housing, retirement villages, nursing homes, and so on.[2] The authors of these studies here, as overseas, 'have tended towards a predictable inventory of the characteristics which are either explicitly or implicitly deemed desirable or undesirable'(Johnson, 1978: 101-2).

Personal relations

This category subsumes a great part of overseas sociological survey research. Family relations have received the most attention, followed by friendship and neighbourhood networks and voluntary associations. Information on the personal relations of older Australians, on the other hand , has largely to be gleaned from surveys with a dominant focus on material factors or from serendipitous information contained in more broadly based sociological enquiries.[3]

Social welfare services

Studies of this type are more narrowly focused than are epidemiological research; they endeavour to locate old people 'in need' of particular services such as Meals on Wheels, home nursing, and so on and/or to evaluate the efficiency of existing services. Some surveys commissioned by the Australian poverty inquiry have this emphasis (e.g. Sach, 1975; Douglas, 1977). Butterworth (1973) has examined inappropriate placement in private nursing homes.

Work and retirement

Though this area has been a principal focus of overseas research, it has received little direct research attention in Australia. The local surveys cited above include some data, such as reasons for retirement, nature of past and present employment, and the like.

Australian research has been almost entirely of the quality of life or social welfare variety, with both concerns frequently evident in a single survey. It has tended to be a-theoretical and heavily value-laden. The 'needs' and 'problems' or older people have been determined according to pre-set 'objective' criteria of what constitutes acceptable housing, satisfactory health, desirable amounts of social contact, and so on. Little attention, and less credence, is given to the older person's *self-assessment* of need. Yet I have presented evidence that professional judgements frequently differ from old people's estimates, not only in relation to what kind of house they should be living in but also in other areas such as health status. One important result of this discrepancy has been the implementation of ill-conceived policies. The community has witnessed, for example, the proliferation of special clubrooms with 'suitable' activities for senior citizens — from which the elderly stay away, in droves.

A major reason for the uncertain value and lack of explanatory power of extant empirical research is the absence of any coherent conceptual framework. There has been very little attempt at theory construction in Australian gerontology. Like their British counterparts (see e.g. Townsend, 1963; Brockington and Lempert, 1966; Carver and Liddiard, 1978), Australian researchers have tended towards *ad hoc* empiricism with an explicit welfare orientation. There has been little quest for sociological relevance. Concepts such as class, kinship and so on have been used, but they have been employed essentially as tools with which to analyze problems and issues thrown up by policy and welfare considerations. American studies on the other hand have been more theoretically oriented. In the United States, major research projects have been conducted in multidisciplinary settings, with psychology the dominant influence.

The principal sociological variable employed in this tradition is the concept of social integration. This construct, ill defined but generally glossed as 'social involvement', 'social contact', or 'social activity', is the basis of the largest survey ever conducted of old people (Shanas *et al.*,1968). The opposite of integration, conceptualized as isolation or segregation, is described in that survey as both the major social problem confronting the aged and the theoretical pivot of research.

The psychological counterpart of integration is adjustment (or 'adaptation', 'morale', or 'mental health'). Attempts to conceptualise the relationship between these two variables lie at the heart of theory construction in the socio-psychological tradition of research on the aged.

Four major social theories of aging have emerged: disengagement theory, activity theory, personality or developmental theory, and symbolic interactionism. Several detailed summaries of the aetiology and development of the major gerontological theories are available (see e.g. Maddox and Wiley, 1976; Hendricks and Hendricks, 1977). This review does not attempt to replicate their thoroughness, but concentrates on those themes and issues of direct relevance to the design and findings of the present enquiry.

Disengagement Theory

The theory of disengagement (Cumming and Henry, 1961) begins from the functionalist premise that society and the individual always seek to maintain themselves in equilibrium and to avoid disruption, and it interprets the progressive loss with age of social roles and relationships as a functional necessity. The theory states 'that the society and the individual prepare in advance for the ultimate "disengagement" of incurable, incapacitating disease and death by an inevitable, gradual and mutually satisfying process of disengagement from society' (Rose, 1968: 185). In other words, a death which has been sociologically and psychologically prepared for is not disruptive of the social equilibrium (whereas the unexpected death of a young person is disruptive). In this view, the integration of the system is seen to be achieved by the withdrawal of elderly people from social roles. The elderly individual also benefits since, by limiting his or her contacts and by lowering commitment to social norms and values, he or she is helped to prepare for death. In the disengagement framework, then, 'successful' aging requires reduced activity and a decrease in affective involvement.

Activity Theory

Opposition to disengagement theory is systematised in the antithetical activity perspective (Havighurst, 1963). Activity theory assumes that a 'successful' old age will be one in which the individual actively engages in forms of behaviour which compensate for his or her lost roles. The central proposition of activity theory, as summarised by Blau (1973) is: 'the greater the number of optional role resources with which the individual enters old age, the better he or she will withstand the demoralizing effects of exit from the obligatory roles ordinarily given priority in adulthood'.

In this view, high morale and life satisfaction are assumed to be correlated with social integration, conceptualised as a fairly high level of involvement in social networks.

Personality Theory

A third theory denies the necessity for any sociologically-oriented explanation of successful aging. Instead, adjustment to old age is seen as the result of individual personality.[4] This life cycle approach conceptualises aging as a developmental process, the outcome of which reflects individual coping styles. Neugarten and her associates (1968: 176-77) maintain, for example:

> People, as they grow old, seem to be neither at the mercy of the social environment nor at the mercy of some set of intrinsic processes — in either instance, inexorable changes that they cannot influence. On the contrary, the individual seems to continue to make his own 'impress' upon the wide range of social and biological changes. He continues to exercise choice and to select from the environment in accordance with his own long-established needs. He ages according to a pattern that has a long history and that maintains itself, with adaptation, to the end of life.

These authors describe four major personality types' of which the 'integrated' personalities are those: 'well-functioning persons who have a complex inner life and at the same time, intact cognitive abilities and competent egos. These persons are acceptant of impulse life, over which they maintain a comfortable degree of control; they are flexible, open to new stimuli, mellow, mature.'

By contrast the 'unintegrated' personalities 'were persons who had gross defects in psychological functions, loss of control over emotions and deterioration in thought processes' (Neugarten *et al.*, 1968: 175-76). According to this theory, the 'integrated' personalities are not necessarily integrated sociologically, in the sense of maintaining social roles and relationships: they may or may not be. They are, however, high in what the authors describe as 'life satisfaction'. Personality itself, and not level of social interaction, is seen as the critical independent variable, 'as the pivotal dimension in describing patterns of aging and in predicting relationships between level of social role activity and life satisfaction' (Neugarten *et al.*, 1968: 177).

Symbolic Interactionism

Proponents of a symbolic interactionist view assert that aging outcomes reflect the reciprocal relationship between the individual and his or her social environment. Aging is conceptualised as a dynamic process which is responsive both to structural and normative contexts and to individual capacities and perceptions.

Society is seen to exist 'as both objective and subjective reality... the individual member of society... simultaneously externalises his own being into the social world and internalises it as an objective reality' (Berger and Luckman, 1967: 149). Symbolic interaction theory 'does not identify particular behaviour, activity patterns, or experiences with old age but rather emphasises the social construction of these in light of interpreted and negotiated interactional encounters' (Estes, 1979: 9). In the social environmental model put forward by Gubrium (1973), for example, life satisfaction is seen to be maximised when there is congruence between normative expectations, individual resources, and subjectively assessed correspondence between these two factors.

Disengagement theory has fallen victim to theoretical and empirical challenges. Critics point to considerable evidence that a disengaged lifestyle is not the only, or even the most common means of adjusting to old age, and argue that the original authors have mistakenly described a socially constructed process as an inherent and inevitable one (see e.g. Hochschild, 1976b).

Activity theory has similarly proved to offer a poor interpretation of the facts. Both disengaged and active lifestyles, it seems, can produce satisfaction in old age, as can a variety of alternatives (Fontana, 1977). In addition to its failure to rally consistent empirical support, activity theory has also been criticised on theoretical grounds. Not all activities provide equal support for a positive self-conception. Nor does the perspective take into account the potentially differential effects on well being of the degree of control which the individual can exert over participation in various interaction contexts (Gubrium, 1973; Hendricks & Hendricks, 1977: 111).

A further criticism can be levelled at both disengagement and activity perspectives. Each is based on an implicit, empirically unwarranted value judgement. Activity theory presumes that:

> at least in modern Western societies, it is better to be active than inactive; to maintain the patterns characteristic of middle age rather than to move to new patterns of old age. In (disengagement) theory, it is presumably better to be in a state of equilibrium than in a state of disequilibrium; and better to acquiesce in what is a 'natural', not an imposed, process of change. (Havighurst, *el al.* 1968, 161).

No wholly adequate personality perspective emerges from empirical testing. Fontana (1977), for example, has shown that personal coping styles in old age may be characterized either by continuity or discontinuity from earlier patterns. There can be little doubt that personality is an important variable in adjusting to old age, but psychologists have increasingly recognised the limitations in explaining behaviour solely in terms of psychological characteristics to the neglect of structural constraints and situational contexts (Maddox and Wiley, 1976: 17).

One attempt to incorporate a dynamic conception of personality within a cultural context has been made by a cultural anthropologist, Margaret Clark (1968). Clark takes as the operational link between culture and personality the set of value orientations[6] which underlie the criteria used by older people as bases for self-esteem. Her analysis is based on a research sample of old people in San Francisco, half of whom had in the past been institutionalised for psychiatric disorder for the first time after the age of 60. The remainder had never been treated for mental or emotional problems. Analysis yielded six criteria of self-esteem in decreasing order of importance: independence, social acceptability, adequacy of personal resources, ability to cope with external threats or losses, having significant goals or meaning in later life, and ability to cope with changes in the self.

However, there were significant differences between the community and hospitalised subjects in the underlying value orientations of each category. For example, concerning independence: 'The community aged want to be independent to avoid inconveniencing others. Among the mentally ill, a fear and mistrust of others makes the goal of independence a defence against malevolence or neglect' (Clark, 1968: 439).

Similarly, the means for achieving social acceptability are seen by the community subjects as 'being congenial, as attractive as possible, pleasant, easy to get along with, and supportive of others', but by the mentally ill as deriving from 'status, wealth, power, or recognition for some talent, special ability, or other outstanding trait; they must command respect from a position of strength'.

Clark observes, 'the value orientations which are associated with the maladapted aged in this sample are strikingly similar to values found by a number of observers to be characteristic of American culture generally' (1968: 440). She concludes:

> patterns of value appropriate to the middle aged in our society are deemed inappropriate (or prove dysfunctional) for the elderly... [and] the accession to the status of old age in American society represents a dramatic cultural discontinuity, in that some of the most basic orientations — those relating to time perspective, competitiveness and cooperation, aggression and passivity, doing and being — must be changed at that stage of the life cycle if adaptation is to occur (1968: 441).

Clark's analysis offers an important corrective to the personality-minus-social context approach. Yet it is incomplete since it fails to specify the conditions under which an 'adapted' or a 'maladapted' response will be made beyond noting that hospitalized subjects had fewer social relationships which is a gesture towards the activity view.

A consensus appears to be emerging among both psychologically- and sociologically-oriented researchers that some kind of contextual approach is needed if a satisfactory interpretation of the variability in aging outcomes is to be achieved (see e.g. Maddox and Wiley, 1976: 17; Hendricks & Hendricks, 1977: 177; Fontana, 1977; Johnson, 1978). Symbolic interactionism, with its emphasis on the meanings which social actors attach to their behaviour and experience, is both theoretically and demonstrably (cf. Fontana, 1977; Gubrium, 1973; Trela, 1971) appropriate to this task.

Opponents of interactionist approaches to the study of social processes and problems traditionally argue that they ignore the issue of power and interest, and minimise the role of structural factors, such as class, in constraining interactional options (see e.g. Gouldner, 1968; Taylor, Walton and Young, 1973; Meltzer *et al.*, 1975). Others (Pearson, 1975; Estes, 1979: 11) counter-argue that such neglect is not *inherent* in symbolic interactionism.

In the following section I compare the symbolic interactionist approach with conventional research strategies in the social psychology tradition. I argue that the only meaningful sociological view of old people is as social actors in the full sense of the term, that is, as persons with unique biographies and diverse resources and needs, who actively participate in the construction of their social reality and make decisions on the basis of personally held meanings. In this process all aged people share a common socio-cultural experience: they are objectively defined as 'old', and that status is loaded with negative stereotypes. At the same time, aged persons are differentially located in the social structure, and hence have differential access to resources and power. However — and this is a crucial point — the consequences of structural constraints on experience and behaviour are not 'given' or predetermined. As Pearson (1975: 115) remarks, structural analysts frequently:

> forget that men also have a psychology, motives and impulses, and (a neo-Marxist) theoretical critique (of interactionist sociology) thus unwittingly perpetuates what the resurrected voice of the deviant imagination had cried out against: the petrification of the human subject, both in theory and in social practice.

I do not believe that the problems of older people in our society can be explained in simplistic, economic determinist terms. Although the political economy perspective I sketched in the previous chapter is an important and necessary corrective to the 'aged as disability group' paradigm, it is not the end but only the beginning of analysis. As Altman (1979: 85-5) suggests: 'While it is easy to demonstrate that there are major gaps to affluence in Australia, it is also clear that this is not the real basis of our discontent. In modern Western societies . . . there is a high degree of misery that does not have simple economic roots.'

Integration: a concept in research of a referent

In social psychology, the most extensively developed research tradition in American gerontology, the key sociological variable is the concept of integration. Most measures of integration are based on frequency of social contacts; thus the opposite of the integrated old person is the isolated old person.[7] In other words, integration appears to be equivalent to 'participation in social life' or, more specifically, to the maintenance of social contacts within an institutionalised framework of social positions or roles. These roles may exist in either formal (secondary) or informal (primary) social structures, though in some cases (such as a work role) both aspects may be involved, as when one's workmates are also one's friends.

It is, of course, possible to make structural statements about the elderly in terms of their participation in the institutions of society. To use a term such as integration is, however, to imply something more about the nature of that participation. It is to make the assumption that such participation is somehow 'good for' the individual, and its absence 'bad for' the individual; or in psychological terms, that social involvement predicts 'adjustment', 'morale', and the like.

Here attention is seemingly given to the subjective experience of aging. However, concepts like 'adjustment' are value laden, using predetermined standards of desirable mental characteristics and lifestyles in later life as independent variables. Along with welfare research which relies on universalistic standards of 'needs', this approach equally 'denies the historical roots of personal "needs" and implies an unrealistic homogeneity . . .' (Johnson, 1978: 106).

Social psychological studies of aging and integration have been dominated by the issue of adjustment to age roles. These studies have largely been formulated within a theoretical framework ideally suited to the 'objective' treatment of social phenomena: the sociology of social systems and roles. The sociology of social systems is centrally concerned with the problem of social order. It is based on a conception of the social system as an ontological reality which is logically prior to individual actors. Essentially, 'the argument is that, since individuals cannot of their own volition create and maintain order, constraint is necessary for society to exist at all . . . Accordingly, society must define the social meanings, relationships and action of its members for them' (Dawe, 1971: 543).

In accounting for the subjective dimension of action, the concept of internalisation comes to be substituted for that of externality and the process is termed 'socialisation'. Thus the actor is seen to be 'on the receiving end of the system', and

> meaning can only be conceptualised by postulating social norms as being constitutive, rather than merely regulative, of the self. That is, the problem of order can only be solved by conceiving of the actor as a reflex of the social system and meaning as a reflex of the cultural system. Far from disappearing, constraint becomes total through internalisation (Dawe, 1971: 544).

This perspective has two consequences. First, it necessarily entails what Wrong (1961) has described as an 'oversocialised conception of man'. Second, if subjective meaning can be derived, through consensus, from a prior characterisation of the central value system, then it does not have to be treated as a significant variable. In the social system perspective, the crucial bridging concept between the social system and the individual is that of role.

Translated into gerontological sociology, the problem of order becomes the problem of integration. To the extent that the elderly life situation involves a loss of roles and an accompanying 'deviation' from core values associated with the various insititutional orders, old people are not integrated. The source of integration is thus located in the social system.

The task of research is to map the distribution of roles among old people in a particular historico-social system. Since the subjective meaning of role performance is already given by the central value system (for example in Western society 'worker' and 'grandmother' are good roles for the individual; 'non-worker' and 'spinster' are not), the total of 'valued' roles becomes a measure of integration.

The concept of role, in fact, accommodates much of gerontology's substantive concern. At the level of macrotheory, Riley, Johnson and Foner (1972: 20) have proposed a conceptual model of age stratification, based explicitly on the Parsonian tradition, which views age as 'a crucial factor in the role structure of a given society'. In this model age 'integrates those of similar age and complexes of roles that are otherwise differentiated' and segregates those of different ages by 'differentiating many of the roles they play'.

Others use the notion of social role as a conceptual framework to analyse the 'social life space' of a particular individual (Williams, 1960; Williams and Wirths, 1965; Williams and Loeb, 1968) or as a vehicle for examining the aging personality (Riegel, 1959). Whether the focus is on 'role involvements and role clusters' (Lopata, 1973), on the consequences of role change (Streib and Schneider, 1971), on the relationship between role and self-conception (Cavan, 1962), on the 'roleless role' of the retired (Burgess, 1960), on 'role exits' (Blau, 1973) or in developing an 'inclusive taxonomy' of role types (Rosow, 1976b), the concept of role is conceived of as an independent variable and as a specific structural element.

The extension of role theory into the study of adjustment during old age was probably inevitable, given gerontology's origin as the study of a social problem. As C. Wright Mills has suggested, the general model for the formulation of social problems was largely shaped by early American sociological notions used to state the 'immigrant problem'. Here the central focus was on problems of integration or adjustment between the immigrant and society, with the former, of course, needing to make the 'adjustment'. According to Mills (1959: 103), the type of person who is judged to be ideally 'adjusted' epitomises small town, middle class, Protestant — and, we can add, middle aged — America:

> The ideal man of the earlier generation of sociologists, and of the liberally practical in general, is 'socialised'. Often this means that he is the ethical opposite of 'selfish'. Being socialised, he thinks of others and is kindly towards them; he does not brood or mope; on the contrary, he is somewhat extrovert, eagerly 'participating' in the routines of his community, helping this community 'to progress' at a neatly adjustable rate. He is in and of and for quite a few community organisations. If not an outright 'joiner', he certainly does not get around a lot. Happily, he conforms to conventional morality and motives; happily, he participates in the gradual progress of respectable institutions.

The notion of the 'adjusted' older person is still largely infused with this doctrine.

Like the concept of role, the notion of adjustment is generally treated as an independent variable. Riegel (1959: 835), summarising the interpretation of adjustment within role psychology, notes that the individual's 'adjustment is dependent on the number of roles, especially standard roles, he knows how to enact. Thus a maladjusted older person may be characterised as one who did not acquire adequate roles for old age during the previous years.'

Kuhlen (1959: 852) suggests adjustment refers 'to the degree to which the organism is in a state of equilibrium not only within itself but also in its interaction with the environment. Since some states may be viewed as representing more or less optimal adjustment, a person may be ... described as being *well* adjusted or *poorly* adjusted.'

Analytically, adjustment may be viewed in terms of two frames of reference: social adjustment, or 'the adjustment of the individual as externally evaluated against formal or informal criteria set by others' (Kuhlen, 1959: 853), and personal adjustment, or the subjective view of the individual. The former framework subsumes the notion of integration as typically conceived, while the latter incorporates the concepts of morale or life satisfaction.

Not infrequently, adjustment is used interchangeably with terms like 'successful aging' (Williams and Wirths, 1965; Williams and Loeb, 1968). To add to the conceptual confusion, such terms are often used without clear distinction between the social and personal framework. Even where the distinction is made, however, the fundamental ambiguity of a concept like adjustment remains (c.f. Treanton, 1962). This becomes especially apparent in studies which attempt to specify the factors related to adjustment in later life, a major empirical preoccupation of social gerontology (Kuhlen, 1959). In this task, the problematic nature of the structural role/adjustment approach is highlighted.

Conceptual and Methodological Problems

Most studies in this area reflect the approach initiated by the Social Science Research Council's Committee on Social Adjustment in Old Age (Pollak, 1948). Several reviewers have noted its influence in focusing attention on social adjustment in old age as the most significant issue for social scientific research and in determining the form which such research should take (Maddox and Wiley, 1976; Riegel, 1959; Kuhlen, 1959). Separate reports dealt with various aspects of personal adjustment (Cavan *et al.*, 1949) and with the issue of older people's roles (Albrecht, 1951a, 1951b; Havighurst, 1952).

Much subsequent research has incorporated an adjustment scale entitled 'Your Activities and Attitudes' prepared by Burgess, Cavan and Havighurst (Cavan *et al.*, 1949). These authors conceptualised adjustment as being dependent on the number of roles enacted by the individual and on the social evaluation of these roles in public opinion. An estimate of personal adjustment was obtained by summing up individual scores of engagement in specific, socially approved activities. Detailed discussion of the results of this and subsequent research is beyond the scope of the present enquiry. However, the substantial criticisms which the instrument and its underlying assumptions have attracted illustrate the inadequacy of the entire role/adjustment orientation.

The Burgess-Cavan-Havighurst scale has been specifically criticised for its circularity (Kuhlen, 1959). The scale 'incorporates some of the variables with which it was to be correlated' (Robins, 1962: 466). Particularly important in this context is the inclusion of de facto measures of social participation in attitudinal scores, and the subsequent correlation of the scores with actual measures of participation (e.g. Pihlblad and McNamara, 1965).

One problem reflected here is the difficulty in separating the social and personal frameworks of adjustment in reality, if not in theory (Kuhlen, 1959). Even if this were possible, however, a more fundamental problem remains. As Treanton (1962) has pointed out, social roles, as defined and prescribed by the environment, do not necessarily affect *either* dimension. There is simply no consistent correlation between personal and social adjustment: 'it is conceivable and, in fact, not infrequently true that a person who is viewed *socially* as a failure or as maladjusted is *personally* quite adequately adjusted or that a person who is judged by others as extremely competent and successful may be an abject failure in his own eyes' (Kuhlen, 1959: 853).

When this problem is confronted in research, the resolution can sometimes only be described as nonsensical. In one study of 'successful aging', for example, the absence of a significant correlation between expressed feelings of life satisfaction and the author's construct of 'success' led to the conclusion that 'successful aging . . . is not always a source of satisfaction to the individual, and one can be successful though miserable' (Williams and Wirths, 1965: 213).

This kind of tortuous reasoning highlights another basic problem with the whole adjustment notion: the intrusion of value judgements. There is an implicit assumption in many of these studies that there is *one* pattern of good adjustment in old age: generally, a pattern which includes wide ranging participation in social activities, especially frequent contacts with children and friends, and a cheerful outlook on life (Kuhlen, 1959).

The situation has been neatly summed up by Videbeck and Knox who write:

> The notion of adjustment to old age is a normative concept, predicated upon some standard of desirability or normality. In the absence of consensus about standards of either normality or of desirability, the usefulness of adjustment concepts is severely restricted. At all times, the use of adjustment concepts requires constant referral back to the implied standards. Taking the leap into normative assumption is neither necessary, nor, in the light of diversity of opinion, desirable. *The behaviour and performace of persons at any stage of the life cycle can be understood without it.* (1965: 38–39 emphasis added)

Adjustment's sociological counterpart — the structural concept of social role — derives from the same theoretical background. The extensive and diverse applications of 'role theory' in sociology generally have been well documented and reviewed (Biddle and Thomas, 1966; Sarbin and Allen, 1968; Turner, 1962).

The structural view of role which dominates empirical gerontology is concerned mainly with the content, organisation, and consequences of roles and their relationships to groups and institutions (Streib and Schneider, 1971: 4). This tradition of role analysis has been widely criticised, and the principal points of attack correspond, not surprisingly, with the shortcomings previously identified in the notion of adjustment. Social structural role analysis, it is argued, neglects the importance of the individual, overemphasises role conformity and stability, and emerges as a kind of normative determinism (Turner, 1962; Blumer, 1962; Komarovsky, 1973).

The concept of role was originally developed within quite a different sociological tradition (Mead, 1934) where it depicted 'a tentative and creative interaction process' (Turner, 1962: 37). In this view, structural features such as social roles are seen to set conditions for action but not to determine it (Blumer, 1962). In this interactionist perspective, behavioural outcomes are not assumed to correspond with pre-set normative conditions; they are, rather, situational and problematic. The focus of explanation is on the individual.

The Sociology of Social Action

In contrast to the sociology of the social system, the sociology of social action is centrally concerned with the problem not of order but of control. The possibility exists for actors to exercise control over their situations by imposing upon them their own definitions. 'Society is thus the creation of its members; the product of their construction of meaning, and of the action and relationships through which they attempt to impose that meaning on their historical situations' (Dawe, 1971: 551). Or, as Berger has expressed it: 'People not only live in institutional structures, they also perceive these structures, reflect about them, and try to understand their own location in them. Their definitions of the situation become a social reality that has, in turn, its own effects on the institutions concerned' (1971: 216). In this perspective, integration enters at the level not of the total social system but at that of the individual actor and, through the concept of control, of the interaction system.

In an action framework the concept of central meaning replaces that of central value in the system perspective. Its basic referent is not the system but the actor, who can be seen to integrate his or her different situations (work, family, etc.) and life experiences around an overall life meaning. This in turn provides him or her with goals and definitions specific to each situation.

The notion of control introduces into the analysis both the dimension of action (to control a situation is to impose meaning upon it by acting upon it) and of interaction (to control a situation is to impose one's definition upon the other actors in that situation): 'The concept of control refers essentially to social relationships whose properties cannot be reduced to the individual definitions and courses of action from which they emerge; it integrates actors into interaction systems' (Dawe, 1971: 549).

Here a critical point for research emerges. The properties of these interactions cannot be prejudged. There can be no assumption of consensus (or, for that matter, of conflict). The role of either of these in a specific interaction setting is an empirical question.

Essential to the symbolic interactionist perspective is the view that human beings construct their realities in a process of interaction with other human beings. It follows that the focus of enquiry must be on action (which arises out of meanings which define social reality) rather than on behaviour. The mere documentation of interpersonal contacts does not constitute an account of interaction, though it is frequently assumed to. Questionnaire surveys generally short circuit the explication of the subject's acts by placing them within a category, an act associated with family, say, or an act of friendship. The meaning of the act for the subject and the other(s) is assumed to be given by the nature of the category. However what is taken: 'to be merely the repetition of the same physical action may imply totally different meanings to those concerned according to the way in which they define each situation. By concentrating on the behaviour itself, it is possible to miss totally its significance to the people involved . . .' (Silverman, 1971: 564). For example, if the married daughter of an elderly widow defines the weekly dinner with her mother as an unpleasant duty, the significance of the interaction to all the participants is vastly different than if it were the congenial family get-together of conventional wisdom.

Silverman suggests that anthropologists who study cultures different from their own may feel most strongly the difficulty of grasping the subjective significance of actions because they occur in an alien culture, but that this problem is also frequent in one's own society. If, as some social scientists maintain (Rose, 1965a; Clark, 1968), the elderly do in fact orient their lives at least partially on the basis of a different set of values from those of other ages, the problem is even more comparable to that of the anthropologist. In any case, the meaning of action is an empirical question, and not to be assumed *a priori*.

Meanings are socially sustained, but man defines the social world as well as being defined by it. Action and interaction are shaped and made understandable by the individual in terms of 'typifications' (Schutz, 1964) of the social world. These arise from the ultimate of social 'givens', our language. Yet society, its roles and institutions, are not an 'ontological reality which determines the behaviour of its members' (Berger and Pullberg, 1966: 67). On the contrary, norms, positions, and roles are simply the frameworks within which human interaction occurs. Thus the actor's individual biography is important in shaping his or her particular pattern of behaviour, and there is an element of choice in role playing which implies the possibility of change through interaction.

We cannot assume, for example, that the role of Senior Citizens Club member entails a unitary set of responses by certain actors to being, and perceiving themselves as being, old people. Far less can we assume that joining such an association is the manifestation of an incipient 'aging group consciousness' among the elderly (Rose, 1965b) or among a particular socio-economic stratum of them (Wild, 1978). If anything, in Australia at least, membership of such clubs is defined *by the participants* as signifying aloneness, and not age *per se*. In other words, belonging to a Senior Citizens Club (or any other phenomenon) may give the outward appearance of conforming to certain socially given expectations associated with the role of an old person. In fact I will show there are a range of motives underlying such apparent conformity. Rather than assuming the existence of pre-set attitudes and responses to various life situations of the elderly, research should therefore aim at uncovering the sets of orientations that mediate between individuals and their responses to a situation.

Finally, it must be borne in mind that: 'The subjective meaning need not necessarily be the same for all the parties who are mutually oriented in a given social relationship . . . 'Friendship', 'love', 'loyalty' . . . on one side, may well be faced with an entirely different attitude on the other' (Weber, 1947: 119). There may exist different definitions of situations, whereby: 'conformity to the expectations of other partners . . . is not generated by shared values . . . (but) derives from the attempts of certain actors to attain their own personal ends and is merely tolerated by others (Silverman, 1971: 573).

Here too the possible role of coercion, that is the ability of one participant to impose his or her definition of the situation, cannot be overlooked. This necessary corrective to the postulate of consensus is important when analysing the social worlds of the elderly, particularly when dealing with their interaction with non-peers, whether they are family members or voluntary welfare workers. A situational outcome may, in fact, turn on competing systems of interpretation.

Integration Reconceptualised

In this study, I propose to employ integration as an analytic construct which subsumes the two key concepts of a distinct sociology of social action: the concepts of meaning and control. It is not associated, in my framework, with any normatively-based idea of adjustment. The opinions of elderly people themselves are taken here as the only measure of life satisfaction, 'success', 'morale', and the like. Nor is there any quantifiable 'degree' of integration: *all* social actors integrate their individual biographies and different life situations in terms of a central meaning which 'makes sense of' their existence and circumstances. The research task is to describe the principle of integration used by each actor as it derives from and provides meaning for his or her life history and present situations. Any regularities that emerge in the central meanings of different elderly subjects can then provide the basis for a descriptive typology of integrative principles.

Central meaning is analogous to what Anthony Wallace (1961) refers to as the 'mazeway'[8] and Kurt Back (1976) as the 'necessary path'[9] of an individual. This concept subsumes and organises those subjective dimensions of experience variously referred to as appearance, self, other, generalised other, and world view. It enables us, in other words, to conceptualise key aspects of individual variability or 'personality' within an environmental context.

Those aspects of the environment most relevant to the development and understanding of individual life meanings are symbolic interaction processes. The social classification of the individual is 'a precondition to the development of individual traits and the complex of self and personality' (Back, 1976: 406). In the present context, the way in which old age is classified in the Australian socio-cultural system is clearly a critical variable.

At the same time, individuality is preserved, or modified, in the context of groups most relevant to the person. Social groups such as family, friends, and voluntary associations stand in complex interrelation to each other as networks in which the elderly participate for different purposes (c.f. Back, 1976: 407). Central meaning, then, has a topological counterpart in the concept of social life space or situation (c.f. Wallace, 1961: 19).

Consideration of the ways in which actors are integrated into these interaction systems introduces the concept of control. The location, nature, extent, and sources of control in any particular system are questions for empirical analysis. However, it is possible to conceptualise more precisely the relationship between control over one's environment on the one hand and the range of physiological, psychological and social characteristics of the individual on the other.

The notion of social behaviour as exchange provides the necessary framework. While symbolic interactionism clarifies the nature of the interrelationships between individual and society, exchange theory 'provides a more specific plan to investigate concretely why given actors act as they do in given social situations' (Singelmann, 1972: 415). The notion of social behaviour as exchange is a familiar one to social anthropologists. It can be traced at least to the work of Mauss (1954), and his classic statement that 'interaction between persons is an exchange of goods, material or non-material'. The sociologists' tradition derives from the more recent constructions of Homans (1961), Blau (1964), Emerson (1962, 1972) and others.[10]

As far as aging is concerned, the centrality of exchange in the relationships of older people has long been recognised. From his review of the then available ethnographic data, Leo Simmons argued that the key variable in aged status and security lay in the nature of the relationships that old people maintained with other generations, in particular, in their ability to maintain reciprocal relationships. Here biology and culture combine to afford or deny the older person those assets or resources with which to reciprocate services performed.

Recently, Dowd (1975) has put forward an explicit theory of aging as exchange. In Dowd's exchange framework, interaction between individuals or groups is conceptualised as attempts to maximise rewards and minimise costs, both material and non-material. Interaction is maintained because — and only as long as — it is rewarding; that is if the actors 'profit' from it. The concept of profit embraces both instrumental and affective gratification.

Power derives from imbalances in the social exchange, that is, when one participant values the rewards to be gained from the interaction more than the other. In other words, one interactant achieves power through the inability of the other to reciprocate. The latter is in a position of dependence: need satisfaction is contingent on compliance.

In theoretical terms, the relation is 'balanced' when 'both parties in the exchange relation are equally dependent upon each other (that is to say, they both are equally desirous of the rewards offered by the other and have similar outside resources from which to obtain the reward)...' (Dowd, 1975: 588-9). Several mechanisms of rebalance are potentially available to the dependent partner. Dowd conceptualises these as:

1. Withdrawal, in which the less powerful interactant reduces his or her motivational investment in the rewards offered.

2. Extension of power network, whereby alternative sources of the rewarding behaviour are cultivated.

3. Emergence of status of the less powerful partner under new conditions.

4. Coalition formation by the less powerful to deny alternative sources of goal achievement to the more powerful.

As a social group, the 'aged have very little to exchange which is of any instrumental value' (Dowd, 1975: 590). The result, Dowd argues, is that the only available social currency which the aged can utilise in exchange relations (outside of the rebalancing mechanisms mentioned above) are esteem and compliance.

The great value of an exchange orientation to the study of aging lies in the multidisciplinary origins of the exchange model, its dynamic emphasis, and its ability to incorporate processes of role and resource allocation in the interaction among individuals in both psychological and sociological terms. Attention to the social environment in which action and interaction occur is a necessary corrective to determinism, of either a sociological or psychological variety.

The literature on aging and personality contains an important clue for the analysis of cost-benefit considerations in later life. The need for autonomy, Kuhlen (1959: 859) suggests, emerges in old age as a particularly salient motivation. Clark (1972: 272) describes the 'almost frantic quality' with which her elderly subjects 'spoke of the necessity of preserving complete autonomy in order to preserve self-esteem'. In Western culture, she argues, self-reliance is imbued with pervasive moral significance. Yet elderly members tend to be denied access to those resources with which independence is typically sustained. Clark's data show that those older people who can maintain 'the semblance of self-reliance . . . have higher morale and self-esteem than those who cannot' (1972: 273).

My own data lead to similar conclusions. The model of integration I have employed permits an even more precise conceptualisation and measurement of the relationship between the social environment, individual biography, and the capacity for control. It also offers a dynamic perspective through which the consequences of stability or change in any of these elements for life satisfaction can be explained.

Summary

Integration is most frequently operationalised in gerontological research in terms of objective measures and correlates of social participation. The inadequacy of these measures to account for the subjective dimension of experience is apparent within the literature itself.

The structural approach to integration derives from a system-oriented perspective of the relationship between individual and society. Concepts such as 'role' and 'adjustment' are not sufficiently sensitive to individual variability, and reflect an underlying normative determinism.

I propose instead a model which focuses on the social actor and sees behavioural outcomes as situational and problematic. The key concepts in this model are meaning and control. Personally held meanings are the product of interaction between individuals, with their unique biographical experiences, and the social environment.

The environment includes both social classifications and particular social networks in which the individual participates. A crucial dimension of integration is the amount and nature of control he or she can exercise in these interaction systems. The need for autonomy must be taken into account as part of the cost-benefit motivations underlying particular forms of social action and interaction in later life. Qualitatively sensitive research methods are demanded by this perspective.

This is not to suggest that there are no structural regularities which confront all elderly people as objective conditions of their existence and which may thereby give rise to objective regularities of behaviour. The unfavourable social classification of age itself impinges on the everyday experience of aged persons in both conscious and unconscious ways, forming a central element in the meaning systems of individuals.

In Chapter 2 I described the main features of this socially constructed 'reality' about the aged and examined the structural conditions which give rise to and maintain it. The rest of this book employs the meaning/control model to show how this social construction becomes actualised in the behaviour of elderly people and incorporated in and through their subjective experience.

The following section continues to explore the broad socio-cultural environment in which all aged Australian are located, but the focus shifts to the effects of negative stereotyping on the self-conceptions of elderly people themselves.

The Subjective View of Old Age

In Chapter 2 I described how the dominant Australian culture encourages a pessimistic and unfavourable image of aging and old people. The significance, in the present context, of this social distribution of 'knowledge' about old age lies in the ways in which the aged themselves participate in it. As Berger and Luckmann (1967: 149) point out, 'society exists as both objective and subjective reality...the individual member of society...simultaneously externalises his own being into the social world and internalises it as an objective reality'. How, then, do old people view themselves and other old people?

Aged Australians, according to Hutchinson's (1954: 21) survey, 'do not in general regard old age as a period of their lives to which they look forward'; old age is something to be postponed as long as possible, and 'passing' as younger than one's actual years is a desirable experience: 'Altogether, old age, both in prospect and in actuality, is felt to be a distasteful necessity with few pleasing features to redeem it'. This is a view shared almost exclusively by my own informants. Old people are overwhelmingly aware that they are the targets of negative stereotypes (Kastenbaum and Durkee, 1964b; Kalish, 1977).

Several studies address themselves to the question of the subjective definition of age and its relationship to other variables, such as chronological age and self-conception. An early study was that of Tuckman and Lorge (1954). They asked 1 032 people of all ages to classify themselves as young, middle aged, or old. All respondents under 30 described themselves as young. The designation middle aged increased from age 30 to 60. A small proportion of those aged 60 and over classified themselves as old. Beyond 80, only sightly more than half (53 per cent) were calling themselves old, while 11 per cent described themselves as young. The authors concluded that self-classification is a function of self-concept and that a critical factor in the process is the acceptance of, and stereotyping of, the cultural attitudes toward aging.

In a more recent study, Ward (1977) asked 323 subjects aged 60 and over if they thought of themselves as young, middle aged, elderly, or old. The two most frequently selected choices were 'middle aged' (44.8 per cent) and 'elderly' (55.4 per cent). Shifts in age identification from middle age to elderly were found 'to be related primarily to age-related deprivation, age, health, activity, and employment status' (1977: 229). There was no relationship between age identification and attitudes (positive or negative) toward old people in general.

Other studies[11] support the suggestion that there is some relationship between chronological age and subjective age, but the former alone is not sufficient to determine an individual's self-definition as old. People are more likely to begin to define themselves as old following an age-related crisis such as worsened health, lowered financial status, institutionalisation or other loss of independence, retirement and widowhood. Thus stereotypes of old age are negative and are shared by the aged themselves, but such sterotypes are not directly related to subjective age identification.

Conceptualisations of the Aged

The sociological and psychological consequences of negative age stereotyping have been variously interpreted in the literature. Several perspectives emphasise the construction of social reality and the power of non-aged groups to enforce definitions unfavourable to the aged.

The Aged as a Minority Group
Several researchers have suggested that the aged should I
minority group. Palmore and Whittington (1971) suppc
pointing to the following factors: the aged are negatively stereo₁,ₑ
there is a widening gap between old and young in economic, social,
and residential terms; the aged suffer discrimination in various areas,
such as employment, obtaining loans, etc.; and they are developing a
unique subculture.

In similar fashion Breen (1960: 157) argues:

> In many respects the aged show characteristics of a minority group.
> They are subject to categorical discrimination, they have relatively
> high visibility, and, in many parts of our society, they constitute a
> functioning subgroup. Stereotypes are held about the group, and
> individuals are judged thereby. Prejudice is not uncommon,
> especially in industry, where persons over age 40 are discriminated
> against in employment practices. Thus, the ingredients necessary to
> the development of minority group status are present for the aged.
> The characteristics commonly attributed to minority groups as a
> result of such categorisation may be expected to develop among
> older persons.

There are a number of difficulties with conceptualising the aged as a
minority group. Streib (1968) argues that the aged can only be considered as a statistical aggregate or social category which is internally
differentiated along various lines, such as those of social class. The
nature of intergenerational relations, he maintains, is obscured rather
than clarified by transferring a term denoting life time group membership, such as minority group, to a situation which each individual, if
he or she lives long enough, will eventually enter.

Another problem with the minority group concept is the fact that
old age is a universal experience, whereas characteristics such as
'blackness' and 'femaleness' are not. Thus old age may be viewed and
feared by a non-aged white male in a way that these other features
need not be.

Streib (1968: 36) suggests that the minority group concept is as in-
applicable to old people as it is to women. Paraphrasing de Beauvoir's
comments on women, he writes:

> The aged are not a minority group for they have no past, no
> history, no religion of their own, and unlike the proletariat, they
> have no solidarity of work and interest. They are not herded
> together in the way that creates community feeling among the
> American Negroes, the ghetto Jews, the workers of Saint-Denis, or
> the factory hands of Renault. They usually live dispersed among

the young, attached through residence, housework, economic conditions and social standing to other people. If they belong to the bourgeoisie, they feel solidarity with the old of that class, not with proletarian old people; if they are white, their allegiance is to white men, not to Negro old people . . .

Streib's position, however, seems to deny *a priori* that age itself can operate as a segregative principle, and hence suggests that integration is achieved (or not) by individual old people on the basis of other characteristics they possess, such as wealth. While old people do not form a homogeneous group, it seems absurd to suggest that they constitute merely a statistical category in the same sense that, say, redheads do.

Old age as a 'deviant' status: labelling theory

Berger and Berger (1976) have suggested that old age might usefully be viewed within the framework of the labelling theory of deviance.[12] Old age, in a youth and health preoccupied society, is socially defined as a 'deviant' condition and consequently the individuals so labelled must confront the various forms of stigmatisation that such a label entails. 'The stigmatisation at least involves placing the victim in a separate social category in order to ease the psychological difficulties of those having to deal with him' (Berger and Berger, 1976: 360).

Within this perspective, Rosow (1967) has conceptualised the effects of negative *social* evaluation on *self*-evaluation. He argues from his data that the perception of the invidious attributes attached to the label 'old' leads to attempts by individuals to avoid applying the label to themselves, even though others so label them. Acceptance of the label would constitute an admission that the negative stereotypes were indeed applicable.

This is a valuable insight, and the labelling perspective offers several important correctives to the study of old age (Maddox and Wiley, 1976). In the first place, the labelling framework shifts the emphasis in studies of 'deviant' behaviour from norm-violation to the processes by which certain behaviours and attributes are defined as 'deviant' (Becker, 1963; Goffman, 1963). Moreover, consideration is given to the viewpoint of the individual 'deviant' actor, rather than to the consequences for the system of his or her behaviour: 'Partly this involves concern for the effect of stigmatisation on 'deviants' themselves, in terms of their reactions to labels and stereotyped views of others' (Ward, 1977: 227).

The literature on negative age stereotyping demonstrates that old age is a stigmatised status. Following Goffman (1963), Ward (1977: 227) characterises old age 'as a combination of abominations of the body (loss of physical attractiveness, crippling chronic diseases, etc.) and blemishes of individual character (dependency, diminishing intelligence, etc.)'. This stigmatisation is likely to have a substantial impact both on the actors' conception of themselves and on their interaction with others.

It seems that the relationship between age labels, age identification, and self-conception is a complex one. A study which focused on the psychological impact of age labels (Ward, 1977) found no relationship between age identification and attitudes toward old people. The variables found to be causally related to age identification were: health, age, and age-related deprivation. These factors too, *and not the age identification label itself*, were correlated with low self-esteem. Those with negative attitudes toward old people, regardless of whether or not they labelled themselves as old, also had lower self-esteem. Overall, 'attitudes toward old people are in fact the best predictors of self-esteem when all of the variables are considered simultaneously' (Ward, 1977: 230).

Ward draws out the implications of his findings in terms both of the experience of aging and of the application of the labelling perspective to old age. Given that acceptance of the label 'old' was not related to attitudes toward old people, he suggests:

It is likely that persons come to identify themselves as middle aged, and continue to do so through continuity and habit. Change in that continuity, due to retirement, health problems, etc., leads to age identification shifts regardless of attitudes toward growing old. Thus, resistance lies in perceived personal consistency, rather than in the perceived traits of old people.

The label could still be important in the sense of fulfilling a 'gatekeeping' function — those who reject or avoid the *label* do not feel the force of the stigma.

This brings labelling down to the personal level of self labelling and the meanings held by the individual regarding possibly stigmatising identities. Again, the age identification label studied here was not important in this regard — it did not affect the relationship between negative stereotypes and self derogation. (1977: 231).

The significance of labelling at the personal level, Ward concludes, is as yet unclear, possibly because the *appropriate* labels are more subtle and implicit than research categories have thus far allowed. However, his data do indicate a link between personal attitudes (negative self-conception) and social stigmatisation:

general labelling of this group as stigmatised appears to have an effect (on the self-image of older people) . . . The results of this study seem indicative that a 'stigma' approach would be fruitful in studying personal reactions to ageing, but that the labels which are generally studied may have little importance. Application of labelling theory requires sensitivity to the meaningfulness and interpretations of specific labels for the individuals involved. The impact of being labelled must be sought at the personal level and viewed in terms of personal experience and meanings (1977: 232).

Similar considerations have been stressed by Brubaker and Powers (1976) in their analysis of negative age stereotyping and self-definition. They point out that events popularly identified as traumatic markers of the transition into old age status are not necessarily viewed as negative by the aged themselves.[13] They suggest that survey research designs — the dominant method in later life studies — do not tap the truly relevant interactional dimension of daily experience. Equally importantly, they argue that the self-concept held *before* old age is potentially significant to later life self-perception: 'individuals selectively evaluate elements of a situation to maximise congruence between the self and the situation. As it relates to age perceptions, aged individuals selectively evaluate the state of being old so as to agree with the self-concept...' (1976; 444).

Important theoretical and methodological considerations emerge from the labelling perspective. First, power relations are inevitably at work in defining 'normality' and 'deviance'. Conceptualising stigmatised statuses, such as old age, in terms of objective criteria is inappropriate and normatively biased. As Becker (1963: 9) remarks: '... deviance is not a quality of the act a person commits, but rather a consequence of the application by others of rules and sanctions to "an offender". The deviant is one to whom that label has successfully been applied; deviant behaviour is behaviour that people so label.' Labelling theory provides a framework within which the stigmatised individual can be treated as subject, rather than object.

However, the full implications of labelling theory have not yet been applied to the study of old age. Regardless of whether meanings for the label of 'old' come from the society or from the potentially opposing attitudes of a subculture, 'the *personal* impact of labelling depends upon the personally held meanings for the label... the impact of age identification, as a potentially stigmatising label, on self-esteem... depend(s) on the personal meanings attached to age identification labels' (Ward, 1977: 228).

Old age as stigma
Old age is meaningfully viewed as a stigmatised attribute, one to which invidious meanings are attached by society at large and by the individuals who 'enter' the status. But objective indicators of the

status have different meanings attached to them by individuals, and one needs to distinguish analytically between a 'generalised' and a 'personalised' view of old age (Brubaker and Powers, 1976).

'Typifications' (Schutz, 1974) provide an important means of structuring situations for individuals. Social organisation, in other words, enters into action by supplying fixed sets of symbols which people use in interpreting their situation. A person 'does not necessarily see himself as others see him, yet his self-evaluation cannot stray too far from the status accorded him by others if he is to maintain his ordinary social relations' (Martin, 1957: 31n). Thus, while behaviour must be interpreted against the background of a socially constructed framework of meanings, specific behavioural outcomes are situational and problematic.

Interaction occurs with various 'others', aged and non-aged. The presentation and evaluation of self may well be affected by the composition of the audience and the extent to which it facilitates or limits what the individual can be seen to be (Goffman, 1959). Recent research in fact suggests that the reference 'other' influences the definitions attached to various 'objective' indicators of old age status (Bultena and Powers, 1976). Whether aged individuals compare themselves and their situation to young people, to other particular old people, to the abstract category of 'people my age', or to their own former selves has an important bearing on their capacity to control a favourable self-image and, it seems, on their satisfaction with life.

The conceptualisation of old people as a category of persons who share a particular social stigma allows these important lines to be pursued. It clarifies the group/category argument: all old people do not constitute a social *group* in the strictest sense, but they are nonetheless disposed to individual group formaton and relationships by virtue of their membership in this stigmatised category (c.f. Goffman, 1963: 36). The work of Erving Goffman (1963) provides an excellent framework for discussion of old age stigma. The rest of this chapter focuses on the reality for invividual old people of their stigmatised situation, as those who are 'disqualified from full social acceptance' (Goffman, 1963: 13). I shall begin to examine the ways in which old people cope with their 'spoiled identities'.

Goffman describes three types of attitudes that are held by 'normals' towards someone with a stigma. First, by definition the individual is marked off as a different kind of being. Exclusion from full social acceptance is based on this assumption. Often the behaviour of the aged is interpreted as 'evidence' that they are not fully mentally competent. Their own assessments of wants and needs are considered less valid than those of 'objective' non-aged outsiders. As a result, the aged are often treated as less than social equals. At committee meetings of the Old People's Welfare Association, the elderly club representatives are present not to take part in management decisions but to make and serve the tea and sandwiches.

Not infrequently, an analogy is drawn between the social competence of old people and that of children. The Senior Citizens Club staff expressed great consternation, when there was a choice of main courses for lunch, that the members would 'squabble' over who got what. The elderly themselves recognise this tendency for non-aged to hold such stereotypes. An 80-year-old widow related to me the following experience. When her refrigerator broke down, she telephoned the manufacturer to enquire about repairs. Although she is fully alert mentally, her quavery voice betrays her age. When she explained that a large hole had rusted through the back of the machine the clerical assistant said: 'Now, dear, you're sure you didn't put that hole there yourself? Do you use a knife to make it defrost faster?' My informant replied that of course she didn't do such a foolish thing and the clerk told her she was 'a very *good girl*'.

A handbook outlining 'appropriate' games and activities for Senior Citizens Centres (Tolhurst, n.d.) echoes the theme. Suggested activities are of the 'children's party' variety. For example:

The Latest Fashion Divide members into pairs and then supply each pair with several large newspapers, scissors, and lots of pins. One member then has to dress his partner in newspaper. You will be surprised how effective some of the outfits will be. You can supply glue too but this could become messy . . . (p. 31).

Jumble Sale Ask all members to bring a bundle of old clothes, including all different pieces such as dress, coat, trousers, hat, gloves, etc. Get them to stand in a circle each holding his bundle. Play some music and get everyone to pass their bundles clockwise. As soon as the music stops tell everyone to put on the clothes they find themselves holding. This will cause tremendous fun (p. 31).

The booklet concludes: 'Remember . . . do not measure success by the beauty of the handicrafts or the quality of the singing or musical group. It is not the perfect piece of handicraft or the successful concert that matters — it is the satisfaction and happy time all have enjoyed while doing it' (p. 37).

A second characteristic of normal attitudes toward the stigmatised is construction of a 'stigma theory, an ideology to explain (their) inferiority and account for the danger (they) represent, sometimes rationalising an animosity based on other differences . . . ' (Goffman, 1963: 15).

I have already discussed the extent to which the popular conception of aging as a time of decreasing efficiency is supported by a biological decline model, a model which is socially convenient but which does not always tally with the facts. Goffman suggests a stigma theory is frequently associated with the tendency for non-stigmatised 'to impute a wide range of imperfections on the basis of the original one, and at the same time to impute some desirable but undesired attributes...' (Goffman, 1963: 15–16), such as the attribution of a 'sixth sense' to the blind.

Brubaker and Powers (1976) argue that not all stereotypes of old age are negative. This has been true historically, and similar images seem to inform contemporary 'positive' stereotypes of old people. Today, as in the past, there is a conception of the 'virtues' of old age. Patience, especially with children, is seen as a characteristic of old people, as shown by the popularity (among the non-aged, at least) of 'foster-granny' schemes. In fact the aged are widely seen as being ideally suited to a 'caring' role for dependent groups of all kinds, including the handicapped and other, frail old people. Such a role is not highly valued within Western culture, yet the aged are supposed to welcome the opportunity to be 'useful', and to perform such tasks without payment or at minimal rates.[14] It is common to impute to them a 'special' affinity for young children. The aged themselves apparently have little desire for close association with young children. This does not deter non-aged professionals from devising schemes to bring the generations together.[15]

Face-to-face contact with *non*-aged people presents problems of uncertainty as to how the aged individual will be identified and received and, if his placement *is* in a favourable category, whether 'in their hearts the others may be defending him in terms of his stigma' (Goffman, 1963: 25).

This sort of 'well-meaningness' leaves the stigmatised person as uncertain of what others are 'really' thinking about him or her as if he or she had been ignored. At one committee meeting of the Old People's Welfare Association the chairman alluded to the activities of 'our club, as I like to call it, and our members, as I like to call them...' the implication being, 'even though that's not what they *really* are'. Later in the same meeting, following a number of speeches in which no mention at all had been made in introductions of the presence of actual club members, the vice-president opened her address with 'Mister chairman, distinguished guests, ladies and gentlemen and (pause) Miss Martin, the president of the members' committee'. The pointedness of this belated inclusion merely highlighted the condescending attitude adopted toward the 'old dears'.

In this kind of situation, the stigmatised person is likely to feel that the usual scheme of interpretation for everyday events does not apply to him or her. Minor accomplishments, Goffman suggests, may be assessed as signs of remarkable and noteworthy capacities. For a blind person:

> His once most ordinary deeds — walking nonchalantly up the street, locating the peas on his plate, lighting a cigarette — are no longer ordinary. He becomes an unusual person. If he performs them with finesse and assurance they excite the same kind of wonderment inspired by a magician who pulls rabbits out of hats. (Goffman, 1963: 26).

Old people who simply perform in a socially competent manner frequently arouse this kind of attitude. One voluntary helper at the Senior Citizens Club discussed a 68-year-old widower, noting that he was clean, well dressed, and possessed an easy, confident social manner. 'You know', she said to me with some astonishment, 'you would really have no worries about taking him anywhere'. Similarly, anyone who performs basic physical feats like mounting stairs or elementary tasks like doing one's own laundry is regarded as 'absolutely amazing'.

Interaction with the non-aged involves even more difficulties when the interaction occurs in a welfare setting. The old person is doubly stigmatised, as old and as a 'charity case'. Some of the consequences are illustrated in Chapter 5.

Coping with Spoiled Identities

The pivotal fact of stigma is that the stigmatised individual tends to hold the same beliefs about identity as 'normals' do. Shame, therefore, becomes a central possibility given the knowledge that one possesses a 'defiling' attribute. According to Goffman (1963: 19), the 'central fact of the stigmatised individual's situation in life...is a question of what is often, if vaguely, called 'acceptance'. Those who have dealings with him fail to accord him the respect and regard which the uncontaminated aspects of his social identity have led them to anticipate extending, and have led him to anticipate receiving...'

There seem to be several ways of attempting to cope with age stigma:

Passing
For a few, a face lift or other cosmetic procedure may be utilised in the attempt to pass. For others, lying about one's age serves the same purpose. When I first met my neighbour Miss Schmidt she told me she

was 70. After I had known her for some months she admitted that she was really 81. 'I can tell you now that you know me', she said, 'but the trouble with telling most people your age is that they start to treat you like it'.

Most elderly people attempt to cope with stigma by coexisting with the non-aged, and either rejecting[16] or (more commonly) accepting the basic social attitudes toward old age in general but denying their applicability to themselves.

Denial
The aged people I interviewed clearly recognised that other people defined them as 'old'. They were very much aware of the negative stereotypes which attach to that label, and also of the fact that many of their contemporaries attempt to deny that they belong to the category. Members of the Bayside Heights Senior Citizens Club invariably responded to my comments about the small number of people who used its facilities along similar lines: 'People don't want to join because they don't want to see themselves as senior citizens'.

However, those who actually belong do not define their *own* membership in these terms. The need for 'company', and to 'save cooking' were the main reasons given for their attendance. Loneliness, too, is an acceptable justification for belonging. At the Senior Citizens Clubs Rally I attended in Adelaide several groups of interstate club members with whom I spoke remarked bitterly that they had had to include associate members to 'make up the numbers'. One woman said that a certain associate 'doesn't belong here. The clubs are for the widows, the lonely ones. She has a husband and children'.

Other reasons given for joining also denied that age itself was a factor: 'A neighbour of mine works as a volunteer here. She suggested I should come along after my wife died. I felt obliged to, you know, I didn't want to seem ungrateful for her concern' (widower, aged 68); 'My life would have been completely different today if I hadn't broken my leg. A volunteer picks me up, so it's the only way I can get out' (single woman, aged 74); 'My friend joined and asked me to keep her company. It's not really my cup of tea' (widow, aged 70).

Alternative definitions of 'old'.
This kind of cognitive dissonance enables club members both to explain their fraternalisation with old people and, at the same time, to support a belief that they themselves are not 'really' old.

But the facts of their existence — the required acknowledgement of being a senior citizen in *society's* terms, the almost exclusive company of others who are regarded as old — must be reconciled with the non-stigmatised view which they hold of themselves.

To further this aim, many old people employ a definition of age which enables them to maintain distance from a stigmatised category to which, in outsiders' eyes, they objectively belong. Old age is invariably defined as a *mental* and not a chronological phenomenon. Being 'mentally old' implies that one has little or no interest and involvement in life, a sufficiently vague definition to permit an individual to see his or her own lifestyle as evidence that he or she is not really old. I heard a woman differentiate herself from her elderly neighbours in these terms although, from what she herself told me, they appeared to engage in comparable activities. This definition enables even those who are already segregated among the objectively old — Senior Citizens Club members, residents of retirement villages and even nursing homes — to avoid self-identification as 'old'.

One guest speaker at an annual general meeting of the club talked about the iniquities of age segregation and mentioned various proposals to establish age-integrated communities. I asked a number of members about their reaction to this idea; in every case the answer was along the lines of, 'Well, I would like it, but the others are mentally old and couldn't cope'.

Cognitive distancing can be interpreted as an integrative element: through it, the aged are seen to be exercising *control* over their construction of reality; in some cases, it is the last vestige of autonomy. In the face of severe objective deprivation, individuals actively continue to integrate their identity around a set of meanings which provide them with the most favourable self-image possible in the circumstances:

> A person is 'old'... when he is so regarded and treated... and when he himself has read the culturally recognised individual and social signs symbolic of membership in the generation of elders. *The only matter of individual choice open to the old person has to do with whether he wishes to accept or postpone belief in his new identity and act accordingly.* (von Mering and Weniger, 1959: 280, emphasis added).

The brief excerpts from case studies presented below highlight the extent to which elderly people perceive the negative stereotyping of old age and the desire to distance themselves from the category. I have chosen accounts of nursing home inmates[17] and retirement village residents[18] since the self-conception of these people offer a dramatic illustration of the power of a selective definition alone to buffer the individual in the face of the most extreme objective manifestations of 'oldness'. These accounts also testify to the prominence of autonomy in the needs hierarchy of elderly people.

Case Study — Mr Reilly Dave Reilly, now 87, has been in the Bayside Heights nursing home for two years. Formerly he lived alone in a flat. After a fall he was hospitalised and then discharged to the home on the advice of welfare and medical workers. He hates being there because of the lack of 'things of my own' and the loss of his independence.

Dave was married briefly in his youth, but his wife left him because 'She was alone too much' (he was a travelling salesman). They had no children. His only living relative, a brother, visits him once or twice a fortnight. Ideally he would like to live in a retirement village unit, where 'you can be your own boss'. He resents his dependence on the nursing staff.

In earlier years he gave no thought at all to what he would do in retirement. 'I suppose I thought it would be pretty dreadful not to have anything to do so I just put it out of my mind.' The future now is just 'waking up every morning and one morning you won't wake up.'

Despite the objective lack of autonomy, Dave says that mentally he is still the same person he was when he was a young adult. 'You're not old until you can't do things any more.' He still defines himself as 'more young than old — the nurses think I'm terrific for my age.' He believes that old people have learned from experience to be 'open', 'honest' and 'friendly'. But it has not brought happiness. 'You just get cast aside.'

Case Study — Mrs Cook Gladys Cook, 78 and widowed, has been in the nursing home for two and a half years. She has three sons, all of whom live in Sydney. Only one visits her regularly. She was one of the few old people I spoke to who expressed a desire to live with a child. She would like a 'granny flat' but says the council 'won't let you build one.'

Gladys says she only feels old 'when I'm sick. I know I am old, but I don't think I act it. People always tell me I don't look my age.' She started to think about getting old when she turned 60. She 'can't think of anything' that makes old age better than youth. The future holds little interest or promise, and she would very much like to leave the home: 'I just don't feel that I *belong* here.'

Case Study — Mrs Price Emily Price, a 78 year old widow, has been in the nursing home for only three months. She had been living with one of her three married daughters but 'when I got sick it was too much for her'. The daughters take turns to visit her every week, but she only sees her grandchildren on her birthday and at Christmas.

She defines herself as 'young at heart', though she recognises that others see her as old. Poor health is her main concern: the restriction of activity was an aspect of aging that she had 'never really thought about before'. She insists that as soon as her health permits, she will 'get out of here'.

Case Study — Mrs Russell   Ninety-two year old Marjorie Russell has been a resident of the nursing home for more than 10 years. Her husband, a retired businessman, had died some 15 months earlier. She was in reasonably good health, with no major disabilities. A married son and a married daughter both live in Bayside Heights, less than a kilometre from the family home. Life without her husband was 'intolerably lonely',she said. 'I found myself ringing Beth [daughter] and Jim [son] at all hours. They were very good, but I dreaded becoming a burden on them. I knew my health wouldn't hold up forever, so when they suggested the (Bayside Heights) home, I thought it would be a good idea.'Both children and their spouses visit her every week. However, she rarely sees her grandchildren. 'They are too busy to come', she explains, 'and anyway what could we talk about? I'm an old woman and they have different interests.'

Unlike the others, Mrs Russell insists that being in the home is not incompatible with being independent. Her husband left her well provided for, and she pays for everything she needs. She has a private room with her own colour television set, and continues to operate accounts at a number of department stores and specialty shops in the area. Staff not only share in her regular purchases of luxury food items, but also get expensive gifts at Christmas. Undoubtedly the deference and special consideration I observed them paying her are not unrelated to this. She spends most of her time watching television, but does not socialise with other residents: 'They're all a bit senile.'

Case Study — Mrs Hughes   Nancy Hughes, an 81-year-old widow, has been living at Bayside Heights Retirement Village for 10 years. She was widowed in her 40s and took a clerical job from which she retired at 60. Her only son is in the Navy and she sees him infrequently, though he writes to her about once a month and 'he never forgets my birthday'. Her late sister's children live in the area and she sees them once or twice a month.

Retirement has brought her a freedom, which she values highly, from the restriction of an office job. The only cloud on her horizon in this respect is the deterioration in her vision. She describes herself as 'young for my age' and says people don't believe her when she tells them she is 81. It has only been in the last couple of years, she says, when her eyesight started to fail, that she began to think of herself as old.

She sees herself as a sociable and helpful person: 'I like to do what I can for people', and she socialises regularly with fellow residents. A close friend, also a widow,lives nearby. She describes Bayside Heights as the 'ideal' place for her, and describes herself as 'just as happy as I've always been'.

Case Study — Miss Coleman Mona Coleman, now 78, has been living in the Village for two years. She had a high school education and worked all her life as a secretary. She never married — 'I just never met the right man, but it didn't really worry me.' She took care of her widowed father, a retired businessman, until he died 15 years ago. When she moved here she sold the family home, invested the proceeds, and receives a comfortable income.

She enjoys the freedom of having fewer responsibilities now that she is retired. The possibility of poor health overtaking her is the only limiting factor she foresees. She interacts daily with friends in the village, and is perfectly satisfied with her present situation. She reads widely. She thinks of herself as 'young in spirit', and believes others see her as younger than her age.

Summary

As Berger and Luckman (1967: 183) have noted,"the micro-sociological or social-psychological analysis of phenomena of internalisation must always have as its background a macro-sociological understanding of their structural aspects". This chapter argues that the macro-sociological phenomenon of particular salience for analysis and understanding of personally held meanings in later life is the set of cultural attitudes, values and beliefs I have referred to as age stigma. This social classification of the individual manifests itself in the structures within which old people experience their reality as social beings.

The stereotypes of old age are predominantly negative. Old people as a group are characterised as dependent and obsolete, and as having little if anything of value to offer to independent adults. This view is tempered by the attribution to them of 'positive' but *unrewarding* traits. Objective characteristics which label people as old are not necessarily central to individuals' definitions of themselves. The subjective meanings attached to the label are more important. Even the most severely deprived old person (in objective terms) can define old age in such a way that he or she avoids a self-identification of 'really' old. By controlling their definition of reality, though they can objectively control little else, they continue to integrate their experiences around a set of meanings which define them as 'normal', that is, as young (at heart). Sadly, old people must often thereby identify their own peers as not 'normal': *somebody* has to be old, for society defines such a status, but it need not be themselves. Some of the ramifications of this phenomenon for aged peer relations are treated in Chapters 6 and 8.

On an immediate, personal level, aged persons confront socio-cultural structures simply as an interactant in the daily routines of life, as a consumer of the public media, and in many cases as the client of governmental or charitable welfare services. More abstractly, they confront 'the whole social structure that provides the rationale of these practices...' (Connell, 1978: 196).

Yet structural factors represent only one side of the social coin. The dimension of personal meaning must be examined if we are to grasp the nature of old people's social relationships in contemporary society. The concept of age as stigma provides a framework within which the meaning component can be fruitfully analysed.

Surveys of age identification are unlikely to tap the critical distinction between the awareness, in objective terms, that one is 'old' and the cognitive strategies which enable individuals, subjectively, to define themselves as not 'really' old. This duality is central to the interpretation of older people's behaviour in various interaction contexts.

As Mary Louise Williams, a retired school teacher, noted in her autobiographical account of going to live at a retirement centre: 'It is one thing... to visit and endeavour to cheer the senile, and quite another suddenly to be classed as one of them' (1976: 313).

Notes

1. It is here neither possible nor necessary to review the entire output of gerontological research over the past few decades. Others have reviewed the historical development of social gerontology as a field of study (Tibbitts, 1960a; Hendricks and Hendricks, 1977; Maddox and Wiley, 1976), and several comprehensive handbooks on aging and the social sciences have been produced (Tibbitts, 1960b; Burgess, 1960; Binstock and Shanas, 1976). An inventory of research findings up to the late 1960s is also available (Riley and Foner, 1968).
2. Much of this literature is written by and/or for architects and planners: it is not sociologically oriented. See for example Australian Council of Social Services (1974); Australian Department of Social Security (1974); Australian Institute of Urban Studies, Task Force on Housing for Australia (1975); Brotherhood of St Laurence (1957); Carter (1971); Dargaville (1974); Foster (1970); Gates (1968); Green (1971): Heath, Murcutt, and Davis (1965); Hodges (1977); Hoekstra (1976); Housing Commission of Victoria (1966); Johnson (1969); Lamb (1971); Municipality of

Willoughby Retirement Community Committee (1971); Pegrum (1975); Platten (1970); Pound (1975); Pudney (1973); Robjohns (1972); Sach (1975); Sorrell (1972); Toon (1975); Twibill (1970); Weinholt (1973); Weir (1966); M.Weyland (1975); Wilson (1975); Woodrow (1975).

3. A major three to five year research project on Aging and the Family was launched in April 1980 by the Research School of Social Sciences, Australian National University.

4. As Wallace (1961: 7) points out, no single definition of personality is universally accepted nor universally useful. The fundamental character of the human self and its persistence as a unity despite development and change throughout life is one of the core problems of modern philosophy (Sartre, 1956). At least one major attempt has been made to analyse human aging as an existential phenomenon (de Beauvoir, 1970). Others have discussed the aging process through a phenomenological consideration of the measurement of time (Hendricks and Hendricks, 1976). And few gerontologists would deny full understanding of the aged individual demands a life history perspective. Yet such an approach generally falls outside the substantive scope of specific research areas and the sensitivity of quantitative methodologies (Bromley, 1974). The majority of research reports are nonetheless organised implicitly or explicitly around notions of individual continuity and/or change (B. Bell, 1976). Operationally, this concern has been most usually expressed within a single substantive domain, ranging from leisure activities (Fontana, 1977) to friendship networks (Blau, 1973). At the other extreme are all encompassing life-cycle theories (Neugarten, 1968) whose very scope precludes empirical grounding (c.f. Fontana, 1977: 109). In other words, various theories are supported by a common model of aging and personality, though they tend not to focus explicitly on the characteristics of the configuration itself. An important exception is Back's (1976) analysis. His review of existing theories of aging isolates the common elements of the underlying model.

5. A variety of approaches to 'personality type' have been used in the literature on successful aging. Four or five types are generally delineated, occassionally with different types being identified for men and women. Cumming and Henry (1961) delineate five types for men (focused active mastery, achievement doubt, adaptive retreat, fixed conformity and ego defect), and five types for women (externalised personal mastery, internalised passive mastery, externalised domination, internalised rigidity, and externalised ego defect). Gutmann (1968, 1976) employs four 'mastery' types for men (active, passive, constricted and magical). Havighurst, Neugarten and Tobin (1968) have also developed four types (integrated, unintegrated, armoured-constricted and passive dependent). In all these approaches, a value judgement is required to convert the concepts into a view of successful aging (Williams and Wirths, 1965: 4).

6. Defined as 'a perception of reality, including notions of cause and effect, that influences the selection from available modes and ends of action' (Clark, 1968: 438).

7. Shanas and her associates (1968: 274) employ four such 'measures of social interaction or integration' and describe four related categories of

isolated elderly people: persons living alone; among those living alone, persons who had had no human contact on the day previous to the interview; persons who declared themselves to be often alone; persons who had no surviving spouse, children, siblings or other relative, or who, if they had one or more relatives in these categories, had not seen any within the previous seven days.

8. According to Wallace (1961: 16), 'Mazeway is to the individual what culture is to the group. Just as every group's history is unique, so every human individual's course of experience is unique. Every human brain contains, at a given point in time, as a product of this experience, a unique mental image of a complex system of objects, dynamically interrelated, which includes the body in which the brain is housed, various other surrounding things, and sometimes even the brain itself. This complex mental image is the mazeway. Its content consists of an extremely large number of assemblages, or cognitive residues of perception. It is used, by its holder, as a true and more or less complete representation of the operating characteristics of a "real" world.

9. In an analysis of theory and method in the study of personality and social behaviour in old age, Back redefines the basic problem of developmental social psychology through analogy with some tenets of modern theoretical biology. Briefly, Back suggests that the conceptual problems of developmental biology are similar to those of the social scientist. Both seek to recognise the identity of the organism whether from the seed to the full grown plant, or from infancy to old age. Biologists have coined the term 'chreod' or necessary path to describe the identifiable units of an individual organism which persist through time. Change of a limiting kind will evoke compensatory mechanisms while maintaining the pre-existing identity. Catastrophic change, on the other hand, will lead to the development of a new chreod. In the same way, 'People act conservatively, attempting to keep a self-image undisturbed, even when subjected to many jolts; in changed conditions, as after bereavement, the maintenance of the self-image may lead to novel looking kinds of behaviour, and in this sense conservation is the basis of innovative behaviour. The maintenance of the self through this conservative function can be defined as a chreod maintaining itself through the vicissitudes of life crises. Catastrophic changes occur when it is not possible to maintain the chreod and a new constellation has to be found' (1976: 405).

10. A systematic review of exchange theory is provided by Singelmann (1972). It should be noted that I do not here adopt the approach suggested by Singelmann of integrating symbolic interactionism with exchange theory. For criticism of this suggestion see Abbott, Brown and Crosbie (1973).

11. See, for example Blau, (1956), Kastenbaum and Durkee (1964b), Kalish (1977). The differential timing and impact of the transition to old age for males and females has been noted (Bell, 1976).

12. There is a considerable literature on this topic. For a seminal treatment see Becker (1963). Gouldner's (1975) scathing attack on 'underdog sociology' is widely cited. The most insightful and balanced discussion is found, I believe, in Pearson (1975).

13 Menopause for women and retirement for men are striking examples. See Neugarten (1976).

14. The Report of the Committee on Care of the Aged and Infirm (Holmes, 1977) is exemplary.

15. For an illustration of the high valuation placed on intergenerational contacts by the non-aged see M. Weyland (1975).

16. For those who adopt a rejecting militancy, a particular set of problems arises: 'in drawing attention to the situation of his own kind he is in some respects consolidating a public image of his differentness as a real thing and of his fellow-stigmatised as constituting a real group. On the other hand, if he seeks some kind of separateness, not assimilation, he may find that he is necessarily presenting his militant efforts in the language and style of his enemies... His disdain for a society that rejects him can be understood only in terms of that society's conception of pride, dignity and independence' (Goffman, 1963: 26).

17. For discussions of self-conception among institutionalised elderly people see Coe (1965) and Anderson (1965).

18. Several accounts of retirement housing projects are available. See especially Hochschild (1973).

4 Research Site And Method

I have now outlined the broad theoretical framework within which my research was conducted. No single perspective can equally claim to accommodate all significant aspects of a social phenomenon. It is important to stress at the outset, however, that this unifying theme emerged from the data itself. At the beginning of the fieldwork period, my principal empirical focus was merely on the structure and content of old people's relationships with their kin and with each other. As the task of data collection progressed, it became clear that there was a commonality underlying the experience of the most diversely situated elderly informants. The commonality lay in the perception of negative stereotypes attached to old age and in the manifestation of cognitive and behavioural strategies whereby aged individuals attempted to cope with them.

Subsequent analysis of the literature confirmed the general significance of this phenomenon. The data I have collected enabled me to fill some important gaps in, and to suggest linkages between, various perspectives which have emerged in the literature on aging.

A brief account of the actual research project in Bayside Heights follows. First, the reasons for choosing the method of participant observation with open-ended interviews is scarcely separable from the decision to subscribe to a certain theoretical framework. The questions I was asking were about meaning in the everyday lives of elderly people. The sociological tradition centrally concerned with such problems — symbolic interactionism — provides two alternative approaches to the nature of the empirical task: the 'objective' testing procedure of the 'Iowan' school and the subjective or humanistic paradigm of the 'Chicagoans' (c.f. Meltzer *et al.*, 1975).

Undoubtedly my background in anthropology predisposed me to the latter. At the same time, however, its potential value was enhanced by awareness of the limitations and inadequacies of the extent gerontological data, in particular the failure of 'objective' indices to tap the meaningful dimension of behaviour. With few exceptions, the empirical data of gerontology have been derived from questionnaire surveys and statistical items. As a lone student researcher, I had neither the human nor material resources for a truly large-scale study of this kind. In any case, like many anthropologists (c.f. Basham, 1978: 299–325), I have strong reservations about the value of such an approach, particularly in the present context.

Several researchers had already pointed to limitations of the present evidence and highlighted crucial knowledge gaps. The most frequent complaint about the extant data is that it fails to tap the subjective aspects of behaviour. As Plath (1972: 137) points out, statistical comparisons which ignòre the structure of meanings which people attach to behaviour are always potentially misleading. The acuteness of the problem was highlighted with respect to the family relations of older people, a substantive field I was particularly keen to explore, (see Chapter 7).

Gross measurements can tell us that certain patterns exist; they cannot tell us what they mean. They can tell us *how many* kinds, but not *what* kinds of relationships an elderly person maintains. There will, for example, be different consequences for integration if a relationship is maintained either because of a sense of obligation or through genuine affection. Some of the literature on age peer relations also draws attention to methodological limitations of this kind (See Chapter 6). Intimacy, a qualitative dimension, is a crucial variable in the analysis of friendship (Lowenthal and Haven, 1968).

These considerations led me to employ participant observation with open-ended interviews as my principal research tool. Other factors influenced the choice of a research site.

The Research Site

The municipality of Bayside Heights[1] is a long established, but still eminently fashionable, residential area. Its suburbs cluster on the harbour foreshores of Sydney. The name I have chosen for it is intended to suggest the air of scenic charm and genteel respectability which characterises the area.

Within 20 years of the city's founding, parts of Bayside Heights had become popular with picnickers are sightseers. By the 1820s, the first of many stately mansions had been established in the choicest locations by wealthier citizens. Nineteenth-century accounts brim with descriptions of 'showplace' residences, 'luxuriant gardents', and 'dazzling social functions'. The 'leading men of the day' — businessmen, professionals and politicians — lived here and formed 'a snug coterie of society'. Less well situated sections were for a time occupied by market gardens. 'Populous villages' sprang up among the estates, and rapid growth followed the construction of a tramway line from the city.

The western or city end of the present municipality, however, has its origins in rather different circumstances. Most of its early residents were working class renters of small tenements and terraces.

Stately homes continued to be built in the fashionable section until the turn of the century when the original estates began to be sold and subdivided. After World War I, the city end fell into decay and disrepute, but the end of the last war witnessed changes in both areas and the beginnings of status convergence. The old terraces were restored and the 'slum' underwent a process of gentrification from which it has emerged, in the 1970s, with some of the highest land values in the city. At the same time, a boom in the construction of multi-storey home units transformed the eastern skyline. These single units commanded prices in excess of spacious homes in many other suburbs.

Today, in terms of the usual criteria of prestige — size of allotment, size and appearance of dwelling, landscaping, views, absence of industry and of ethnic minorities — Bayside Heights is among the city's most desirable and exclusive residential addresses (Congalton, 1961).

The choice of Bayside Heights as the research site was dictated by a number of considerations. These sprang in turn from the kinds of theoretical questions I was asking and from the nature of the anthropological method, both of which suggested the desirability of a locality-based study rather than a more broadly-based sample survey of the city. Given this, there were practical reasons for selecting informants within the boundaries of an official local government area. Most census and other statistical data are presented in this form, and most services for the aged are organised on a municipal basis. This particular municipality manifested a happy convergence of demographic, ecological and social variables. Like Canada's Crestwood Heights (Seeley *et al.*, 1956), Bayside Heights is in many ways a 'critical', in the sense of 'crucial' community[2] for the sociological study of old age.

Urban studies (Starr, 1972; Toon, 1975; Robb and Rivett, 1964; Pollard, 1970; Gibson, 1970) reveal that the relative sizes of aged strata and the characteristics of the aged population show significant variations from one local area to another. In line with certain Australian urban demographic trends (Howe, 1977), Bayside Heights has a disproportionately high percentage of older residents. This has come about since World War II as the result of two factors: the general aging of the population and the movement of younger people out of the area which, in recent years, has produced a net loss of population.[3] In 1976, 18 per cent of the municipal population were of pensionable age, compared with a city-wide average of 12 per cent (Australian Bureau of Census and Statistics, 1976 census, preliminary figures). Apart from a scattering of coastal and inland resort areas which have, in recent years, become the target of aged retirement migration, it is precisely areas like Bayside Heights — the 'more affluent and better serviced areas of the city . . .' (Howe, 1977: 9) — that are the areas of aged concentration.

To date, the few studies of aging which have relied in part or wholly on participant observation as a method of data collection have been confined to populations in such conveniently age-segregated settings as nursing homes or retirement communities (c.f. Ross, 1977; Fontana, 1977). The type of age concentration found in Bayside Heights offers a theoretical vantage point which these settings do not. Rosow, for example, has postulated:

> four conditions under which the aged may be socially integrated into normal (i.e. age-heterogeneous) neighbourhoods. Old people may be integrated to the extent that: (1) they are long-term residents; (2) they are in a relatively stable, unchanging neighbourhood; (3) their neighbourhood is socially homogeneous, especially for social class and racial, religious, and ethnic minorities; and (4) the person's local primary groups of family, relatives, friends, and neighbours are still reasonably intact. But to the extent that these conditions are not met — and people are recent arrivals, the neighbourhood changes or is socially heterogeneous, and their primary group supports melt away — then their chances of becoming alienated from the social environment increase. (1962: 333)

All four of these objective conditions may be met in Bayside Heights, and my sample includes people in this situation. Equally importantly, it is possible to examine in the same locality the lives of those who fail to meet one or more of these conditions.

Certain ecological factors further enhance the value of Bayside Heights as a research location. It contains, in addition to the full range of housing types (from luxurious family dwellings to cheap boarding houses), significant pockets of age segregation in its various guises: several retirement 'villages' and hostels, a geriatric hospital *cum* day-care centre, a hospice, and several nursing homes (Table 7). The age-segregated can thus be compared to those living in the "normal" community within the same geographic area. The municipality also operates Meals on Wheels, emergency housekeeping, home help and home nursing services, and two Senior Citizens Clubs.

Finally, as a social structure, Bayside Heights fills a major empirical gap in the Australian gerontological literature. Most researchers have

Table: 7 *Special Accommodation for the Aged in Bayside Heights, 1977*

Type of Accomodation	Sponsoring Organisation	Number
Retirement units	Church of England	216
	B'nai B'rith (Jewish)	
	Parents Home	31
	Methodist Church	12
	Presbyterian Church	58
Hostel beds	Church of England	143
	Presbyterian Church	40
Nursing home beds	Private establishments	
	(State registered)	159
Geriatric hospital beds	State government	108

tended to concentrate on those sectors of the aged population most in need, economically and/or medically (Howe, 1979). At the time I began my research, little was known about the process and nature of aging among Australians whose only or major 'problem' may simply have been old age itself.

Thus Bayside Heights seemed to provide an ideal location for studying non-needy aged people in a setting which maximised opportunities for social integration as it is usually conceived. The site also afforded a choice of venues for participant observation. These factors obtained in about half a dozen municipalities within the city. The final choice of Bayside Heights rested upon happenstance: I had lived in the area for four years, and continued to do so during the initial stage of data collection. The fieldwork was conducted from December 1976 to August 1978.

Method

Participant observation
This kind of data was collected in a variety of settings. I played bridge, joined in 'coffee mornings', and was even invited to a few dinner parties. However, the most important venues for participant observation were the Bayside Heights Senior Citizens Club, where I worked as a voluntary helper, and the Meals on Wheels service for which I became a regular 'runner'.[4]

During my initial canvasing of the municipality I had visited both of these establishments, as well as the geriatric hospital and day-care centre, the hospice, the Church of England retirement village, the Presbyterian hostel, and a 39-bed nursing home. I interviewed staff and obtained background data from them. The Club, I felt, would provide a good setting in which to observe peer interaction, while the Meals on Wheels service offered the opportunity of studying a 'needy' population in a decidedly non-needy area. Both venues had the advantage of giving me a 'legitimate' reason for being there.

At the Senior Citizens Club I had the ideal situation. My job was to serve lunch and morning and afternoon teas. Despite my repeated explanation that I was 'doing a study of older people in the area', my helping activities seemed to be taken as the only necessary justification for my presence. In between the focal points of each day's activity — indoor bowls, craft, euchre or housie — there were long stretches of unfilled time. The members themselves simply sat and chatted in small groups: I joined them. Gradually I got to know well several of them. I was invited to their homes 'to see photos of the grandchildren'. Sometimes I was asked in for a cup of tea after driving a member home. I also attended annual meetings of the Club members and of the voluntary organisation which runs it. In September 1977, I travelled to Adelaide for the first (and so far only) National Senior Citizens Clubs Convention and Festival.

Meals on Wheels was a less satisfactory venue for participant observation. Time was at a premium (the meals had to be kept hot for the recipients at the end of the run), and there was little opportunity to do more than note the old person's appearance and living conditions and exchange a few words. Some of the other volunteers I worked with seemed to know a good deal about the old people's backgrounds, especially those who had been involved in the service for many years. Initially, I found out as much as I could from them and from the service's executive officer, who gave me access to the files. After I had been on the service long enough to become familiar to the recipients, I began trying to arrange interviews with the elderly people themselves.

As the literature had predicted, a large number of these old people were very much alone in the world. But many were not. Quite a few had sons, daughters, and other relatives living in the city, often very close by. Quite a few were obviously in poor circumstances. About one in ten lived alone in cramped, unserviced and often filthy rooms in private 'guest houses' where they struggled with chronic physical ailments to maintain a sad independence. Others, remnants of their former working class community, rattled around in terrace cottages, whose peeling facades contrasted starkly with the chipped-back sandstone and carefully nurtured hanging plants of their 'trendy' neighbours. But some were obviously suffering no such reduction in their circumstances: their large elegant cottages with manicured lawns, or harbour-view apartments gleaming with silver services and antique china, made a strange background to the dented aluminium trays that conveyed a lunch of shepherd's pie and canned peaches. From the outset, the interpretative value of 'objective' characteristics was clearly problematic.

Collection of life history material — interviews
Since my aim was not to provide further statistical information or to specify rates and frequencies of behaviour, I did not attempt to obtain a representative sample. The old people I interviewed were contacted in fortuitous fashion. Two early informants were my neighbours, several were the relatives of friends, or friends of friends. I met others at the Senior Citizens Club, through the Meals on Wheels service, or in institutions. Some in turn introduced me to others in their social network.

The case study technique, utilised so effectively in family research by Ernest Burgess (1973), Mirra Komarovsky (1940), Elizabeth Bott (1971), Peter Townsend (1963), and others, seemed indispensable as at least one method of obtaining the necessary kinds of qualitative data. Life histories from 45 elderly people were collected during lengthy, unstructured interviews in the person's home. At least two, and in most cases three or more, sessions of several hours each were involved.

The interviews did not follow a rigid format, though I attempted to secure for each individual the three kinds of data which Else Frenkel-Brunswick (1968) describes as a life inventory. These were:

1. The 'external events' of the individual's life, the significant elements of social action. This included a list of the dimensions of behaviour or the different fields of activity in which the person participates (such as work, family, friends, hobbies, travel and so on).

2. The 'internal reactions' to these events. These subjective data include beliefs, values and norms relating to events and activities.

3. The 'accomplishments and productions' of the individual's life, or the relation of the course of life to its objective results. Here I included statements about what each person saw as the sources of satisfaction — or lack thereof — in his or her life.

Apart from this, the principal concern was to ensure that the data I obtained were not an artifact of an interview structure in which *a priori* decisions had been made as to what was 'important'. As far as possible I was determined that this should be decided by the older people themselves. These life histories were then individually analyzed and compared with each other.

Quality of interaction with different subjects varied widely. With a few I enjoyed a warm and easy rapport. Our 'interviews' were wide-ranging, with frank converstions on subjects of mutual interest. These informants were all women, relatively well educated (if not formally, they were informed and thoughful), and they understood more clearly than others what my project entailed.

I had the strong impression that ours was a two-way traffic of information. They were seeking, with varying degrees of clarity, a deeper personal understanding of themselves and others close to them, and of the world which was inexorably leaving them behind. Those with families sought my opinion and advice on particular issues. Mrs Chevalier was 'taking sides' with one of her granddaughters who had chosen to live with a man without marriage, much against her mother's (Mrs Chevalier's daughter) wishes. Through me, I felt, Mrs Chevalier was attempting to gain some greater insight into the world view of this younger generation — its norms, values beliefs. Over the period of our acquaintance I loaned her various books and articles on subjects in which she had expressed interest (from material on the Grey Panthers to Anne Summers' *Damned Whores and God's Police*). These were all read and discussed at length. For others, like Mrs Streetfield, I represented a link to the formal institutions of society around which, until recently, her own life had substantially revolved. Miss Schmidt, on the other hand, had few social ties and those which she did maintain offered no intellectual satisfaction. On this plane she existed in a solitary and self-sustained world. She apparently found in me a rare opportunity to share her unspoken world view. This group of women came to take a sense of personal participation in the project. They introduced me to their friends, cut out newspaper articles they thought might be of interest, and so on. They spoke freely of their feelings and fears. To a far greater extent than with other informants, I entered into their personal world.

A few others I interviewed were openly suspicious and guarded in their responses. The most reluctant group were the Meals on Wheels recipients. Although I had only two outright refusals of my initial request for interviews (both from men), on several occasions I called, after an interview had been in principle agreed upon, to find that the potential interviewee was 'just on my way to doctor' (in dressing gown), or was 'busy at the moment' and 'couldn't really say' when another appointment would be convenient. Whether this reluctance was due to fears that I was investigating their circumstances in some official way, or because of the stigma of being on a welfare service, or for some other reason, I find impossible to say with certainty.

The attitude of the majority of my informants however, fell between these two responses. In many cases they were quite happy to be interviewed. In others they were neither particularly interested nor distrustful — it was just something to do. The data I obtained from this group were often rich in factual detail.

The case histories evoke differential responses (from myself no less than other observers) in terms of how 'happy' or 'successful' some lives appear in contrast to others. This kind of subjective assessment, based on contemporary personal and cultural values, is unavoidable. It is also part of the tendency to treat old age and old people as a *social* problem, rather than a *sociological* one, and to approach the study of aging from a value-laden perspective.

As a result of minimal structuring, the processes of both data collection and analysis were at times frustrating.[5] My early field notes are studded with comments about respondents telling me the same story two or three times, or going over ground already covered in previous interviews. It was not until I completed a number of interviews and sat down one day to record my third session with Mrs Kraus that I became fully aware of just what it was that I had collected. The notes began: 'More tales of death and depression today', and go on to her description of the recent death of a neighbour, the widow's grief, the funeral and other depressing details which had occupied the greatest part of our three hour conversation. I looked back over the notes from the previous two meetings with her. On our very first acquaintance, we had not spent more than five minutes together before she fled the room in tears after telling me about her husband's death some five years before. I subsequently heard all the details of his sudden heart attack, the trip to hospital, the news of his death, the funerals, the later and equally sudden death of his two brothers, *their* funerals, and so on. I was shown into what had been his study: everything was there, just as he left it. Every week, on the hour the hospital telephoned word of his death, she lights his bedside lamp. She played their favourite music for me, and cried. Every conversation I had with her was dominated by death, grief and loneliness.

At the time I had been re-reading Gregory Bateson's *Naven*. These words in the Epilogue struck me with their full significance for the first time.

> When I came to the task of fitting my observations together into a consecutive account, I was faced with a mass of the most diverse and disconnected material.... I had collected...not isolated facts, but facts in little bunches: the facts in some bunches were grouped on a chronological basis, and in other bunches they were grouped on a structural basis, and so on. No one system of organisation ran through the material, but in general my groups of facts had been put together by my informants, so that the systems of grouping were based upon native rather than scientific thought. (Bateson, 1958: 259)

I realised that what I had collected was precisely this kind of information. My informants were telling me the way the world appeared *to them*, and what, *to them*, were the most salient features of it. Mrs Kraus's obsession with the memory of her dead husband and with her own sense of grief and loss *were* the parameters of *her* construction of reality. Yet it could all have been summed up neatly in a single statistic: Marital Status: Widow.

Notes

1. All names of places and people are fictitious. Some minor demographic and life history details of subjects have been changed.
2. I use the term 'community' here in a very loose sense. As an abundant literature attests, the concept of community has been the subject of a long and inconclusive debate in sociology (see Bell and Newby, 1971), and it is not necessary for me to add a further convolution. Suffice it to say that I am not studying a locality, but rather the manifestation of certain institutions within a particular geographic boundary which is conveniently labelled a 'community'. It is unnecessary for my purposes whether or not its inhabitants share a 'sense of belonging' or any other attribute which is said by some to define 'community' on a non-territorial basis. This would itself constitute a research question.
3. This aging of the population has been mistakenly interpreted elsewhere (Wild, 1977; 1978) as the result of retirement migration to the area.
4. Background information on the Meals on Wheels service is provided in Chapter 5.
5. When collecting data I was guided by many of the practical suggestions put forward by Glaser and Strauss (1967) for a 'constant comparative method' of qualitative analysis. As far as possible, I recorded everything I saw and heard. At regular intervals I reviewed my field notes and attempted to generate appropriate conceptual categories which would subsume various statements and events (Glaser and Strauss, 1967: 36-9). In this way, I gradually became sensitised to the meaningfulness of certain kinds of data for my elderly subjects, though its importance had not initially been apparent to me. In a retrospective account, the process of data analysis naturally appears much more systematic and logical than it did at the time. As Fontana (1977: 1972) points out, 'people and events do not carry labels advising the researcher about their importance as data...', and the search for conceptual categories and meaningful relations among them was an elusive and at times frustrating task.

5 Welfare Services and the Aged

Policies for the aged in Australia reflect the prevailing socially constructed 'reality' that aging is a period of decline, poverty and dependence. Thus, they fall easily within the scope of a broader welfare ideology that locates the aetiology of, and solutions to, social problems within the sphere of individual action.

I have argued that dominant attitudes towards the aged tell us more about underlying political, economic, and social structures which largely determine the life chances and conditions of elderly people than they do about any intrinsic aspects of the aging process. Because they fail to address structural issues, our social policies have done little to improve the situation of elderly citizens. Instead, help to the aged has come to be defined in terms of what Estes (1979) has termed a 'services strategy' for needy individuals. The need is treated as if its cause lies within the individual — he or she is improvident, lacks a family, or is simply 'naturally' infirm. However, as Estes has shown, the benefits of a services strategy accrue principally to the dominant institutional order and its representatives, rather than to the elderly themselves.

Once the problem has been defined in terms of an identifiable set of needs, unique to and widespread among the aged, the provision of various services constitutes tangible evidence to the public that its officials are taking meaningful action to alleviate it. Underlying structural inequalities are not only obscured, but actively reinforced by defining and treating the elderly as a different and homogeneous outgroup with special needs that can be met through a separate network of services. The consequences for the elderly are stigmatisation and segregation. Agencies and service providers on the other hand benefit from the legitimation and expansion of their activities.

Not only do such policies generate dependency, they also foster a bureaucratic form of social control over aged clients. As Estes (1979: 25) points out: 'The use of terms such as *help* symbolically removes the political connotation of power . . .' that is inherent in service roles. She argues further:

If the aged are cast as deserving because they are caught in a situation beyond their control, the service strategies ... tend to define the aged as passive dependents who must be 'helped'. An explicit definition of the aged as responsible for their own plight (and therefore somehow immoral) is absent, but the a-symmetrical power relationships involved in the giving and receiving of services (as opposed to an adequate income that would permit the aged to negotiate society in a more equal position) are scarcely based upon a conception of the aged as dignified individuals with incontrovertible rights in society. (Estes, 1979: 30)

This situation is exacerbated in Australia by the strong association between welfare services and 'charity'. Old-age welfare has a long history of participation by voluntary, charitable bodies (Kewley, 1965; Hamilton-Smith, 1973; Jones, 1979). 'Charity work' is itself an expression of the stratification system (most voluntary workers come from successful middle-and upper-status families)[1] and of class-linked values; the dominant theory is that of 'self-caused poverty' (Jones, 1977: 83).[2] Thus, Jones (1977: 83) suggests, voluntary agencies 'are likely to be more sensitive to their donor supporters than to their clients, with whom there are usually large class barriers'. This frequently goes with a tendency to force clients to play submissive, humiliating roles.

A study of community aid centres in New South Wales (Horowitz, 1975: 15), reports for example that volunteers tend 'to adopt over-simplified and middle-class attitudes towards social problems', and quotes excerpts from interviews with volunteers in which clients are morally condemned as 'inadequate people' and as being in difficulty 'because of their own stupidity'. There is a typically low level of participation in decision making by clients themselves (Duigan, 1975: 38).

Attitudes towards *aged* clients may be tempered somewhat by the tendency which Jones (1977: 89) reports for Australians to classify the aged as 'deserving' of welfare support (in contrast to 'dole-bludgers', for example). Nevertheless, he points out (1977: 76): 'In a society that places a high value on self-reliance, hard work and thrift, those who obtain aid from others will be subject to some degree of stigma.' Different types of anti-poverty measures, he continues, are coloured by different degrees of stigma, with in-kind services being particularly high on a 'sense of shame and degradation that comes from public admission and display of poverty' (Jones, 1977: 82).

Through participant observation, I investigated in detail the operation of two major welfare services for the aged in Bayside Heights — the Meals on Wheels service and the Senior Citizens Club. As a 'runner' for Meals on Wheels and a voluntary helper at the Club, I gained invaluable insight into the interaction of voluntary and paid workers with clients and with each other, as well as their perceptions of, and attitudes toward, the aged. These findings are described later.

This research method also yielded data about clients' participation which rested uneasily with prevailing theoretical frameworks used to interpret the meaning of such services for older people. In particular, the use of a voluntary association model for old people's clubs emerged as entirely inappropriate. This is dealt with in a subsequent section.

For the moment, I will focus on the behaviour and perceptions of Meals on Wheels workers. I show that the operation of age stigma cuts across social class boundaries and acts as an independent organising principle in the perceptions of the non-aged. This in turn has important consequences for the self-conception and social interaction patterns of the aged themselves.

Meals on Wheels

Meals on Wheels is a service which provides sick or disabled people, primarily the elderly, with regular meals in their own homes. This may be on a temporary basis — during convalescence following discharge from hospital, for example — but the majority of recipients on any service are the housebound elderly who will continue to receive meals as long as they remain in their present circumstances. The service is defined as part of the solution to the problem of institutionalisation: those old people who have difficulty in caring for themselves in their own homes should be supported by such domiciliary services which enable them to remain as independent as possible, in familiar surroundings. Eligibility for the service is proven by a doctor's certificate. There is no means test.

Persons who receive a home meals service are likely to be among the frailest of the non-institutionalised aged population. Data from the cross-national survey (Shanas *et al.*, 1968: 119) show that the proportion of old people who have difficulty in preparing a meal is much smaller than the proportion who report difficulty with any other household task. Only a tiny fraction of all elderly people (in Britain, about one per cent) receive meals through a welfare service. A greater number are in fact unable to prepare meals themselves, but few of these depend on social services. Instead, help comes from primary sources, notably relatives. Significantly, a very low proportion (no more than 5 per cent) of aged persons in my survey who received help with meals did so from a relative *outside* the household. As I discuss more fully in Chapter 7, the idea that the extended family, rather than the household, is the functionally relevant unit for elderly persons is highly problematic.

Table 8 *Bayside Heights Meals on Wheels Recipients: Marital Status*

	Male No.	%	Female No.	%
Married[a]	9	23.68[b]	6	6.52
Widowed	16	42.11	67	72.83
Single	13	34.21	18	19.57
Divorced	0	0	1	1.09
Total	38	100.00	92	100.01

a In all cases, both spouses received meals on wheels.
b The wives of three elderly men are in nursing homes.

Table 9 *Bayside Heights Meals on Wheels Recipients: Household Composition*

	Male No.	%	Female No.	%
Lives alone	31	81.58	73	79.35
With spouse only	6	15.79	6	6.52
With others than spouse	1[a]	2.63	13[b]	14.13
Total	38	100.00	92	100.00

a One elderly man has a lodger.
b One woman lives with her son; the others with sisters, who also receive Meals on Wheels.

Table 10 *Bayside Heights Meals on Wheels Recipients: Location of Nearest Relative*

	Male No.	%	Female No.	%
Same dwelling	7	18.42	18	19.57
Bayside Heights	10	26.32	16	17.39
Elsewhere in Sydney	4	10.53	11	11.96
Outside Sydney	0	0	5	5.43
No contact	17	44.74	42	45.65
Total	38	100.01	92	100.00

Not surprisingly, the majority of Meals on Wheels recipients in Bayside Heights are in the 'old-aged' bracket: fewer than 9 per cent are aged under 70 years, while more than half (53 per cent) are over 80. Most have been receiving service for more than two years. Tables 8, 9 and 10 show something of the family and residential status of recipients.

In 1970 the commonwealth government introduced the Delivered Meals Subsidy Act, which subsidises services conducted by voluntary organisations and local governing bodies on the basis (in 1978) of 30 cents per meal with an approved Vitamin C supplement and 25 cents for each other eligible meal. Recipients are charged for meals at a rate set by the individual service; in 1978 it was 60 cents per meal in Bayside Heights. Apparently this charge almost covers the cost of the food. Other expenses are generally met from money raised or donated to the local service. To receive the commonwealth subsidy the service must be registered as a charity with the Chief Secretary's Department and must serve meals five days per week, excluding weekends and public holidays.

A hot two-course midday meal is provided in Bayside Heights. Diabetics are catered for. Meals are cooked at a large public hospital and delivered to the service's headquarters where they are heated up and packed. Voluntary helpers working on a roster system distribute the meals. Volunteers provide their own transport. Usually two people make the rounds — the driver and a 'runner' who makes the actual delivery and serves the meal.

Descriptions of the service[3] continue to stress the dual aims envisaged of the project at its inception — a food service and a social service — a project designed to combat not only malnutrition but also loneliness. From my experience as a volunteer in Bayside Heights it appears that the latter aim is given, in practice, a very low priority. Rarely does the volunteer spend more time with the recipient than is necessary to dish out the meal — certainly less than five minutes between entering and leaving the house. Logistically, this is unavoidable, even if some volunteers wished to do more (and I did not meet many who seemed so inclined). A problem-free runs takes at least two hours; longer if the volunteer does not know the run well, if parking is difficult, if an emergency occurs, and so on. The whole procedure is quite exhausting, particularly on a warm day and if helpers are themselves in the older age bracket (as is typically the case). It is also important that recipients get their meals as hot as possible, and delays adversely affect those at the bottom of the list.

In 1972 some 4 million meals were being supplied annually in Australia. While no exact figures were available, the Hon. W.C. Wentworth, M.P., estimated then that 'an expansion to 6 million meals a year would adequately meet Australian needs' (Second Reading Speech, Delivered Meals Subsidy Bill, 1972). Between 1970 and 1972 the value of commonwealth matching grants to the states for delivered meals rose from $196 000 to $338 000 (Dixon, 1977: 153).

Provision of Meals on Wheels is the principal activity of the Bayside Heights Voluntary Community Service (B.H.V.C.S.), an organisation set up 'for residents by residents' about 15 years ago. Apart from a paid administrator, assistant, and two kitchen employees, the service is entirely voluntary. It receives the commonwealth government's delivered meals subsidy and Bayside Heights Council provides a grant of $8 000 per annum and free premises. A fund-raising committee, the Friends of the B.H.V.C.S., was formed in 1976. Local clubs and prominent individuals make regular donations.

Meals are prepared five days a week (Monday to Friday). Capacity is about 100 meals per day, though the actual number served is usually something less than this. The municipality is divided into four 'runs', each of which is covered by two volunteers — a driver and a 'runner'. A few volunteers come every day or at least several times a week, but the vast majority do only about one day a month. Shortage of helpers is a constantly recurring problem. All the volunteers for this service live in Bayside Heights and all, with the exception of one or two men who accompany their wives, are married women in their late 40s, 50s and 60s[4]. The paid supervisor, a widow in her 50s, also lives in the area.

There are identifiable cliques among the volunteers. The largest is based on the local Church of England women's group. Several other women responded individually to newspaper advertisements for additional help and then introduced their friends. Some volunteers have neighbours who are clients and occasionally they organise husbands and friends to carry out odd jobs for their elderly neighbours.

As Martin (1957: 33-34) has pointed out, this kind of women's activity in social and service groups is a vehicle for expressing class values and maintaining class differences. The cliques themselves are linked through common memberships of the volunteers and/or their husbands in exclusive clubs (the annual get-together of volunteers is held at a Bayside Heights sailing club), through other forms of charitable work, and as a result of having children and/or grandchildren at certain private schools which the wealthy of Bayside Heights traditionally patronise.

Most of the volunteers have been, or still are, involved in other charity work. One woman remarked that Meals on Wheels was 'more satisfying' than other charity work she has done because 'you actually get to meet the people you are helping'. Another became involved in order 'to say thank you God' for having had enough money to keep her own aged mother in an expensive nursing home. A third breezily remarked that after she finishes the delivery run she can go and play golf at an exclusive club 'with a clear conscience'.

The pervasiveness of class consciousness was reflected in their attempts to 'locate' me when I joined the service. I was invariably asked not *whether* I had attended one of two expensive private girls' schools, but *which* one I had attended. During the period of fieldwork, class consciousness was also focused in an attempt to maintain community closure (Weber, 1947: 136) in the face of state government plans to incorporate Bayside Heights municipality with an inner city, low-status council. For several weeks after the proposal was announced, volunteers' conversation was dominated by the subject, and several became active in organising a petition to oppose the scheme.

The attitudes held towards the service's clients — many of whom come from the same class background as the volunteers — were characterised by attempts to rationalise the discrepancy between family status and welfare dependence. This was accomplished by classifying recipients in terms of several interrelated dichotomies which permitted their stigmatised position to be explained as the result of personal failings.

Volunteers were contemptuous of the fact that obviously wealthy old people were receiving the service. Thus a basic dichotomy was between the wealthy and the poor. Many of the latter were working-class aged people from the former 'slum' end of the municipality. Superimposed on this division was a categorisation into the personally unworthy and the personally worthy. One expression of personal worth was the state of cleanliness of the household.[5] Before I set out on my first run, the service coordinator told me that a particular section which included mainly wealthy elderly women in large and imposing houses was 'the most devastating'. 'Wait till you see the conditions they live in', she said. 'Dirty old newspapers on the table... I wouldn't ask for a glass of water in any of them.' By contrast, she suggested I would find that 'the little old pensioners' kept their terraces spotlessly clean, always had neat tablecloths laid out, were well dressed, and so on.

This (objectively false) distinction was combined with an evaluation of clients' personality and character. The wealthy generally were classified by volunteers as 'the cantankerous ones', who 'fuss over things they won't eat' and are least likely to pay promptly for their meals though they can best afford to. The poor, on the other hand, are 'the real sweeties'. A further distinction between the 'ungrateful' and the 'grateful' parallelled this classification. All of the recipients whom I heard described by various volunteers as 'ungrateful' were wealthy. Either or both of two things was meant by 'ungrateful': those who resisted the service by taking themselves off at regular intervals or by leaving meals uneaten were 'ungrateful', as were those who did not display a submissive attitude when meals were delivered, such as the woman in a luxury apartment block who tried to have the volunteers use the service entrance. By contast, all those described as 'grateful' were in poor circumstances and made appropriately deferent comments about how 'wonderful' the volunteers were.

This attitude permitted the volunteers to place a cognitive distance between themselves and the recipients of similar status background, and to substitute sympathy for empathy. As one voluntary worker expressed it: 'I feel sorrier for the ones in A (exclusive suburb) than in B (former working-class area). There seems to be more solidarity among the working class — they rally round one another, whereas I think those in their A units probably never see anyone.'

Thus the stigmatisation inherent in the receipt of in kind welfare services is compounded for aged clients by the stigmatisation of age itself.[6] This was also apparent in the operation of the Bayside Heights Old People's Welfare Association, a voluntary body set up as a registered charity in 1957 which administers both the Meals on Wheels service and the Senior Citizens Club.

Organisational responsibility is vested in a committee made up of municipal councillors and members of local service organisations, notably the Bayside Heights Lions and Rotary Clubs. In common with voluntary welfare groups elsewhere in Australia (Duigan, 1975), the latent function of the Welfare Association is status advancement for its own members. Committee members have high levels of participation in voluntary organisations of various kinds. They are self-avowedly motivated by the ideal of 'community service'. Yet clients do not participate in decision making, and committee members have little actual contact with them. Again, this is not unique to Bayside Heights (Duigan, 1975).

Interviews with committee members and attendance at general meetings showed clearly that this latent function superseded the manifest function of service to the aged in the community. At one meeting of the Welfare Association the mayor's speech was devoted to a propaganda broadside against plans recently announced by the state (Labor) government to amalgamate Bayside municipality with the city council. 'Bayside is known as a privileged area', he said. 'We want to keep it that way. If the scheme goes ahead we will be subsidising the rest. Rates will have to go up.' There were audible ripples of shock and concern from the audience. Similarly, the obstensible focus of activities, the older residents of the municipality, scarcely rated a mention in the president's speech, which was devoted to the achievements of Rotary International. When he did mention the Senior Citizens Club, he referred to it as a 'home'. He had obviously never been there, and did not even know where it was. The rest of the proceedings consisted of reports of fund-raising activities.[7]

Senior Citizens Club users were represented at the Welfare Association meetings by four women from the Members' Committee. Significantly, they sat in the audience and not on the rostrum with the 'real' committee. One elderly lady fell asleep and snored audibly throughout the proceedings.

Denial to the aged of normal adult status extends to club activities. An analysis of this institutionalised expression of age stigma shows that the elderly react to and cope with the devaluation of self in a variety of ways. In the literature, old people's clubs are conceptualised as voluntary associations (Riley and Foner, 1968; Rose, 1960). Participation is taken as an index of integration: membership is seen as a status conferring attribute, as well as a sign of meaningful social activity. In the discussion which follows, I argue from my observation of the Bayside Heights Senior Citizens Club that this model is inappropriate and that the meaning of membership in a club specifically for the elderly is not at all related to the functions assumed to apply to it. A more appropriate model, at least for the Club I observed, is suggested.

Aging and Voluntary Associations

A sizeable body of sociological literature on the phenomenon of voluntary associations dates from the 'breakdown of the family' debate of the 1940s.[8] Basically it was devoted to testing the proposition that formal organisations had begun to replace the traditional primary group supports of family and neighbourhood. Research, however, failed to reveal any consistent correlation between lack of primary relations and voluntary association membership. There *is* a link between formal group affiliation on the one hand and community status on the other, but it is in the opposite direction to that predicted. There is now substantial agreement in the literature (Babchuk and Booth 1969) that:

1. Affiliation is directly related to social class (the highest rate among professionals, the lowest among unskilled workers).

2. Membership rates increase with length of residence.

3. Married persons are more likely to be members of such groups than are the single.

4. Men are more likely to be members than are women.

5. Home ownership is positively associated with membership.

By comparison, the relation between aging and voluntary association membership has received rather less attention. Early studies, which suggested that aging is characterised by declining activity, were taken as support for disengagement theory (Cumming and Henry,

1961). This view is not universally accepted (Rose, 1960), and some data indicate stability and continuity in memberships, at least up to very old age (Cutler, 1977). The lack of a clear-cut relationship between age and club membership is suggested by at least one Australian study (Wild, 1974).

Consistent correlations do emerge in other respects and these are in line with the general trends reported for voluntary association participation at other age levels. Significantly higher rates are reported for older people of higher socio-economic status and for married people (Riley and Foner, 1968).

Clubs for the Elderly: Assumed Functions

As I have suggested, the participation of older people in *age-graded* organisations, such as Golden Age or Senior Citizens Clubs, presents some anomalies as far as general trends in voluntary association membership are concerned. The data are limited, but there is fairly consistent evidence that the usual social class and marital status indices of voluntary association membership are reversed in clubs specifically for the elderly.

A major American study (Rosow, 1967) found that 24 per cent of working-class subjects but only 6 per cent of middle-class subjects participated in Golden Age Clubs. In an English community (James, 1960), membership of clubs for older people is reported to be largely a working-class phenomenon. The author of a Melbourne survey (Sach, 1975: 46) writes that such organisations 'are prominently patronised by low income groups'.

It seems also that married couples are *under*-represented in old people's clubs. The majority of members are female (Trela, 1976), and widowed (Townsend, 1963). Townsend (1963: 144) reports that married women in a London working-class area sometimes belonged to old people's clubs, 'but, when they did, rarely [did] their husbands also'. In Bayside Heights, the majority of Senior Citizens Club members are elderly unmarried women (Table 11).

Table 11 *Bayside Heights Senior Citizens Club: Marital Status of Members*

Marital Status	Male		Female	
	No.	%	No.	%
Married	11	30.56	15	7.77
Widowed	18	50.00	145	75.13
Single	7	19.44	33	17.10
Total	36	100.00	193	100.00

These discrepancies between the composition of age-graded and non-age-graded organisations in later life have received little attention from researchers. On the contrary, impressionistic discussions may even assume that the conventional social-class linkage is operative (Wild, 1977; 1978).

Theoretical treatment of the phenomenon of old people's clubs has focused instead on two major issues: the function of such organisations, especially their role in 'adjustment' in old age, and the question of age segregation as a factor in the development of an 'aging group consciousness' and sense of solidarity among the elderly. In both cases, serious doubts can be raised about the adequacy of interpretation.

The most systematic presentation and discussion of data on organisations for older people is that of Rose (1960). He suggests that there are three reasons for the proliferation of voluntary associations in modern society. Each of these factors, he argues, has special significance for the participation of the elderly.

First, membership is a status-generating mechanism. This, he argues, is important for older people in a society where age does not automatically bring higher status. Second, the voluntary association can be seen as a substitute for the extended family and integrated community in a highly mobile society. Rose argues that the voluntary group oriented to the elderly 'arose as an institution in response to the withdrawal of the interest, support, and social life previously provided to the elderly by the extended family' (1960: 693). Third, the increasing diversification and specialisation of modern society creates a need for limited purpose groups 'that can bring together significant numbers of people who are likely to have a single interest in common but other interests greatly diversified' (1960: 668). The aged, he suggests, are likely to experience special difficulty in finding others of the same age and interests. They are more likely to suffer restricted mobility and to lack an expressive outlet through family relationships. Thus, he asserts (1960: 691), the values of membership for elderly people extend beyond sociability to, 'a sense of personal identification with a group. Everyone has to identify himself as a certain kind of person, and one significant kind of identification in our society is as a member of a certain association.' Australian discussions echo the view that 'clubs give the elderly person a feeling of belonging to a group again' (Donovan, 1960: 37).

As in other aspects of gerontological research, a key focus in studies of voluntary associations is the evaluation of participation as a factor in keeping the aged 'mentally healthy' or 'adjusted'. Most of the literature implicitly or explicitly supports activity theory; that is, a high rate of participation in formal group activity is seen as a contribution to 'successful' aging (see p. 53). Typical of the findings reviewed by Rose (1960) and by Riley and Foner (1968) are those of Havighurst and Albrecht[9] (1953: 340) from their study of elderly people in 'Prairie City':

> It is clear that those people who continue to be active in associations are happier and better adjusted than those who do not. The average adjustment scores of those who belong to associations are considerably higher than the scores of those who do not belong... we cannot say that we have proved that a person who belongs to no associations would become happier and better adjusted if he joined a club. While this seems a reasonable conclusion, we can only treat it as an assumption that seems reasonable and worth acting upon.

Bull's and Aucoin's (1975) data, on the other hand, indicate that health and status characteristics are more potent predictors of life satisfaction in old age than is participation in voluntary associations, which shows a *non*-significant relationship to life satisfaction when controlling for the effects of health and status. Thus correlations between voluntary association participation and adjustment may be tapping more significant underlying variables, or it may be that here as elsewhere objective measures of 'adjustment' correlate poorly with subjective experience.

Whatever the case, a fundamental problem with the adjustment/function perspective remains. If participation in old people's clubs is so 'good for' the elderly, why do they stay away — in droves?

Only a tiny minority of older people belong to special clubs for the aged. Figures of one to five per cent have been reported in American studies (Riley and Foner, 1968: 508), with a high of 12 per cent in a London working-class area (Townsend, 1963). The situation in Australia appears, from the limited data, to be similar. Local studies (e.g. Hutchinson, 1954; Fink, 1973; Duigan, 1975) report very low rates of utilisation of, or desire for, clubs and centres for older people. Among Richmond (Victoria) pensioners, only 12.9 per cent belonged to a club of any kind. Of these 40 individuals, 10 were members of an elderly citizens' club. The researchers note that although the 'existence of such clubs is widely known, membership is small and utilisation even smaller' (Dewdney and Collings, 1965: 86). Attendance at the first Australian National Senior Citizens Clubs Festival in Adelaide in 1977 was so disappointing that organisers abandoned plans for a second rally.

Explanation of this 'elderly apathy' is heavily value laden, if not in fact ageist. Rose (1960: 689) sees it as just part of the 'problem' of 'getting the elderly involved'. Many older people 'seem to want things to be done *for* them, and even expect things to be done *to* them, rather than having things done *by* them'. Many are unwilling to 'make an effort', and specialists require better techniques to 'heighten motivation': 'More knowledge is needed of how to get older persons ego-involved in programmes designed for their benefit' (1960: 690).

In the club I studied, the supervisor frequently voiced similar complaints about the apathy of members: 'It's impossible to get them involved in anything new'; 'only a few are interested in new activities'; and even (from a voluntary helper) 'I wouldn't go near most of them [the members]; only a handful have the right attitude to what the Club can do for them'.

In summary, formulations about the function of old people's clubs posit a series of problems: problems which clubs supposedly alleviate, and problems which are in the process of amelioration by clubs. The first are structural problems arising from social changes which are believed to have a particular impact on the aged. The second involves the 'whole problem of getting a lively sense of psychological participation on the part of the aged, and, in general, the *proper* orientation toward participation . . . ' (Rose, 1960: 690, emphasis added).

The problems, of course, belong to the old people. The inexorable and inevitable march of history is responsible for their present state and, if only they will cooperate, the efforts of the non-aged on their behalf will alleviate their situation. Why, then, do the aged seem unwilling to cooperate? Why do so few of them seek out the meaningful companionship of their age peers in clubs specially designed for their use? And of those who do join such organisations, why do they not seem to participate with the 'right' spirit? And why, given the dominant egalitarian ethos in American and Australian society, are the aged encouraged to segregate themselves from the wider community in the exclusive company of their age peers?

Aging Group Consciousness?

This last feature of old people's clubs has in fact been the starting point for a different kind of analysis; one which takes the existence of age-graded organisations as part of a broader subcultural development. One of the central elements in this development is seen to be the emergence of shared political concerns. Advocates of the aged frequently cite the increasing number of political organisations connected with the aged as evidence that such a subculture is an imminent possibility, if not already a reality. The history and present functioning of such groups has been widely discussed in the American context (see e.g. Hudson and Binstock, 1976; Binstock, 1976) and some attention has been devoted to the subject in Australia (Ellis, 1981).

In this broad context, a central assumption is that age alone is or can be the basis for a cohesive identity and common action among older persons for political purposes. The facts, however, suggest otherwise. Overwhelmingly, the political concerns of the aged reflect socio-economic and regional interests, which militate against the emergence of any common age-based issues. With Rosow (1967), Binstock (1976: 230) emphasises the reluctance of the more affluent aged in particular to identify with a stigmatised category. He in fact argues that '[t] he prospects of the poor aged for substantially improving their situation through politics may lie in the development of identity ties, not between them and other elders, but with persons who are disadvantaged by circumstances similar to their own' (such as young unemployed, racial minorities, the physically handicapped, and so on). However he is justifiably doubtful about the prospects of such a common identity as 'deviants' actually developing.

The role of Senior Citizens Clubs in subculture development has been portrayed in positive terms by some American writers (see e.g. Hess, 1976c) and in Australia. Building on Rose's subculture theory, Wild (1978: 169) has argued that the recent growth of Senior Citizens Clubs and other age-graded organisations in Australia represents the incipient development of an 'aging consciousness and solidarity'. Wild believes that this is part of a broader pattern of self-segregation of elderly middle-class persons from the community which denies them status in its own terms. Thus he asserts (1978: 160) that it is only the middle-class Australian aged who 'cooperate in the formation and development of senior citizens centres', while the lower stratum aged do not participate at all.

As I have already shown, this class-linked distribution, while it applies to participation in non-age-graded organisations, is not characteristic of Senior Citizens Clubs. Further, the suggestion that development of such centres is *initiated* by the elderly is inappropriate in view of the way in which these clubs are actually organised, a point I shall return to. These factual errors aside, is there evidence that participation in Senior Citizens Clubs fosters aging group consciousness and a sense of solidarity? Impressionistic sources certainly support the idea. Ford (1979: 99), for example, suggests that old people's clubs 'will invariably' "stick to" their own members who become infirm through age or illness . . . '. There is overwhelming evidence, however, that age is not a sufficient basis for sociability, let alone for group solidarity and individual identification. Considerable dissension has been shown to exist within clubs for the elderly, the causes ranging from personality differences to class and cultural divisions (Rothchild,

1954). Even where the social class backgrounds of members are homogeneous, solidarity is highly problematic, as Bowen's (1959) account of the first old people's club opened by the Sydney council testifies. The membership was drawn from a 'slum area' in which the provision of a decent meal was felt by organisers to be an important need. Bowen (1959: 69) found that members displayed no sign of 'effective cooperation', or a 'sense of community'; an attempt at self government was unsuccessful because some members felt 'they could not trust their own kind in positions of authority'.

Other findings are equally anomalous. From a large-scale study of community structure and aging, Taietz (1976: 221) concludes that, 'senior centre members do not differ from non-members in age identification or in a preference for organisations exclusively for the elderly. Whatever their reasons for joining the senior centre may be, solidarity with the aging and identification with them are not strong reasons.'

Far from elderly club members exhibiting interpersonal loyalties and bonds of affection with their age peers, Arth's (1962) data suggest, senior centre members tend to be characterised by a general mistrust of others and a dearth of close relationships.

Clearly a different perspective is needed to make sense of old people's participation in age-graded organisations. Most importantly, explanation cannot begin from the asumption of identity between the nature of the group and the individual self, as is implied in the assertion that clubs give old people a sense of belonging and identity. This is the question, not the answer, and is especially crucial in a consideration of organisations exclusively for the elderly. The fact that old people's clubs have little appeal for the elderly reflects their attitudes towards such establishments. As Dewdney and Collings (1965: 86-7) remark of Melbourne pensioners: 'There is a widespread feeling among the elderly that to belong to such clubs is to be stigmatised'.

I have already suggested that the identification of an old person with the stigmatised category of his age peers is inherently problematic. Old people's clubs are doubly stigmatised. First they carry the legacy of their origins as 'soup kitchens' for the poor (c.f. Leanse, 1977), a legacy reinforced by their contemporary integration with various community welfare services for the dependent aged (c.f. Holmes, 1977). At the same time, membership constitutes public identification with a social category which is stigmatised in its own right (Rosow, 1967: 322).

The sociological analysis of a setting which brings together significant numbers of elderly people in this way must take this fact as its starting point. According to some interpretations, we are expected to believe that the effects of age stigma are limited to *creating* such organisations, but do not reach inside them. I shall demonstrate that this is not the case. In addition, by replacing *a priori* assumptions about group identification and normative notions of adjustment with a conception of aged social actors as stance-taking entities who construct and attempt to control their definitions of the situation, I will illustrate the diversity of meanings and functions which actually characterise participation in an old people's club.

A Reinterpretation of Function

Rose's interpretation of the function of old people's clubs is based, as we have seen, on three major assertions: that membership is a status-generating mechanism; that voluntary affiliations replace extended family life; and that clubs provide a sense of identity. Each of these

Table 12 *Bayside Heights Senior Citizens Club: Living Arrangements of Members*

	Male		Female	
	No.	%	**No.**	%
Alone	22	61.11	134	69.43
With spouse only	9	25.00	13	6.74
With relative other than spouse	3	8.33	33	17.10
With others	1	2.78	7	3.63
With others & spouse	1	2.78	1	0.52
Nursing Home	0		1	0.52
Hostel	0		4	2.07
Total	36	100.00	193	100.01

Table 13 *Bayside Heights Senior Citizens Club: Location of nearest Relative of Members*

	Male		Female	
	No.	%	**No.**	%
Same dwelling	13	36.11	46	23.83
Bayside Heights	10	27.78	43	22.28
Elsewhere in city	8	22.22	48	24.87
Outside Sydney	2	5.56	7	3.63
No contact reported with relatives	3	8.33	49	25.39
Total	36	100.00	193	100.00

assertions is problematic. First, membership in age-graded organisations carries stigma, not status. Second, the growth of senior centres
cannot be seen as a response to the disintegration of the extended
family, which was never a widespread feature of Western social
organisation. In any case, though the majority of club members live
alone (Table 12), more than half the men and 46 per cent of the
women have a relative living with or near them; a further quarter of
both sexes have contact with at least one relative outside the
municipality (Table 13).

Finally, the conspicuous failure of old people to participate in these
associations suggests that the supposed socio-emotional functions
may not coincide so neatly with members' motivations.

A fundamental feature of old people's clubs which Rose and Wild
fail to take into account is the fact that they are not organised *by* old
people, but *for* them. Australian Senior Citizens Clubs follow the pattern of those locally organised groups known in America as 'Golden
Age' Clubs. These and similar euphemistically titled organisations
('Borrowed Time', 'Cook County Grandmothers', and so on) vary in
content, organisation and sponsorship, but have in common a broadly
recreational function and the fact that they are financed and organised
by the non-aged. The latter is seen by some commentators on clubs for
the aged as prerequisite for their 'success'; Mannes (1954) writes, for
example, that 'self government is inadequate and a trained and
tolerant staff imperative'.

I suggest that the explanation for both the organising activities of
the non-aged on behalf of the aged and the lack of elderly 'cooperation' must begin from recognition of the fact that in modern society
old age is perceived and defined as a social stigma. In a functionalist
sense, the terminal demotion[10] from normal adult status to old age
presents as much of a 'problem' for society as for the individual
undergoing the transition. Somehow the elderly must be induced 'to
accept the great injury that has been done to their image of
themselves, regroup their defences, and carry on without raising a
squawk...' (Goffman, 1962: 490). In Goffman's terms, the aged in
modern society have to be 'cooled out'.

Cooling Out the Elderly

Cooling out is a term in criminal argot which refers to the terminal
phase of a confidence game. In order to prevent the 'mark', or
'sucker', from complaining to the police, one of the con operators (the
'cooler') stays with him to offer consolation and divert his anger. An
effort is made to define the situation for the mark in a way that makes

it easy for him to accept the inevitable and quietly go home. According to Goffman (1962: 486): 'Persons who participate in what is
recognised as a confidence game are found in only a few social settings, but persons who have to be cooled out are found in many. Cooling the mark out is one theme in a very basic social story.'

If a mark in the larger social scene is someone whose reasonable expectations have been disappointed, then the aged indeed have a lot to
squawk about. They are involuntarily deprived of a range of roles and
involvements and made in return something that is considered a lesser
thing to be. This is the real crux of talk about 'loss of roles' in old age.
The loss inevitably alters both the conception the losers have of
themselves and the conception others have of them:

> For the mark, cooling represents a process of adjustment to an im-
> possible situation — a situation arising from having defined
> himself in a way which the social facts come to contradict. The
> mark must therefore be supplied with a new set of apologies for
> himself, a new framework in which to see himself and judge
> himself. A process of redefining the self along defensible lines must
> be instigated and carried along; since the mark himself is frequently
> in too weakened a condition to do this, the cooler must initially do
> it for him. (Goffman, 1962: 493)

The use of the cooling out metaphor, I suggest, highlights one of the
important functions of institutions for old people in modern society;
the Senior Citizens Club, for example, can be seen a social agency for
cooling the elderly out. For society, it is functional that the aged come
to define themselves as no longer properly belonging to their former
positions and to accept an altered status and a changed reference
group. Physical segregation clearly facilitates this process. The more
the aged become institutionalised, the easier it is, too, for the non-
aged to define them as a different kind of human being and to thereby
protect themselves from remorse and guilt.

As one enthusiastic commentator on the welfare function of old
people's clubs innocently remarked: 'Perhaps unique to the senior
center is the opportunity it provides for older persons to learn to be
gracefully dependent. In the group setting with their peers, retired persons can learn that it's not a disgrace to be dependent' (Leanse,
1977: 326).

In other words, the latent function of the Senior Citizens Club in its
role as a segregating agency for the age-stigmatised is the generation
of new self-conceptions on the part of members. If it cannot, as I
argue, appropriately be analysed as a 'voluntary association', how is it
to be conceptualised for sociological purposes?

Goffman (1961) has suggested that 'total institutions' are par-

ticularly effective mechanisms for generating assumptions about identity. The ideal type of total institution refers to 'a place of residence
and work where a large number of like-situated individuals, cut off
from the wider society for an appreciable period of time, together lead
an enclosed, formally administered round of life' (Goffman,
1961: 11).

The encompassing or total character of such establishments is symbolised by the physical barriers set up to the outside world and
characterised by the consequent unity of normally separate life
spheres: sleep, play and work. In a total institution, all activities occur
in a single space and under a common authority: inmates are treated,
and required to act, as an undifferentiated group; all aspects of daily
life are scheduled and bureaucratically imposed from above; and 'all
activities are brought together into a single rational plan purportedly
designed to fulfil the official aims of the institution' (Goffman,
1961: 17).

The bureaucratic organisation of total institutions produces a caste-
like cleavage between staff and inmates: social distance between the
two groups is typically great, and each conceives of the other in terms
of narrow stereotypes. Authority is vested in the staff who, according
to Goffman (1961: 80), operate in 'a special moral climate', their activities and approach to inmates being governed by the institution's
particular 'rational perspective'. This includes an *a priori* devaluation
of the personal and social worth of inmates.

The incompatibility between total institutions and the basic work-
payment structure of our society means that work within the institution does not proceed from the usual motivations nor does it have the
usual structural significance attached to it. Sometimes only minimal
or no work is required.

Among the consequences flowing from this combination, two are of
special interest in the present context: the modification of self-
conception on the part of inmates, initially through a process of 'strip-
ping' or mortification of the self, and the particular form of social
control which total institutions facilitate. The former aspect has, in
fact, received some attention from gerontologists studying old people
in nursing homes (Anderson, 1965; Coe, 1965).

None of the actual institutions Goffman describes shares every one
of his defining characteristics. The distinctiveness of the ideal type of
total institution rests rather on the intensity of expression of many of
these features. Thus it has proved possible to analyse institutions
along a continuum of severity of 'total' characteristics and to
demonstrate that 'depersonalization' effects vary directly with this
dimension (Coe, 1965). In these terms, the Bayside Heights Senior
Citizens Club can be analysed as a total institution.

'Total' Characteristics of the Senior Citizens Club as Institution

Physical and social segregation

The club building is physically and socially segregated from its environment. It stands well back from the street, screened by a stone fence, a fringe of trees and a wide lawn from contact with passers-by. Special arrangements must be made if a member wishes to bring a visitor for lunch. On special occasions (Christmas, Senior Citizens Club Week) a local school is prevailed upon to provide a choir or similar entertainment for members. Visits may be specially arranged from time to time to or from other Senior Citizens Clubs. Thus there is relatively little interaction with the wider community, and what does occur is neither spontaneous nor informal. The social segregation of the Club was dramatically signified when it held an Open Day for the public: nobody came.

Class and status considerations on the part of the Welfare Association Committee further reinforce the isolation of the group. The external and internal appearance of the clubroom reflects its socio-economic milieu. The building has a pleasing design and is set in spacious, well tended grounds. Inside it is bright and sunny, with sweeping views of lawn and trees. In addition to the library, facilities include a piano, raised stage and public address system. The kitchen, where meals are kept hot and morning and afternoon teas are prepared, is equipped with modern stoves and dishwasher. Glass walls around the supervisor's office insulate her from the more noisy activities (such as housie) without impeding surveillance.

The contrast which this establishment affords to most senior citizens centres in the metropolitan area was commented upon by an official of the NSW Council on the Aging, whose job takes her to a different club every few days. 'This place has "Status" written over the door', she remarked. The difference between Bayside Heights Senior Citizens Club and a much older centre at the city end of the municipality was often stressed to me by staff and officials of the Welfare Association. The older centre began as a 'soup kitchen', and is still patronised by low-income elderly and aged migrants.

The Bayside Heights Club attracts fewer than 2 per cent of the municipal population of pensionable age. Only 30–40 people actually attend on a given day. Despite this small membership, rigid residence requirements are enforced for prospective members by the Welfare Association, effectively excluding those from 'undesirable' areas. The members themselves told me that they would welcome an influx of 'new blood'. The members' appearance reinforces the air of genteel respectability. Most of the few male attenders wear a suit and tie; at minimum, 'neat casual' slacks and jacket are the order of the

day. Women come in tailored suits or print dresses; hats are ubi-
quitous.

My first impressions of the Club thus indicated that here indeed was
a limiting case of old people's centres: a strongly middle-class
establishment using a typically working-class pattern of participation.
In a short time, however, some of the veneer had begun to peel away.
As my work at the Club proceeded, I noticed that the elderly ladies'
attire did not vary week after week. Their outfits were always neat and
clean, but they were always the same. Until I got to know most of the
regulars by name, I referred to them in my notes as 'the white hat',
'the blue suit', and so on.

Scheduling

A schedule of activities is arranged for the members by the superintendent: indoor bowls on Mondays, craft on Wednesday mornings,
euchre Thursday afternoons, and housie on Fridays. She also
organises an occasional stamp drive for the local hospital: 'They love
to feel that they're being useful', she told me, 'but they would never
do anything about it themselves'. Members' role in scheduling activities is largely limited to showing apathy in attendance, whereupon
the activity is curtailed. A physical fitness class folded through such
lack of interest.

Even the election of the members' own committee and the running
of their annual general meeting are orchestrated by the supervisor. At
these meetings, the Club president in theory should control the proceedings, but at the meetings I attended, the supervisor conducted the
meeting, cueing the secretary and treasurer to present their reports but
allowing the president to *appear* to be in charge.

Absence of socially valued activity

Apart from the stamp drives and donation of the craft group's han-
diwork to the Welfare Association's annual charity stall, the Club offers no opportunity for socially meaningful activity. For most of the
time, the Club appears as 'a kind of dead sea' (Goffman, 1961: 68).
Relief from the tedium is found in what Goffman (1961: 67) refers to
as 'removal activities, voluntary unserious pursuits which are sufficiently engrossing and exciting to lift the participant out of himself,
making him oblivious for the time being to his actual situation'. The
passion with which most regular attenders engage in the sessions of
cards, bowls, and/or housie contrasts dramatically with the unevent-
ful stillness of regular Club life. When no organised activity is taking
place, most members simply sit around and talk.

The incompatibility between Club life and the work-payment structure of society is further reflected in the token nature of payment for

items which the Club provides (50 cents for a hot, two-course meal, 5 cents for a cup of tea). Some members seek a toe-hold on an externally valid definition of self as a 'normal' (that is, not a 'charity' case) by off-handedly rejecting a few cents change.

Staff-member cleavage
The staff on a given day consists of the salaried superintendent and kitchen-hand and two voluntary helpers who are middle-aged local women rostered for one or two days a fortnight.

Interaction between staff and members is severely restricted. Staff take their lunch and afternoon tea together at a separate table after the members have had theirs. Although many of the volunteers know at least several members by name, and occasionally something of their circumstances, I did not in 18 months observe any staff person sitting down at a table with members to socialise. On one occasion a regular volunteer and I were the only non-members on the premises. When I sat down to chat with some members I knew, she reluctantly joined us (the only alternative being to stand or sit somewhere conspicuously alone). She was obviously ill at ease, and took the first opportunity to leave. Staff initiated interaction is limited to a service role, such as driving a frail member home. With one or two exceptions, members show considerable deference in approaching a staff person with a request — to ask for a sandwich in preference to a disliked hot meal or for coffee rather than tea (coffee is considered too expensive and is doled out only on request).

On another occasion I was chatting with an elderly member whose granddaughter used to go to school with the daughter of Mrs Baker, a volunteer helper. The member called Mrs Baker over and began to chat with her about this common experience. The acquaintanceship was, however, not comfortably acknowledged by Mrs Baker. She did not sit down, and excused herself almost immediately.

A rational perspective
Goffman has suggested that the staff in total institutions operate in 'a special moral climate', their activities within it and their approach to the inmates being governed by the institution's particular 'rational perspective'.

The avowed goal of the Club is to provide a meeting place for the aged and lonely members of the community. It sees itself as part of the solution to the 'social problem' of old age, as a benefactor to the needy. This role is seen as essentially custodial and diversionary rather than ameliorative. What the staff sees as 'good for' old people reflects a conception of old people and of appropriate standards for their welfare.

The organisation of club life defines the aged as people whose social needs will be met by socialising with fellow aged and by participation in diversionary pastimes. Once again, the popular stereotype of the 'good' old person is promoted: members are expected to be 'friendly and sociable', and almost indiscriminately so. The supervisor strongly disapproved of 'cliques' and the practice of 'saving seats' for particular people. She tried hard, though without success, to get members to 'circulate more'.[11]

In similar vein, a telephone enquiry from the son of a prospective member elicited the response that if his mother was a sociable, friendly person she would have no trouble 'fitting in'. It was implied that if she did not possess these characteristics to a marked degree, the Club had no place for her.

Stripping

The process of becoming a Club member entails an admission procedure which parallels, in kind, if not in severity, the curtailment of one's self as an ordinary member of the community described by Goffman for other sorts of total institutions. The supervisor writes out a card for each new recruit which contains, in addition to basic items such as name and address, details not normally considered polite or even relevant in other circumstances, such as one's age and next of kin. Members thus see themselves defined from the beginning as people who should not expect the usual respect for privacy in personal matters and who are likely to find themselves incapable of handling their own affairs.

Providing such information is not mandatory; however, refusal to divulge such intimate details is interpreted as, at best, an unwarranted lack of cooperation. At worst, it may suggest that the person is not fully *compos mentis*. On one occasion a female member's[12] continued absence provoked concern and a visit to her home revealed that she was suffering some mild derangement, characteristic of the aftermath of a slight stroke. Her symptoms could also be interpreted as the result of an alcoholic binge. After discussing the situation, staff decided that the latter view was more likely to be correct. 'I always thought she was mentally unstable', the supervisor said. 'She refused to give her age or any information about her background when she joined.'

Social control

The staff-member split is characterised by stereotypes on the part of most members towards staff, but these are not typically negative or hostile. On the contrary, staff (including volunteers) are described by almost all members as altruistic and deserving of gratitude for the services they perform. I was frequently and sincerely told that the supervisor was 'a wonderful person', and was myself often thanked in terms like: 'You're such a good girl for doing this for us'.

Staff are generally portrayed by and among members as having the interests of old people sincerely in mind, as their 'protectors' to a large degree or at least as mediators with the wider world. Their authority is not questioned. This extends to relatively minor and peripheral representatives. For example, the driver who conveyed a busload of members from several Sydney clubs to Adelaide for the National Senior Citizens Clubs Convention told me that he would prefer old people as passengers to any other group: 'They make my job so much easier. If I tell them to jump, they jump'. The constant expressions of gratitude he received from his passengers represented far more than mere acknowledgement that he was performing his job competently. It highlighted the extent to which old people are usually ignored.

That the non-aged may have less altruistic motives for their service (such as payment, status recognition, or simply filling in time) does not appear to be relevant. The stigmatisation of old age, in other words, seems to be internalised to the extent that some kind of personal sacrifice on the part of the non-aged is seen to be inherent in any interaction with the elderly. Only once was a contrary view expressed to me. At the 1978 annual general meeting of the Welfare Association I asked a member, a European-born widow, what she had thought of the proceedings. 'It's all bull', she said quite vehemently. 'It's just something to fill in their [the committee's] time'. I tried several ways of getting her to elaborate on this remark, but she would not be drawn and seemed embarrassed at having expressed such an opinion.

These attitudes, coupled with the definition of desired and undesired conduct on the part of members in terms of a personal morality, facilitates a 'benevolent dictator' form of social control. A particularly striking example of this occurred during the preparations for the state government-sponsored Senior Citizens Week. The Club had been asked to send four representatives to a Government House garden party, and a ballot was organised to select them. The result produced considerable bitterness among the losers, and the supervisor delivered a castigatory speech. It went something like this:

I want to talk to you today about something that has caused me a great deal of unhappiness, something which I would have hoped I would never have occasion to address. We have always been a happy, friendly group, and I intend to see we stay that way. Word has come to me that certain remarks are being made about the four people who have been chosen to go to Government House. You know there was a ballot; it was fair and democratic, conducted at the annual general meeting for all to see. Now just because sort of manners you have, is no reason for this kind of behaviour. I am deeply shocked and upset and I'm sure that most of you would join me in deploring the mean-mindedness of a few.

The speech was punctuated with murmurs of approval and loudly applauded by the members present. Watching the proceedings, I could only compare the style and tone of the address to that of a kindergarten teacher and the response to that of naughty but remorseful children.

Thus members are 'caused to *self-direct* themselves in a manageable way ...', (Goffman, 1961: 83). This translation of behaviour into moralistic terms reflects the broader stereotype of elderly people as something less than social equals and the internalisation of this perspective by the aged themselves.

Of particular importance in this context is the fact that the Club is formally and informally connected to various welfare agencies concerned with the elderly, and is thus in a position to affect aspects of members' lives outside its walls. It can, for example, nominate any member to become a tenant of one of eleven subsidised apartments in the local retirement village. These places, otherwise prohibitively expensive for many, are much sought after, and will only be filled by members considered suitable in terms of the institutional perspective. Staff are also in a position, by virtue of their 'expert' status, to place considerable pressure on a member, whose capacities (physical and/or mental) are deemed wanting, to move into a more sheltered (and by definition dependent) environment. In this way, frail Mrs Brown was induced to give up her flat (where she employed a housekeeper) and move into a hostel. The supervisor handled all the arrangements. The unhappy results of that move are described later.[13].

The Meaning of Participation Reconsidered

Clearly membership of this old people's club cannot be conceived as a status-conferring attribute, nor does it provide a favourable self-identity. Why, then, do old people join at all?

My observations suggest that loneliness (which is not precluded, it seems, by the availability of children and other relatives) and/or inadequacy of resources (functional capacity and/or income) for alternative forms of social participation (and in some cases for obtaining a decent meal) are the most common motivating factors. To many, the Club is a 'last resort' for the satisfaction of basic needs for simple human contact, if not for survival itself.

Detailed analysis of my data suggests that a typology of members can be drawn up along three main dimensions:

1. Persons who attend the Club daily or almost daily (regulars) and those who attend less than once a week (irregulars).

2. Those who participate in socialising and/or one or more organised activities (participators) and those who do neither; that is, whose participation involves little more than ritual greetings and a minimum of 'small talk' (non-participators).

3. Those whose orientation to the Club is primarily expressive, and those whose orientation is primarily instrumental.

The following categories emerge:

1. *Regular participators, expressively oriented* About 15 women fall into this category. They are all single or widowed and have a fixed income, in most cases an old-age pension. For them, the Club is overwhelmingly the focus of their social existence. More than half of them live in Club-sponsored units in the local retirement village. One lives in a church hostel, and four live alone in rooms or flats. Although they eat at the Club every day, I have characterised their participation as expressive because this is not the sole, or even primary reason for their attendance. The woman in the hostel has her meals provided, and the others have both the capacity and the facilities to cook for themselves. Some take part in at least one or two activities (usually cards or housie); the others simply sit and chat. They participate eagerly in exchange visits with other clubs and in sponsored activities for 'seniors'.

2. *Regular participators, instrumentally oriented* Almost all of the other regulars fall into this category which includes the only married couple designated as regular attenders. None of this group attends the Club all day. About half come for the meal alone, and leave as soon as it is finished. I have called them participators because they sit at the same tables with the same clique every day and clearly maintain more than a minimum level of sociability. This segment includes some of the regularly attending widowers for whom cooking represents a new and relatively problematic experience. The hot meal is also the main attraction for the couple: the wife is somewhat mentally confused and is incapable of preparing a meal.[14] For the rest, the organised activities constitute the main reason for belonging to the Club. Several of them, for example, play carpet bowls with almost professional seriousness, participating in inter-club and even national competitions. Not all of this group live alone; a few live with relatives, and two sets of friends share dwellings. Most of the others appear to have at least one special friend with whom

they maintain frequent contact outside the Club. Several, including the married couple, live in the retirement village.

3. *Regular non-participators, instrumentally oriented* Several men fall into this category. One of them, a widower whose situation will be detailed shortly, participates in ways that more closely resemble the activities of staff than of other members.

4. *Irregular non-participators instrumentally oriented* Miss Schmidt[15] typifies this category. She attends about once a fortnight, either because she doesn't feel like cooking that day, or to use the equipment during the crafts morning. She never stays to socialise, and told me emphatically that there is no-one in the Club with whom she feels compatible.

The majority of the Club's nominal members attend so infrequently, if at all, that I was unable to get a firm picture of them. They appear to drop in for an occcasional meal or a special occasion, such as the Christmas party or an inter-club bowls competition.

The real sociological interest, however, lies in a fourth distinction which crosscuts these three. Following Goffman (1961), I term it a distinction between primary adjustment and secondary adjustment. It is this dimension which provides insight into different reactions on the part of old people to the cooling out process.

Primary and Secondary Adjustments

Total institutions can be viewed as places for generating assumptions about identity. 'To engage in a particular activity in the prescribed spirit is to accept being a particular kind of person who dwells in a particular kind of world' (Goffman, 1961: 170).

Regular participators engage 'in the prescribed spirit'. For them, a chance to be publicly recognised representatives of the Club at ceremonial occasions organised 'for Sydney's Senior Citizens' (such as the Government House garden party or the annual Senior Citizens Convention) is eagerly accepted. In Goffman's terms, they have a 'primary adjustment' to the organisation. These old people seek self-validation in other ways, which I describe in the following chapter.

For others, such participation would be unthinkable. For them, social recognition of themselves as part of the age-stigmatised category symbolises a demeaning role which they personally reject for themselves. As Goffman (1961: 70) suggests: 'To forgo prescribed activities, or to engage in them in unprescribed ways or for unprescribed purposes, is to withdraw from the official self and the world officially available to it. To prescribe activity is to prescribe a world: to dodge a prescription can be to dodge an identity.'

The ways in which an individual stands apart from the taken for granted role and self sanctioned by the institution are termed 'secondary adjustments':

> Walled-in organisations have a characteristic they share with few other social entities: part of the individual's obligation is to be visibly engaged at appropriate times in the activity of the organisation... This obligatory engrossment in the activity of the organisation tends to be taken as a symbol both of one's commitment and one's attachment (to a social entity), and, behind this, of one's acceptance of the implications of participation for a defintion of one's nature (Goffman, 1961: 161–2).

Thus distance from the self implications of affiliation with the Club can be expressed by remaining visibly uninvolved in Club activity. There are two or three men who, after lunch, remove themselves from the tables (where everyone else remains sitting) to some armchairs in a corner where they read in silence. They do not socialise, even with each other, nor do they participate in any of the organised diversions. In this way they abjure identification with the membership at large.

The non-obligatory nature of participation in Club life facilitates this kind of defaulting to the extent that, for those members who wish to resist the self-definitions that are institutionalised within its walls, the Club functions primarily as a service centre. However, to attend at all entails a manifest acceptance, albeit a temporary one, that one is indeed the sort of person for whom the institution exists. Failure to participate 'in the prescribed spirit' is therefore a *passive* kind of secondary adjustment. For these regular non-participators, the extent of participation reflects no more than the extent of their need for a particular service and the lack of alternatives available to them.

Certain structural arrangements also facilitate an *active* form of secondary adjustment. Jim Fletcher, a 68-year-old widower, has filled a structural niche in the establishment which allows him a measure of control in defining his own situation. This control is unavailable to other members.

Case Study — Mr Fletcher   Jim retired from his job as an accountant three years ago. His wife died shortly after, followed by his only surviving sister. His only daughter, a 29-year-old unmarried school teacher, shares a house in Bayside Heights with friends. Jim would like to see her marry and settle down, because 'when I go there will be no-one'. There are some relatives but 'we're not close'. Once or twice a fortnight his daughter spends the night at his flat: they go out for a meal and he drives her to school the next day. He can cook 'a bit of meat and veg', but sometimes eats out at a restaurant. Although he tries to keep in touch with old friends who live elsewhere in the city, he does not see them often. Most of his companions are new-found friends. After his wife died, he joined the local Rugby Union Club and, through the coaxing of a neighbour who is a voluntary helper, the Senior Citizens Club. He now has a number of friends at the Rugby Union Club, but his most frequent companion on outings (to films, shows, and the like) is a same-age widower who lives in his apartment block. He has made no friends at the Senior Citizens.

Jim has put himself on the waiting list for a private hostel in the area because, he says, 'I didn't think I'd be able to stand cooking forever'. He envisaged a wait of about 10 years, but they contacted him recently and offered him a place. 'They're trying to even up the sexes', he explained. 'Of course I refused — that won't be for a long time yet'. He would not consider moving to Bayside Village: 'There would be no point unless I wanted to sell the unit and have more money. But what would I spend it on?'

Last year he went alone on a package tour to Europe. He would like to go again, and says his daughter wants to go with him. He does not want to remarry: 'I like my privacy. There's a widow in the apartment block I take to the Club occasionally, but it's only a superficial friendship'. The secret of 'being well' in later years, he maintains, is to 'keep active'. He does not like to think of himself as a 'senior citizen' — 'although I suppose I am. I'm old enough to belong here, but sometimes I look around and wonder what I'm doing here with all these old fuddy duddies'. He says that mental age and not chronological age is the important thing: 'All old people are of different ages mentally'.

At the Senior Citizens club, Jim's business expertise has been put to use: he has become a kind of honorary bookkeeper *cum* organiser, arranging bus trips and other outings for members, though he never goes along himself. These activities are highly valued by staff: 'He's a real gem', the supervisor told me.

In return, Jim is accorded a considerable reduction in the social distance that typically prevails between members and staff. His interaction with staff is characterised by a degree of equality that I did not observe in any other case. It is symbolised not only by a conversational style free of deference/superiority overtones, but also by the fact that certain matters deemed unsuitable for members' knowledge are freely confided to him. He alone of the members was told about Mrs Walton's 'drinking bout' and visited her when the supervisor was too busy to go. His competence and self-assured gentility seem to strike some volunteers as incongruous with this status as an objectively 'old' person. 'You know', one helper commented to me with apparent surprise, 'you could take him anywhere'.

In other words, Jim has been relatively successful in retaining a kind of status that is valued in outside life. In conversation he disassociates himself from his fellow members, a separateness symbolised by his organising activities. He takes no part in the ordinary round of Club life, invariably sitting alone with his books. His Club activities can be seen as a 'substitute for the business day' (Mannes, 1954), which was the focus of his life until comparatively recently. Significantly, he told me that for some time after his retirement he would visit his old work place from time to time to 'keep in touch'. But one by one the old familiar faces disappeared, and he stopped going.

The structural arrangements which support Jim Fletcher's secondary adjustment to the Club take a variety of froms. First, it is necessary to remark upon the *unofficial* status of his position. Club members annually elect the usual complement of office bearers. He is always suggested for nomination, and always declines, just as he declines every other opportunity to represent the Club officially (at the Government House reception, for instance). Clearly any such publicly legitimated representative role implies an identification with the sort of image of self which is anathema to him. Elected officials must operate within a framework which derives from and supports the institutionalised conception of members. In addition, a representative role makes it incumbent upon the occupant to appear at mixed gatherings, such as the annual general meeting of the Welfare Association, at which the stigma of old age is symbolically expressed.

Jim brings to his role three valued 'resources': relatively young age (68), unimpaired physical capacity, and male gender. Within the Club, each is a scarce commodity; in combination they are prerequisite for performance of the role. In terms of age, health, and mobility (via his car) he is closer to staff than to the majority of members. In addition, he was personally known to one of the volunteers prior to joining, hence his introduction to the Club and to other staff was atypical and immediately set him somewhat apart. By cultivating a role which is primarily an extension of staff activities, and by assiduously avoiding anything other than superficial social relations with members, he has managed to maintain this separateness.

The expressive component of life is fulfilled in activities external to the Club. The Club provides him with an outlet for more intrumentally oriented activities. Psychologically, then, the role of 'mediator' enables him to minimise the dissonance between his positive image of self and his negatively valued manifest status as a Senior Citizen. The institutional relations that characterise the Club provide a niche or in Wolf's (1966) terms, an 'interstitial position', whereby a member whose personal and social attributes are both similar in kind to those of staff and a source of prestige among members can 'work the sytem' and escape some of the more demoralising aspects of old age stigma. It is at these points of secondary adjustment, whether active or passive, that the ability of the institution to define the situation of members is weakest.

Summary

The Bayside Heights Senior Citizens Club manifests many of the attributes of a total institution. There is an embracing conception on the part of staff and of the wider welfare agency of what a Senior Citizen is and needs. The overt behaviour and expressed attitudes of some members suggest that they share, to a considerable extent, this image of old people.

For the regular participators, for whom the spare round of Club life constitutes the major social outlet, an array of world-building activities has developed.

A general theme of being *in* but not *of* the institution characterises the irregular attendance of many members, and the deliberate nonparticipation of others. Even among those I have described as primarily adjusted to the institution, almost all participate keenly in one or more of the 'removal activities' whereby the environment is temporarily displaced. Whether through a game of cards, housie, or solitary reading, the element of control over one's definition of self and situation is briefly restored: 'whatever else they accomplish these practices seem to demonstrate — to the practitioner if no-one else, that he has some selfhood and personal autonomy beyond the grasp of the organisation' (Goffman, 1961: 275-6).

For others, the barrier is drawn not so much between one's self and the institution, but between one's self and one's fellow members. Refusal to participate beyond the minimum level required to satisfy certain instrumental needs is not in itself a source of satisfaction, but functions rather to express distance from those with whom one would thereby be identified: a self-maintaining rejection of age stigma.

The importance of these arrangements for the structure of the self cannot be over-emphasised in studies of old age. The tendency of gerontologists to define an elderly individual's social being in terms of the various groups to which he belongs — family, friends, or whatever — represents an extension of a widespread sociological predilection: 'The simplest sociological view of the individual and his self is that he is to himself what his place in an organisation defines him to be' (Goffman, 1961: 280). Thus a member of a Senior Citizens Club would be defined as a person who embraces the manifest purposes of this kind of social establishment or, on a higher level of abstraction, as one person among many who have developed a common aging consciousness and solidarity.

However, as this discussion has shown, in an old people's club as in any other social organisation, individuals find ways of maintaining some distance between themselves and the identities which others assume them to have. Given the fact that old age is a granted status (de Beauvoir, 1970: 100), that the aged as a stigmatised social category are the *objects* of society-wide patterns of social control, it is easy to understand why individual old people come to be defined by the groups in which they participate. In the logic of role theory, definition by the group = identification with the group = gratification of *a priori* 'needs'.

Far more valid for sociological purposes, and for gerontological reseach in particular, is initially to define the individual 'as a stance-taking entity, a something that takes up a position somewhere between identification with an organisation and opposition to it . . . ' (Goffman, 1961: 280). In this way, the interaction of an elderly person in a particular social network can be analysed without prior assumptions about group identification or normative notions of adjustment.

The existence of special clubs for old people points to the presence of a problem for society as much as for individual old people. We have developed agencies for cooling out the elderly and an ideology of their nature which justifies such a process. The total institutional aspects of this old people's club makes it a particularly effective place for generating assumptions about identity which in turn facilitate the cooling out process. We must not assume what the reaction to this process will be. Old people after all *are* people, not problems. As Goffman has remarked in a broader context:

> Without something to belong to, we have no stable self, and yet total commitment and attachment to any social unit implies a kind of selflessness. Our sense of being a person can come from being drawn into a wider social unit; our sense of selfhood can arise through the little ways in which we resist the pull. Our status is backed by the solid buildings of the world, while our sense of personal identity often resides in the cracks, (Goffman, 1961: 280).

The refusal of some Meals on Wheels recipients to display the submission and deference which seems to be expected of them can also be understood in this light, as can the attempt to have volunteers use the service entrance. Keenly aware of their stigmatised situation, they are simultaneously adamant that the individious stereotypes do not apply to them personally. Their behaviour, interpreted by others as 'ingratitude' or 'apathy', is much more appropriately understood as an attempt to define themselves as 'normal'. Deprived through physical and/or financial adversity of the power to exercise autonomy over some aspects of their life situation, they yet strive to retain control over their *definitions* of that situation: they are not welfare cases, but equal participators in a routine social interaction.

This perspective applies equally to the non-institutionalised aspects of old people's lives, including the patterns of interaction they maintain with their age peers. This is the subject of enquiry in the following chapter.

Notes

1. Significantly, voluntary helpers for services which operate in low status areas tend to come from 'better' suburbs outside the district (Duigan, 1975).
2. On the attitudes of some welfare groups in Hindmarsh, Victoria, Duigan (1975: 35) comments: 'The provision of services by welfare groups with a religious basis is guided both by humanitarianism and by a Christian ethic which seeks to curtail and to relieve the excesses of the lower classes. The two are closely related; for instance, "these people just don't know how to budget". The accusation of unnecessary expenditure leads to a concept of the *deserving poor* by which stringent criterion one can then be sure of not encouraging any type of sloth'.
3. See for example New South Wales Council on the Aging, *Meals on Wheels* (pamphlet, n.d.); New South Wales Council on the Aging, *A History of Meals on Wheels in New South Wales* (pamphlet, n.d.).
4. This age/sex composition is typical of volunters in charitable agencies generally (c.f. Hamilton-Smith, 1973: 58–60).
5. Some researchers also attach great importance to their estimates of 'the degree of cleanliness both of the person and the surroundings' (Sorrell, 1972: 16) as evidence of mental competence.
6. As I mentioned in Chapter 4, many Meals on Wheels recipients in Bayside Heights were reluctant to be interviewed. That stigmatisation is likely to have been an important factor is suggested by other evidence: the attitudes of voluntary workers, the deferent behaviour of some recipients and the attempts by some others to conceal from neighbours the fact that they were dependent on the service (by, for example, insisting on the runner using the service entrance; several others had their meals delivered through a rear lane access).
7. For an examination of goal displacement in the activities of three organisations dealing with planning for the elderly see Estes (1974).
8. See for example F. Dotson, Patterns of voluntary associations among urban working-class families, *Amer. Sociol. Rev.*, 16, 687: 93 1951; R. Freedman and M. Axelrod, Who belongs to what in a great metropolis? *Adult Leadership*, 1 (Nov.), 6–9; 1952; M. Komarovsky, Voluntary

associations of urban dwellers, *Amer. Sociol. Rev.*, 11, 686–98; 1946; W. Bell and M.T. Force, Social structure and participation in different types of formal associations, *Social Forces,* 34, 1956; H.H. Hyman and C.R. Wright, Trends in voluntary association memberships of American adults: replication based on secondary analysis of national sample surveys, *Amer. Sociol. Rev.*, 36, 2, 1971; J. Curtis, Voluntray association joining: a cross-national comparative note, *Amer. Sociol. Rev.*, 36, 1971; M. Axelrod, Urban structure and social participation, *Amer. Social. Rev.*, 21, 1958.

9. It should be noted that at the time of this study there were no clubs in 'Prairie City' specifically for the aged. The conclusion therefore refers to participation in non-age-graded organisations.
10. This expression was suggested to me by Dr Richard Basham.
11. A booklet designed for club supervisors in fact suggests ways to help 'break down ... cliques' (Tolhurst, n.d.: 5).
12. Case history, p. 142–143
13. Case history, p. 143
14. Case history, p. 166–167
15. Case history, p. 186–188

6 Interaction Among the Fellow-stigmatised

The devaluation of self which an old person is likely to experience in social encounters with the non-aged highlights the social — and sociological — significance of relationships which the age-stigmatised maintain 'among their own'. Interaction on the basis of age is not, of course, confined to the later years. People of all ages experience institutionalised age-grading at various stages in their life and, in informal contexts, demonstrate age homophily in their choice of friends (Hess, 1972).

Commonality of interests and experiences is usually stressed as the basis for friendship formation among the aged, and the positive effects on self-conception of peer relations have been proposed (Blau, 1973). In these terms, age segregation comes to be seen as a natural coping mechanism for shutting out those who would discredit one's self (Fontana, 1977). It has also been conceptualised as a condition for, and expression of, an aging group consciousness in which the status of old person can be favourably evaluated (Rose, 1965b).

Rose has argued that the aged constitute a subculture with a partially distinctive value system. He maintains that the development of an aging subculture has proceeded from the increasing separation of older people, both physcial and social, from other age categories. Rose finds evidence for the existence of a subculture in the tendency for older people to form voluntary relationships with others of the same age, reflecting the 'positive affinity' which they feel for each other vis-a-vis other age groups. The content of the subculture is characterised by a partially distinctive status system and, at least among some of the elderly, by an 'aging group consciousness'.

While Rose does not deny that the internal stratification system of the elderly is partially 'a carry-over of that of the general society' (1965b: 30), he suggests that prestige derived from factors such as wealth and occupation will decrease in importance with age, while other attributes will assume greater significance. Physical and mental health and extent of social activity, for example, will have 'special value in conferring status within the subculture of the elderly' (Rose, 1965b: 31). Clark's (1968) study provides some support for this notion of a particular aged value system, as does other research among the age-graded elderly (Hochschild, 1973). Rose's analysis locates the impetus for subculture formation in the rejection of the aged by the wider society. However, the status conferring factors delineated by Rose do not suggest that age *per se* has come to be positively valued, a necessary precondition to the development of a group *pride*, and not just group awareness, which the notion of subculture subsumes (Fontana, 1977). As will become clear in the course of my discussion, common age does not of itself promote social solidarity. Rose is correct in identifying the segregating effects of age stigma, but it is precisely the fact that old age *is* a social stigma which precludes rather than facilitates the development of aging group solidarity.

Certainly the in-group presents the aged individual with a basis for interaction which differs in important respects from the pattern of encounters with the non-aged. But, generalisations regarding the functions of age homophily need to be treated with caution. What cannot be ignored is the concomitant operation of age stigma.

For aged segregation reflects the operation not only of homophily, but of social, political and economic structures which limit interactional opportunities and affect the nature and meaning of interaction itself. Segregation of the aged as clients of welfare services is the most obvious manifestation of this process. But the effects of age stigma also appear in non-institutionalised friendship networks.

Interpretations of the meaning of friendship in old age couched in role theory terms emphasise the structure and composition of the groups or networks in which the individual interacts. The psychological processes involved are taken as given; that is, cognitive and affective features of belonging are assumed to be congruent, *ipso facto*, with the structural arrangements. For the stigmatised individual, however, *ambivalence* is likely to characterise attachment to the stigmatised category, since his 'real group is the category which can serve as his discrediting' (Goffman, 1963: 137).

As DeVos and Wagatsuma (1966) suggest, we can understand a great deal about social integration in terms of the group to which an individual feels he most belongs. However, they point out, the existence of negatively charged symbolic representations of a group can create an expressive dilemma for its members if the reference group is not also the membership group.

In this chapter, I examine the involvement of some older people with their age peers. Patterns of interaction within the Senior Citizens Club are described first. I show that age alone is not a sufficient condition for friendship formation. On the contrary, cliques and dyadic relationships, based on similarity of resources and lifestyles, are differentiating mechanisms by means of which the elderly can distance themselves from the membership at large and, by implication, from the category of 'old people'. These relationships are not stable. The composition of friendship networks is constantly changing, while dyadic ties may alter their character or terminate altogether. I then present data on old age friendships in non-institutional settings and offer an explanation for the patterns observed in the Club and for the dynamics of aged peer relations more generally.

Aged Peer Relationships

Gerontologists have explored the relationships which old people maintain with their peers from four main perspectives: as sources of instrumental assistance; as a factor in 'adjustment'; as a reference category; and in terms of the effects of age segregation.

Age peers as a source of instrumental assistance
Given the research emphasis on material needs of the elderly, it is not surprising that most comprehensive surveys have included questions on the extent to which friends provide help and services of various kinds. The findings summarised by Riley and Foner (1968: 573-4) and original studies by Rosow (1967), Johnson (1971) and Sherman (1975b) suggest that material assistance is one function of friendship, particularly within the neighbourhood. Neighbours are especially important in emergencies and for old people living alone (Prinsley and Cameron, 1979). However, as Rosow has emphasised, it is the family which has institutionalised responsibility in the area of instrumental assistance for its aged members. Friends and neighbours are utilised far less often than are relatives for help and services, and are generally only mentioned as a primary source of assistance by those without available relatives. They are hardly ever a source of financial assistance.

In any case, the provision of help by one aged person to another is part of an interaction process which has more than material consequences. It is a symbolic as well as an instrumental expression and needs to be analysed as such. Something of the significance of this perspective is revealed by two well-known studies which have focused on the qualitative dimension of helping relationships within age segregated settings (Johnson, 1971; Hochschild, 1973, 1976a). These suggest that instrumental assistance between age peers is of two main kinds: balanced exchange in which each interactant remains autonomous and reciprocates any assistance, and non-reciprocal service, in which a physically fit older person offers assistance to a frail one.

Balanced exchange involves the routine exchange of non-substantial goods and services; it is based on a norm of reciprocity, and functions through what Sheila Johnson (1971: 98), in a study of a working-class mobile home community, refers to as 'the mechanism of rough equivalence'. Those unable to reciprocate in kind sometimes employ cash as a medium of exchange. Others, physically and/or financially unable to reciprocate at all, simply withdraw from instrumental forms of interaction (Johnson, 1971: 100).

Arlie Russell Hochschild's analysis of instrumental patterns within Merrill Court, a public housing project for the retired, reveals the existence of both balanced and unbalanced exchange systems. The latter is an important component in the informal status hierarchy that had developed among the residents. The formal hierarchy was based on the 'distribution of honour', particularly through holding offices in the service club. The informal hierarchy was based on the 'distribution of luck', as defined by the residents:

> She who had good health (defined as the result of luck) won honour. She who lost the fewest loved ones through death won honour, and she who was close to her children won honour. Those who fell short of any of these criteria were often referred to as 'poor dears'. The 'poor dear' system operated like a set of values through which a sense of superiority ran in only one direction. Someone who was a 'poor dear' in the eyes of another seldom called that other person a 'poor dear' in return. Rather, the 'poor dear' would turn to someone less fortunate, perhaps to buttress a sense of her own achieved or ascribed superiority. Thus, the hierarchy honoured residents at the top and pitied 'poor dears' at the bottom, creating a number of informally recognised status distinctions among those who, in the eyes of the outside society, were social equals. (1976: 327)

Socio-emotional functions of peer relations

Some attention has been paid in the literature to the role of friendship in later life in adjustment or morale. Rosow's (1967) analysis shows that the primary emotional orientation of older people is toward their families; friends and neighbours rate far lower in terms of expressed identification, loyalty, and closeness. Neither morale in general nor satisfaction with friendships in particular is related to actual frequency of contact. There is, however, some association between the two subjective dimensions: half of those with low morale, but only one-fourth of those with high morale, express desire for more friendships (that is, are dissatisfied with their friendships).

Zena Blau (1973) has argued that friendships with age peers become critical for morale following major role losses through widowhood or retirement. She suggests that 'extensive social activity with age peers constitutes an effective *alternative* for either the marital or occupational role' (1973: 63) and that friends are more effective in this context than are relationships with children: 'because friendship rests on mutual choice and mutual need and involves a voluntary exchange of sociability between *equals*, it sustains a person's sense of usefulness and self-esteem more effectively than filial relationships' (1973: 67).

However, not all interaction between age peers who describe themselves as 'friends' can be interpreted in this way. There are degrees of 'mutuality' and of 'voluntariness', and for some interactants the outcome of such relationships is a *lowered* feeling of usefulness and self-esteem, as later case studies demonstrate.

Further insight into the qualitative dimension of friendship is provided by Johnson (1971: 82-3), who notes that her respondents construed the word 'friend' in vastly different ways, differentiating essentially between 'close friends' and people with whom they were 'friendly'. Other researchers have shown that it is the possession of a confidant or intimate friend which is positively associated with morale in old age (Lowenthal and Haven, 1968). Consideration of the factors responsible for this association brings us to another perspective on aged peer relations — the reference function.

Age peer relations and reference group theory
The personal network of same-age friends, Blau maintains, is critical to the self-conception of elderly people. Her data on subjective age-identification suggest that the most significant determinant of age self-conception is the appraisal of one's social intimates:

> The stability of the network of relationships within a group of friends ... prevents mutual awareness of the gradual alterations taking place among the participants, particularly if these changes do not interfere with a person's ability to share in the group's activities. Consequently, the recurrent gatherings of the same people lend a sense of continuity to each participant's identity. (1973: 108)

Moreover, it seems that the comparative function of age peers is not restricted to the immediate circle of acquaintances. A longitudinal study of older Americans found that favourable comparative evaluations of their situation with that of 'the aged' as a social category were 'as important to the life satisfaction of respondents as were their actual objective positions on various status scales' (Bultena and Powers, 1976: 176). These authors suggest that the social category of 'old people', to which negative stereotypes are popularly attached, emerges in later life as a powerful reference group against which older individuals can compare their own life situations in favourable terms.

As Hess (1976b) has pointed out, the phenomenon of 'pluralistic ignorance' undoubtedly operates among aged people. Pluralistic ignorance refers to:

> the pattern in which individual members of a group *assume* that they are virtually alone in holding the social attitudes and expectations they do, all unknowing that others privately share them. This is a frequently observed condition of a group that is so organised that mutual observability among its members is slight. (Merton, 1968: 377)

These data seem to support Hochschild's assertion that older persons 'compare themselves not to the young but to other old people' (1976a: 329). Analytically, the category of 'other old people' needs to be divided into two subgroups: the semi-abstract notion of 'other people my age', and the immediate personal network. The latter is in turn subdivided into intimates and acquaintances.

Andrea Fontana, on the other hand, suggests that the ultimate reference group is always the non-aged. Retirement communities, he argues, act as a buffer against potential invidious comparisons: 'they can believe that they are still young, as long as . . . they have no blue-eyed, lean, tanned-bodied, freckle-faced youngster around to remind them that what they see in the mirror is a mask that society labels as old' (1977: 29).

Townsend (1968) has in fact suggested that not one but several references may be important in the different orientations of older persons toward one aspect of their life situation, physical isolation. These are: comparison with contemporaries, comparison with preceding generations of aged, comparison with earlier life statuses, and comparison with the statuses occupied by younger persons. Unfortunately the types of reference groups that are used in later life, and their differential importance for the aged, are research questions which have not yet been sufficiently explored (Bultena and Powers, 1976). I shall argue that the choice of reference others is strongly influenced by the operation of age stigma.

Effects of age-segregated environments
Several studies have compared older people living in 'normal', age-heterogeneous neighbourhoods with residents of age-segregated facilities of various kinds (Rosow, 1962, 1967, 1968; Teaff, Lawton,

Nahemow, and Carlson, 1978; Sherman, 1975a). There appears to be a significant relationship between the residential density of older people and patterns of informal association. Two major findings of Rosow's (1967) study of 1200 middle-and working-class Cleveland residents were that the number of old people's local friends varies directly with the proportion of older neighbours available, and that, regardless of the number available, friends consist disproportionately of older rather than younger neighbours.

Sherman (1975a) interviewed residents of six retirement facilities and matched controls in age-integrated housing and found that retirement residents had, relative to their controls, more new friends and visited more with neighbours and with age peer friends. A similar study of public housing sites (Teaff *et al.*, 1978) reports that age segregation shows small but reliable relationships to local participation patterns, as well as to morale.

There is some suggestion, however, that age-segregation effects vary with social class and with amount of role loss. Rosow's analysis (1967) showed that different subgroups of the elderly are most sensitive and responsive to age-density variations. The effects are strongest for working-class rather than middle-class people, and for those with high role loss.

Another study sheds a somewhat different light on peer relations in age-segregated settings. Stephens (1975, 1976) has described and analysed the social world of the aged single room occupancy (SRO) hotel tenant and finds it to be characterised by an impoverishment of social roles and relationships which result in a 'world of strangers'. Peer relationships, especially among the women, were decidedly not supportive. Their attitudes toward each other revolved around hostility, jealousy, and permanent competition for the few available males. Friendships among the women were transient phenomena, lasting only a matter of days, and interaction tended to take the form of one-upmanship whereby each person attempted to establish that her family and background were superior to that of the others.[1]

How is one to explain and reconcile such apparently discrepant findings? Clearly, aged peer relationships are complex, multi-faceted phenomena that simultaneously perform a variety of functions *and* reflect particular social contexts and subjective understandings. We need to look at friendships as systems of meaning, rather than merely as structures. My data show that an exchange theory of social relations can provide the starting point for analysis of elderly people's relations with their age peers. At the same time, however, the perception of age stigma intrudes on network processes in ways which may sometimes undermine the positive functions of old age friendships.

Friendship in Bayside Heights

As part of each case study, I collected information about the people whom my informants thought of as friends: their ages and other demographic characteristics, the history of the association, and the structural features of any networks within which each relationship was embedded. I also obtained observational data on peer relations within the Senior Citizens Club.

In line with research which shows that older people tend strongly to choose friends of the same age as themselves, only one of my informants (Mrs Chevalier) described any non-aged person as a friend. Homophily of friendship in terms of sex, marital status, and social class is also supported. Several respondents, queried about their relations with neighbours, spontaneously mentioned disparities in age and/or marital status as reasons for their failure to interact with certain people in their immediate environment. The perception of status differences was also salient. One resident of the cheaper units in the retirement village described how the owners of the expensive apartments 'look down on' her and her fellow bed-sit occupants as 'just pensioners' and conspicuously fail to mix with them at village functions. Two wealthy informants suggested that I interview their cleaning staff for 'a totally different picture' of old age.

For several elderly women in my sample, social interaction was almost exclusively confined within networks of same-age friends and acquaintances. The majority of these women were residents of the retirement village and/or members of the Senior Citizens Club, though the case study of Miss Jones highlights the extent to which age-segregation can operate within far less visible boundaries.

Friendship Networks in the Senior Citizens Club

A striking feature of relationships among club members was the high degree of differentiation. Far from presenting a 'common front' to the intrusion of stigma through the agency of welfare personnel, the membership was split into a multiplicity of cliques. The same people always occupied 'their' table: after only a few weeks of observation I was able to spot the absence of a regular member by an empty chair. Rules of occupancy were strictly adhered to; only a newcomer would sit in someone else's place, to be informed, politely but firmly, that 'Mrs — always sits there'.

On some occasions, such as the selection of representatives for the Government House garden party, the membership as a whole could become bitterly divided. For the most part though, each clique co-existed peacefully with the others through a kind of polite curtailment.

Social distinctions established in the wider society made their presence felt in Club interaction. One strongly bounded clique comprised four relatively wealthy widows who met at the Club to play bridge. Their social distance from other members was symbolised by their physical withdrawal to the library for this purpose. Whereas all members were always neat and clean in their appearance, these four were conspicuously stylish in their dress. Even this was apparently considered 'dressing down'. As one of the group remarked to me, 'I had a job convincing my friend not to dress up when she comes here. You have to make concessions so you don't stand out too much — I don't wear either of my minks.'

Sex was also a differentiating criterion. About eight widowers were fairly regular attenders, and they exclusively occupied two adjacent tables. The only exception was a very elderly married man who came with his wife and sat at an otherwise all-female table.

Other cliques were based on participation in the only active pastime provided — carpet bowls. Those physically active strove to differentiate themselves not only from the actually infirm, but also from those they saw as 'lazy'. Their motto seemed to be, 'as long as I'm active I'm not old like those others.'

Goffman (1961: 265) suggests that in total institutions cliques provide a means of defining their members as 'normal' and others as 'not normal'. During the period of observation I made a point of sitting down to chat at different tables in turn.[2] Each group invariably compared its members favourably with the others in terms of mental age. Comments like the following were common: 'Personally, we would like to live in a community that had people of all ages in it, but the others here are too mentally old to cope'; 'We keep an interest in life, but these others just want to sit and stare'. Thus elements of the aged value system operate against group solidarity.

At the same time, not all cliques comprised members who viewed each other as equals. Two groups exhibited a caretaking pattern whereby one member, with the approval or at least quiescence of the others, assumed a kind of leadership role. One group was 'led' by a 70-year-old former nurse, Miss Chapman. Although she would occasionally use a walking stick as a result of a car accident, Miss Chapman brusquely took charge of several fellow members — dispensing advice, deciding seating arrangements, and acting as spokesperson for the group ('Mrs — hasn't had her sweets yet, Miss'). Her interaction with staff was not marked by deference and she routinely took it upon herself to assist them to clear tables and help with other tasks.

The other group in this category was led by Mrs Buchanan, a

79-year-old widow. She and her clique were the self-styled 'regulars', attending the club all day, every day and always sharing the same table. When I first began attending the club, her group consisted of Mrs Walton, Mrs Brown, and Miss Lewis. These last two women were very frail, and Mrs Buchanan would see to all their needs, collecting their cups of tea, assisting them to move around, getting taxis for them in the afternoon, making small purchases for them and so forth.

The dynamics of this network during the research period are illustrative of a number of basic themes which characterise patterns of friendship among the age-stigmatised.

Case Study — Mrs Buchanan Mrs Buchanan was born and spent most of her adult life in an interstate capital city. Her father was a prominent 'old family' barrister and politician, her husband a chemist with his own business. 'I had everything one could wish for.' They had one child, Joanne, who had just started university when Mr Buchanan died. He apparently left relatively little money (for reasons she was reluctant to reveal), and Mrs Buchanan could not afford to keep the large family home. Joanne found a job in Sydney. They knew a 'good family' who had moved to Bayside Heights, and Joanne found a flat through them. Mrs Buchanan followed her here and took over the flat when Joanne went to London soon afterwards.

She married an Australian there, and had a child. A year or so later the family returned to Bayside Heights and took a house near Mrs Buchanan's flat. The marriage did not work out. Mrs Buchanan remarked that her son-in-law was 'not our kind of people'. I asked what sort of family background he had, and she replied vehemently: 'None.' His father was a butcher. Joanne returned to London with her daughter. She writes to her mother regularly every fortnight.

For a time Mrs Buchanan continued to live in the flat, which was part of a large house, and became 'good friends' with the elderly woman died Mrs Buchanan could not afford to remain in the flat. She their Sunday meals together, and watched television in the evenings. I found out later from the Senior Citizens Club supervisor that she was in fact employed by this old lady as a companion-help, something which was apparently considered too demeaning to tell me. When this woman died Mrs Buchanan could not afford to remain in the flat. She applied for admission to Bayside Village and lived in a series of cheap rooms in the area until she was offered a place in one of the Club-subsidised units. The only complaint she had about the village was that neighbours were 'always dropping in' and she could not get enough privacy.

Her only income was the pension, from which she payed $23 rent per fortnight. She had furnished her unit with the few things she had left from the old family home. Though rather shabby now, they were of extremely good quality. The unit was sparkling clean and neat, and the kitchen was sensibly, if sparsely, stocked with food. She said she cooked for herself at night, though she had lunch at the Club every day. She was president of the Club for a year before the present incumbent, Mrs Hill, was elected. Mrs Buchanan was once very active in church affairs (Presbyterian) in her original home city, but she did not go to church any more. 'It has a different atmosphere these days', she remarked. 'I talk to God instead.'

When I asked her what sorts of things bring respect for an old person from age-peers, she said, 'Being kind, pleasant . . . and clean.' She attended all the inter-Club functions and was one of the four members chosen for the Government House reception during Senior Citizens Week. On the latter occasion she told me that she was 'used to these kinds of functions' from her earlier years in a socially prominent family.

When I first met her, Mrs Buchanan referred to the other three women as her 'good buddies', though she had only known them for the two years she had been coming to the Club. She continually impressed upon me how much she did for Mrs Brown and Miss Lewis. Mrs Walton, on the other hand, was not infirm, and this relationship was accordingly egalitarian. It did not, however, survive the period of fieldwork.

Case Study — Mrs Walton   Mrs Walton, an elderly widow, lived alone in a Bayside Heights rooming house. Little was known about her personal history at the Club, as she refused to disclose any details about herself when she joined. She told me she had always lived in Bayside Heights, and no-one had ever observed her to have any contact with people other than Club members. When she had her 'turn', the Club superintendent visited her room and found that she had been living in appalling conditions: the windows were coated with grime, eating utensils were unwashed, and the bedclothes had to be destroyed. She eventually and very reluctantly agreed to have the Catholic Brown Sisters come and clean up for her. The perception of this incident by staff has already been described, (see p. 120).

Though staff attempted to prevent other members from knowing about the situation, word spread quickly and the topic provided a talking point for the two weeks of Mrs Walton's absence from the Club. Rumours as to her intemperance provoked expressions of scorn and contempt. During this time a new member joined and Mrs Buchanan immediately invited her to join the 'regulars'. When Mrs Walton returned she expected to resume her old place, but found it usurped. According to the member's own informal social code, her clique should have backed her claims to prior occupancy but no-one, including Mrs Buchanan, did so.

Case Study — Mrs Brown   Mrs Brown, 86, was born in Edinburgh, where her father was a doctor. She met Jack Brown there during World War I and came to Australia three years later to marry him. He became the advertising manager for a major Australian publishing company, and they bought a large house in Bayside Heights. They had two children, a son who died at 11 from a football accident and a daughter who succumbed to pneumonia when still a baby.

Her husband died after a long illness in 1962, leaving her 'a little bit of money . . . well, a good bit really, but I've gone through most of it'. Just three weeks after her husband's death Mrs Brown was knocked over by a hit-and-run driver. She required lengthy hospitalisation, but received no compensation. Since her accident she had not been able to use public transport and had to get taxis everywhere. She was partially blind and badly arthritic. During her husband's illness (he was in hospital for three years) she sold their home and moved to an older style flat not far away.

Her only living relative was a sister-in-law, whom she never saw. A lot of her friends were also dead. She had a number of 'good friends' at the Club, including Mrs Buchanan whom she met there and Miss Martin whom she had known for many years. She paid a woman to come in and do her housework in the flat and came to the Club every day for a meal. She could not manage any cooking, and used to hate the weekends when the centre was closed.

At the time of my first meeting with Mrs Brown she was about to move into a church hostel. The Club supervisor had been urging her to take this step for some time, and she eventually agreed, reluctantly and with misgivings. 'They take all your pension there', she said. 'If you didn't have a little bit of your own you couldn't even buy a paper.' At least, she remarked, her 'good friends' would be able to come and visit her.

They never did. Some months after the move I asked the supervisor how Mrs Brown was getting on at the hostel, and I was told she was very unhappy. A voluntary worker drops in to see her regularly, but no members visit. Even Mrs Buchanan had only been a couple of times, and then only after some pushing from staff. She had not been back since, despite Mrs Brown's expressed disappointment. 'I don't like going to places like that', Mrs Buchanan said to me.

Case Study — Miss Lewis   Miss Lewis, 87, came to Australia from England in 1912. Her mother had died when she was a child and her father remarried. She began working at the age of 11. Since then she had been a domestic servant, a factory worker, and a kitchen-hand. She was employed by a Bayside Heights Club for 33 years, and her residence in the municipality dates from this time.

She had a room in the same lodgings as Mrs Brown, through whom she joined the Senior Citizens Club about 15 years ago. They were part of a small group of single and widowed ladies who used to meet regularly at the local hotel. The others have since died.

Miss Lewis obtained a subsidised unit at Bayside Village through the Club, and furnished it with her $400 share of a lottery win. After five years there she had a bad fall and broke her leg and hip. She was hospitalised for many months and discharged to a church nursing home on the outskirts of the city. 'It was too far away, I was so lonely and unhappy I just cried all day'. After repeated requests she was eventually transferred to the church's hostel in Bayside Heights. When her friend Mrs Brown moved into another church hostel in the area, she asked Miss Lewis to move there too. Unfortunately, there was no extra hostel space, so Miss Lewis was put into the nursing home section.

She was unhappy about the situation, and maintained that she was 'perfectly capable of managing' in the more independent hostel setting. She also found the atomsphere in the nursing home depressing, especially the condition of her fellow residents whom she described as 'a bit mental'. She had to wait for a hostel place, 'for someone to die, I suppose'. She was happiest at Bayside Village, where she could do things for herself. She would have loved to go back, but was resigned to the situation.

On one occasion Miss Lewis and I were sitting at a table with some other members whom Miss Lewis referred to as her 'good friends'. I noticed that in my presence the other women all talked *about* Miss Lewis, though she was sitting next to me and had perfectly good hearing. They made comments like, 'Isn't she wonderful', 'I've never heard her grumble' and 'how old is she anyway?' Mrs Buchanan, her self-appointed 'guardian', was quick to point out that she does things for Miss Lewis. 'I sit with her and take her to the taxi', and so on, though she never visited the nursing home.

Mrs Buchanan did not maintain relations outside the Club with any of these women. Her pattern of association with Mrs Brown and Miss Lewis can be characterised as 'caretaking'. From an exchange perspective the relationship is unbalanced. Neither of these frail old people could reciprocate Mrs Buchanan's services in kind or cash. At a certain point, too, the ties with Mrs Walton were broken. Mrs Buchanan's selection of network interactants and subsequent discarding of them can be understood only in the context of old stigma.

As Whyte has remarked, 'It is only when [a] relationship breaks down that the underlying obligations are brought to light' (1955: 257). Clearly the obligations of Mrs Buchanan's frail friends did not include reciprocation within an exchange relationship. On the contrary, I suggest, it was in their *dependence* that Mrs Buchanan found purpose in interaction.

The element of control is central here. Even when life is spent almost exclusively in the company of others clearly categorised as old, one can still distance oneself from the category by playing the role of helper to the less fortunte:

> Perhaps in old age there is a premium on finishing life off with the feeling of being a 'have'. But during old age one also occupies a low social position. The way the old look for luck differences among themselves reflects the pattern found at the bottom of other social, racial, and gender hierarchies. To find oneself lucky within an ill-fated category is to gain the semblance of high status when society withholds it from others in the category. The way old people feel above and condescend to other old people may be linked to the fact that the young feel above and condescend to them. (Hochschild, 1976a: 329–30)

By carefully selecting those of one's peers with whom interaction will occur, the older person can continue up to a point to define the situation in favourable terms and thus retain a sense of control over his or her own affairs. In an egalitarian relationship, on the other hand, one's fellow interactant has a different kind of obligation — an obligation to buttress, or at least not to discredit, one's 'face'.

In an age-segregated setting, psychological self-interest involves *not* being identified with the category of old people, if not to outsiders then at least in comparison with one's ostensible peers. Individuals are accordingly engaged in competition for a limited and valued resource — a relatively unstigmatised 'face'.

The maintenance of face depends not only on one's own actions but on those of the people with whom one is publicly associated. As Goffman points out, 'in many relationships, the members come to share a face, so that in the presence of third parties an improper act on the part of one member becomes a source of acute embarrassment to the other members' (1967: 42). When the behaviour of one interactant becomes a potential source of loss of face for the other(s), he or she can no longer safely be presented to the world as an equal. The relationship will be suspended or permanently broken or, in some cases, the person may be reinstated in the network at some later date as a 'poor dear', that is, as an object of caretaking activities. (It appeared, for example, that Miss Lewis had, prior to her accident, participated as an equal in Mrs Buchanan's network of regulars. The transition to 'poor dear' status had occurred prior to the fieldwork period.) Mrs Walton was replaced because her loss of face reflected adversely on Mrs Buchanan's projected image.

A similar pattern appeared to be developing within a third network in which caretaking did not figure.

Case Study — Miss Martin   Miss Martin was an extremely active 81-year-old pensioner. She joined the Senior Citizens Club about seven years ago, and had been occupying one of the Welfare Association units at the retirement village for three years.

Her mother died when she was a baby. Her father, a wealthy businessman, employed a housekeeper to take care of Miss Martin, her sister and two brothers. The family was very well-to-do and always lived in Bayside Heights when they were in Sydney. However Mr Martin's business took them throughout Australia and overseas for varying periods of time.

Until her father died almost 40 years ago, Miss Martin had never worked. She just 'played tennis and bowls and went out with Daddy'. He left her a parcel of shares, but the amount was insufficient to live on. For 10 years she was employed as a companion-help to an elderly spinster. Then she got a filing job at a city department store. They retired her when she turned 60, and she could not find another job. The shares, which rendered her ineligible for an old-age pension, were sold on the advice of her brother, along with what remained of the family furniture. From the pension she paid $32 per week for an old dilapidated flat in Bayside Heights which she lived in for 37 years. The landlord refused to make necessary repairs, and she eagerly took up the offer of a subsidised unit in Bayside Village, for which she paid $25 per week. She decribed herself as 'very happy' in these surroundings.

All her siblings were dead. Her only living relatives were a niece (sister's daughter) and grandniece who lived in the area. She was thinking of going to live with this niece when the latter's mother died a few years ago, but decided against it because she 'didn't want to be a burden'. They keep in regular contact by phone and exchange visits once or twice a month.

Miss Martin followed a busy and regular pattern of social activity: bowls at the local bowling club on Mondays, the Senior Citizens Club on Tuesdays, bowls again on Wednesdays, the Club for housie on Thursdays, bowls on Friday, and the Club for indoor bowls on Saturdays. She also participated in any special activities organised by the Club: bus tours, Senior Citizens Week functions, and so on. She was Club treasurer for three years.

The main attraction of Bayside Village, she claimed, was the security of tenure and the knowledge that care would be available if necessary. Her two closest friends lived there and also belonged to the Senior Citizens Club. She had known both of them for many years, and they all decided to join the Club together. One of them was married: they did not become 'close friends' until she was widowed. The other, a spinster like herself, recently had been ill and did not get about much any more. 'She's just giving up' Miss Martin declared to me with some anger. 'She expects other people to do things for her now. But that's no good; you have to do things for yourself.'

She had few kind words to say about her fellow aged in Bayside Village: 'They just sit in their rooms all day. You can't get them involved.' She felt that, 'You're old when you stop doing things.'

Miss Martin did not regard the deterioration in one of her close friends with sympathy; nor did she respond with offers of assistance. On the contrary, Miss Martin was adamant that she would not cater to her friend's growing dependence. Thus the relationship will probably be severed altogether and not transformed into a caretaking pattern. Miss Martin's 'face' was that of a physically active, independent — and definitely not *really* old person — and she did not yet lack sufficient social contexts in which to display this image.

Among the age-segregated in my sample relatively few friendships were anchored in long-term associations reaching back into youth or middle adulthood. For most, the years had taken their toll, and acquaintances were of fairly recent standing. Many friendships had been built on neighbour relations in the retirement village, or through common membership in the Senior Citizens Club. Great value was nonetheless verbally attached to these associations. Short duration of relationships was apparently no bar to the description of new-found acquaintances as 'good buddies' or 'close friends'. Yet in reality these friendships were fragile phenomena. Few seemed able to withstand conflicting demands of self-interest. There was a contradiction between the value placed on friendship and the ease with which the ties could apparently be discarded.

Networks of personal relations which were chronologically shallow also lacked emotional depth, a situation which offers some interesting parallels to the characteristics of personal networks described by Liebow (1967) for a group of street-corner Negroes. In Tally's Corner, Liebow suggests, a romanticised perception of friends is an important source of emotional security and self-esteem in the absence of impersonal, culturally valued resources. Yet the street-corner world is constantly in flux: intense relationships grow rapidly out of casual encounters, and may equally rapidly break down; the component dyads of an individual's network are at varying stages of development or decline; few people are connected by a shared history, so friendship in this social world is inherently weak. This fact, coupled with the array of economic, social and psychological forces which militate against the stability of personal networks in the street-corner world, suggest to Liebow that friendship itself and not particular friends is the principal social commodity:

> Friendship . . . appears as a relationship between two people who, in an important sense, stand unrevealed to one another. Lacking depth in both past and present, friendship is easily uprooted by the tug of economic or psychological self-interest or by external forces acting against it. (Liebow, 1967: 206–7)

Thus the role of age-segregated environments in fostering the development of new relationships among age peers also has its dysfunctional side. The function of new-found friends in the retirement village and at the Senior Citizens Club was to provide companionship and, as with Liebow's street-corner people, to bolster feelings of security and self-esteem. This concentration of like-situated individuals, however, must be analysed in the context of age stigma.

According to Blau (1973), the contribution of friendships to a positive conception of self in old age is related to the duration of the relationship. With friends of long standing, the individual can retain the identity of his or her former unstigmatised status.

Many of the age segregated in my sample had no real knowledge of the personal history of their 'good friends'; they often knew neither their exact ages nor birthplaces. Thus they have not gained a view of the others as whole, multi-faceted beings who were once young and unstigmatised.

The absence of a shared history has special implications for face-to-face interaction, as Goffman (1967) has demonstrated. Such interaction has to be based on a working acceptance of each other's 'line', rather than 'on agreement of . . . heart-felt evaluations' (1967: 11). In the context of old age stigma, even greater significance is attached to a social relationship 'in which the person is more than ordinarily forced to trust his self-image and face to the tact and good conduct of others' (1967: 42) who are in fundamental respects strangers.

Friendship Among the Non-segregated

Yet even some long-standing relationships are not immune to the effects of stigma, as Miss Martin's history shows. These effects may take different forms. Two case studies of non-segregated elderly women show something of this diversity.

Case Study — Miss Jones Miss Mary Jones, 74, lived with her unmarried 77-year-old sister, Betty. Their spacious home and grounds
were maintained by a housekeeper and a gardener. The family moved
to Sydney from Fiji, where their father owned a plantation, when the
girls were in their teens. They cared for their aged parents in this house
until the latter's death. Betty worked as a nurse for a time, and Mary
was a librarian. Two other sisters were married. One of them lived in
Canberra and hadn't been seen for about two years. She had four
children who boarded at local private schools: two of them spent a day
with Mary and Betty at weekends several times a year. The other sister
lived in a nearby suburb. Her husband was incapacitated several years
ago and she was in fairly frequent contact. They shopped together,
and Mary 'help out' in other ways whenever she was asked. This
sister's married son also lived in the neighbourhood and called in occasionally to see if Mary and Betty needed anything done around the
house.

Mary had no physical incapacity, though her sister was somewhat
frail and had difficulty getting about. They lived comfortably on in-
vestments which were handled by an accountant. Mary automatically
received an old-age pension, though professed feeling guilty about this
as she did not need it.

Mary's social life revolved around her membership in an exclusive
local golf club. She socialised there regularly with about 10 same-age
female members. This group also met in each other's homes to play
bridge; Mary played every day. She had only one friend outside this
circle, an unmarried woman she had known for many years. They met
for lunch about three times a year.

Mary felt that she had not accomplished anything in her life. She
envied 'the women of today' who 'have brains and do something with
themselves'. She apologised before our first interview for being 'as
dull as dishwater'. Her sister was unwilling to be interviewed because
she too thought she was 'too dull'. Mary approved wholeheartedly of
euthanasia for old people. I was surprised when she opened our first
conversation by asking me what I thought of it. 'I couldn't bear to be
a burden on anyone', she said.

Though Miss Jones' segregation was not institutionalised, she spent
almost all her time in a world of face-to-face relationships with age
peers. In the absence of other concerns — family, work, self-
improvement, cultural or political activities, and so on — in which to
invest her time and energies, these resources had come to be almost exclusively devoted to maintaining a network of personal relations with
age peers within which diversionary pastimes consume the days. She
did not engage in much instrumental exchange with these friends: the
members of her network were extremely wealthy and did not need

favours from friends; any requirement she may have had for 'odd jobs' and the like was fulfilled by her sister's son, while she in turn provided assistance to his mother.

Despite the long history of acquaintanceship, Miss Jones' level of emotional involvement in her network was low. She would not confide problems or intimate life details to her friends, she told me, since gossip was a major activity of the group. She was 'very fond' of the old friend who lived outside the area, but saw her too rarely for this to be an important emotional outlet.

The most important social goods which she exchanged with her peers were companionship in activities and the acceptance of each other as social equals. No particular member of the network provided an age or sex role model. Miss Jones saw 'the woman of today' as worthy of admiration, but felt she, herself, compared unfavourably with this model.

Only one of my informants, Mrs Chevalier, numbered non-aged persons among her friends.

Case Study — Mrs Chevalier   Despite her 76 years, Mrs Chevalier had no serious physical disabilities. She lived alone in a large, attractive house near the harbour foreshores. It was in need of some repair — there were cracks in some of the walls and a few damp patches near the ceiling. She 'lives' in one cosy room which served as an informal sitting room. The rest of the house — including a large formal dining room — was well kept but rarely used.

Her husband, an accountant, died some 30 years ago. They had three daughters: one lives on the semi-rural outskirts of Sydney where she breeds horses; one is in the country; and the other, until her death some two years ago, lived just around the corner. There are several grandchildren, with most of whom contact is limited to holiday stays. Mrs Chevalier's family-tree stretches back to English and French aristocracy. However her father lost most of his property during the bank crash of the 1890s. The only remaining family legacy is a collection of fine antique furniture imported from England.

In the early years of married life in Bayside Heights her Catholic background set her somewhat apart from the elite Wasp circles of Sydney society. She was 'converted' from her conservative upbringing by the death of a close friend during the Spanish War, the depression, and her service as a Red Cross volunteer during World War II. Her 'leftist' leanings apparently created some friction with her husband, who did not share her political views. As she put it, she was 'just starting to blossom' when he died. After his death she joined the paid staff of the Red Cross, and later worked as a cosmetics consultant. Her interests are wide — theatre, films, reading, and gardening.

Though not formally educated beyond high school level, she is extremely well read, thoughtful, and passionately interested in learning. She is especially fascinated by politics and is socially conscious in a way that has always made her feel a 'misfit' among her circle of friends: for them, the 'socially acceptable' bits of charity work; for her, the socially unacceptable Smith Family. The one friend who shares her political sympathies — Mrs Streetfield — is careful to conceal them in public. Until recently, so did Mrs Chevalier.

The loss of her daughter apparently set in motion a positive consolidation of the 'socially unacceptable' threads of her life. They had been 'very close', spending much of their time together and sharing many activities. The relationship was characterised as much by genuine mutual need as by personal affinity, since the daughter was unhappily married and had few social and emotional outlets.

The bereavement has left Mrs Chevalier 'restless' and lonely, but the final severance of truly close social bonds has, it seems, acted as a liberating factor. She is thinking about moving to Canberra where she has politically like-minded friends. And she has recently gone on a tour of China, an experience which thoroughly vindicated her social outlook. She has no intention of sharing the 'stagnation' of old age that she sees in many of her acquaintances.

It was through Mrs Chevalier that I met both Mrs Streetfield and Miss Jones. Mrs Chevalier sees the lifestyle of the latter as 'typical' of the elite segment of Bayside Heights aged: trivial, insubstantial, and of absolutely no interest for her. She has known Mrs Streetfield for many years, as Mr Chevalier had been the company accountant for the Streetfield family. Shared political convictions form a potentially strong basis for identification between the two women, but they are apparently not personal confidantes. At the time of the death of Mrs Chevalier's daughter, Mrs Streetfield told me, she had 'dropped around a few times to see if there was anything I could do' but she was not close enough to offer emotional support and solace. Mrs Streetfield's emotional energies are largely absorbed by her husband and handicapped child, while her public commitment to conservative politics undoubtedly sets up a subtle barrier to any deeper friendship.

Apart from Mrs Streetfield, Mrs Chevalier interacts with others from this elite Bayside Heights network, whom she had met originally through her husband. Her participation is however restricted to joining in theatre parties and to dining occasionally at exclusive city clubs (though she does not herself belong to any). At the same time, she maintains a variety of other networks.

One is centred on the Smith Family and her former co-workers; another springs from her recently acquired membership of a minor liberal political party; a third, comprising mainly young adults, reflects the cultural interests which have brought her into contact with artists, film-makers,and the like. Some indication of this variety was manifested in the array of guests at a dinner party I attended in Mrs Chevalier's home. In addition to an anthropologist, she had invited a middle-aged woman who worked for the Smith Family, a same-aged widow of considerable wealth, and two teenage neighbours, friends of her favourite granddaughter, who smoked marijuana and made experimental films.

As a result of this diversity, Mrs Chevalier had an assortment of reference groups with which to compare her life, against which to evaluate her worth, and from which to draw role models. Among her fellow aged, the comparison was unfavourable in terms of material wealth. Although she was certainly comfortably off by objective standards, she was relatively deprived in terms of the wealth of her aged friends. When I asked her if there was one thing she would like that she did not now have, she replied 'a little more money to do all the things I like — going to the theatre, travelling, that sort of thing'. On the other hand, she compares the content of her lifestyle favourably with the emptiness she sees in the meaningless social diversions of her peers. She identifies with people who are 'making a contribution', something she can see herself as doing, and something moreover which can occur at any age. Her social affiliations reflect and reinforce her conception of herself as a multi-faceted, committed person whose worth rests on considerations other than age.

When confronted with the reality of old age in her friends, she responded in the same way as Mrs Buchanan. An old friend of hers had had a stroke and been placed in a convalescent home. After several months — 'I felt terrible that it took me so long to visit' — she went there to see her friend. Mrs Chevalier expressed horror at the sight of 'all those pitiful, wizened old people'. She said she dreads 'getting like that. What would I be doing to my children? They'd feel they would have to come and see me.'

The personal experience of being in such a place, she feels, would be unendurable. 'You could only stand it if you were the worst of them.' Her friend, she reported, had in fact 'gone a bit soft. I suppose it's the only way you could endure it'. As a result, she said, conversation had proved impossible, and there was 'just no point' in going back for a further visit.

Summary

In the introduction to this chapter I discussed four important foci of research into aged persons' peer relations: instrumental assistance, socio-emotional support, comparative reference functions, and the effects of age density. The existing data posited a number of correlations of statistical significance between each of these variables and certain social and demographic characteristics of individual old people, and between some of the variables themselves. No consensus obtains in the literature, however, as to how the overall phenomenon of friendship in later life is best conceptualised and analysed.

Two fundamental considerations emerge from my data on peer relations. First, the meaning and function of friendships in later life are multi-faceted phenomena; no single aspect such as exchange, comparative reference or age density is adequate on its own to explain observed patterns of peer interaction. Rather, all aspects are interrelated in a complex 'feedback' system. Second, friendship patterns must be analysed in context and from a dynamic perspective.

Instrumental and expressive categories of behaviour, while analytically distinct, emerge in situational analysis as *meaningfully* related. As Lozier and Althouse (1976: 360) have pointed out in another context: 'An object such as a vase may be useful for keeping flowers, but keeping flowers is useful in other ways; quite literally it may be 'instrumental' for 'expressing' claims for social status or personal style.' It is in these terms that the operation of both balanced and unbalanced exchange relationships needs to be analysed.

In Bayside Heights, balanced instrumental exchange characterises the relationships of social equals, whether intimates or acquaintances. It rarely involves substantial goods or services, and is kept within fairly strict limits: anybody offering or receiving too much or too often is perceived as 'interfering' with others' privacy. This suggests that infractions constitute as much, if not more, a breach of the norm of autonomy and independence than of the norm of reciprocity. The frail aged who lack alternative sources of material assistance, or who cannot afford to pay for needed services, must either withdraw from interaction altogether or enter into an imbalanced exchange with their peers. In return for material help, they can offer only deference and gratitude. The carer responds with condescension and thus receives an emotional fillip: gratification at feeling useful and needed and, most importantly, justification for not defining himself or herself as 'old'. Such a label belongs to the dependent.

Not all elderly people appear willing to adopt a caretaker role even when an opportunity is presented to them. The emergence of status discrepancies within a previously homophilous network or dyadic relationship provokes one of two reactions on the part of those whose status remains unchanged: either the relationship is severed or it is transformed into a caretaking pattern. The former response is illustrated by Miss Martin, who has observed deterioration in one of her intimates and is gradually reducing contact with her. The un-mistakeable signs of 'oldness' in her friend now clash with Miss Martin's own projected self-image as an active, and hence not 'really' old person. For people like Mrs Buchanan and Miss Chapman, on the other hand, the relative deprivation of later years can be partially reconciled by constantly affirming that there are others much worse off than themselves. Mrs Buchanan's helping activities reassure her that she is still 'in control', in contrast to those she helps. In addition, she is keen to take on the role of representative for the Club at mixed age functions, thereby strengthening this view of herself as being at the top of the aged heap, so to speak. In this latter role, she is careful to define events such as the Government House garden party as a continuation of an earlier high status, and not, as it appears to others, a condescending 'treat' for people who do not normally belong in such a setting.

The ultimate function of both responses — maintenance of network homogeneity or caretaking — is the same. Each, in a different way, permits the older person to control the definition of self in favourable terms. It is likely, moreover, that the choice of interaction pattern reflects personal styles of long-standing duration.

Clearly, personal interaction in either an exchange or caretaking context involves comparison with one's own situation. The reference function is in fact implicit in the choice of companions. The personal network of friends and neighbours is thus one potential source of age-sex role models (Rosow, 1967). However, this is not always the case. Miss Jones, for example, does not see any of her friends as people worthy of emulation. She compares her entire cohort unfavourably with 'the women of today'. Her own sense of failure in life, therefore, can be interpreted by her as the result of her generation's unlucky placement in time, and not the product of personal inadequacy.

This suggests that the role of the personal network needs to be considered in relation to other sources of comparison. Both the composition of the network and the age density of the environment are relevant in this context. Sheingold (1973) has drawn an analytic distinction between two dimensions of isolation: network insulation, reflecting the extent to which an individual's *network* is linked, directly or indirectly, with other networks; and paucity of social ties, which relates to an individual's direct contacts with other individuals. He suggests that network attributes may be more important than individual attributes in determining the likelihood of new information reaching an individual.

Mrs Chevalier has exposed herself, through interaction with a wide variety of networks, to different sets of ideas and values, from which she has chosen the elements of a conducive and satisfying lifestyle.

Miss Jones, on the other hand, is locked into an unchanging and narrow world view through her almost exclusive participation in a single network. Both women have experienced a strong sense of disaffection and dissatisfaction. However, whereas Mrs Chevalier has a wide range of life models on which to draw to shape a more satisfactory existence for herself, Miss Jones had no first-hand contact with 'today's woman', who appears as a larger-than-life figure of talent and accomplishment — a mythical being whom Miss Jones feels incapable of emulating.

Some older people approach the selection of their personal network with considerably more resources than others. For those like Jim Fletcher (see p. 125–128) who have no major physical or financial decrements, control can be maintained by choosing friends in similar circumstances and by adopting a formal or semi-formal caretaking role over those already publicly stigmatised as old. He eschews familiarity with the membership at large, and interacts on a personal level only with his daughter and with similarly situated same-age friends who have no affiliation with age-graded organisations.

In later years, the ever-present danger of physical infirmity or death makes the tenuousness of human bonds a tangible reality. There are unspoken parameters beyond which friendships in old age will extend only rarely and with difficulty. The nursing home — the institutionalisation of dependence — places its residents beyond the pale. They are, for even their 'good friends', socially dead.

The survivors must somehow cope with their guilt at failing to meet the cultural expectations of friendship and with the fear for their own fate which the close encounter naturally engenders. Before the former friend can be justifiably neglected and forgotten, it seems, a process of rationalisation may occur in which evidence is found that the person is 'really' dead and no longer a social interactant. Mrs Chevalier's account illustrates this process. She satisfied herself that her friend had 'gone a bit soft' and that visiting was accordingly not justified.

This discussion of friendship has focused primarily on the peer relations of unmarried people in my sample. As I discuss in the following chapter, the bond with highest cognitive-affective salience in old age is the marital relationship. To a greater extent than relations with kin, friendship contains and reflects the element of choice. The dynamics of friendship formation, transformation, and dissolution are accordingly an important key to the self-conceptions and motivations of individual actors, and ultimately to their modes of integration. The absence of a spouse, and the limits which generational differences place on the nomos-building capacity of relationships with children, bring one's age peers to centre stage in the process of defining one's self. Under these circumstances, the dual theme of identification and rejection which characterizes interaction among the similarly stigmatised emerges most forcefully.

Notes

1. Other research among 'disaffiliated' aged populations (Rooney, 1976) suggests that this phenomenon should not be interpreted as a loss of *need* for meaningful personal relationships with increased exposure to the life of a 'social outcast'. Among Rooney's skid row subjects, the proportions of friendless men desiring either friends or casual acquaintances was not related to either age or length of residence in skid row.
2. Considerable status was apparently attached to interaction with 'the student'. On more than one occasion I was made to feel rather like a trophy.

7 Family

Many researchers regard family relations as the principal means by which older people are integrated into modern society (see e.g. Shanas *et al.*, 1968). This view is echoed in government reports and policy statements (see e.g. Holmes, 1977). As I pointed out in Chapter 2, the dependence of aged persons on their relatives, particularly adult children, is rationalised and legitimated on 'historical' grounds, and encouraged in a variety of ways; most directly through a system of payments to persons caring for an infirm aged relative at home.

In this context, the 'preventive effects' of family ties have been widely discussed. This concept refers to the fact that those older people who lack such ties are disproportionately represented among the users of care services and those admitted to institutions, thereby implying that institutionalisation is 'prevented' by family support.

The term 'family' is not generally used in gerontological literature to refer to the conjugal or nuclear unit. The residential unit is generally considered less important as a source of support than the geographically dispersed kinship network or modified extended family, which is often described as the functionally relevant family unit for the majority of elderly people (c.f. Lefroy, 1977; Howe, 1979).

Generalising from data on rates of extra-residential contact with relations and the exchange of services between generations, gerontologists (e.g. Shanas *et al.*, 1968; Riley & Foner, 1968) have argued that the family balances the segregation of old people from the formal economic, social, and political structures of industrial society by integrating them into primary networks of mutual affection and care. It has even been asserted 'that within industrial societies the aged are able to survive only because of the psychological and other supports given them by their families' (Shanas, 1970: 6). Conversely, an absence of family ties is seen as a 'striking factor' in explaining 'the casualties of old age': the institutionalised and the lonely (Lefroy, 1977: 38). The family is said to support its aged members in a variety of ways: by providing direct or indirect economic aid, caretaking of the infirm, and other, practical services, and by fulfilling important emotional needs for affection and self-expression.

Many writers accordingly see the family network as an all-purpose support system for aged members. One prominent theme in suggestions for Australian policy on aging has been the plea to strengthen these ties. The aim of government, Lefroy (1977), Bower (1974), and others assert, should be to supplement the efforts of younger family members, primarily through the extension and expansion of domiciliary services.

In this chapter, case studies showing a variety of family structures are presented. I argue that the popular representation of the extended family, rather than the household, as the functionally relevant unit in the lives of elderly people is misleading. For most older couples, the most significant emotional bond in life is the marriage relationship. Extended family networks, on the other hand, are institutionalised around specific and limited dimensions of social action. Beyond these, non-conjugal family roles are ambiguous and vaguely defined. This lack of clarity means that, in practice, the roles of adult family members relative to aged parents will be determined by structural and situational factors — most importantly, by the distribution of resources and the dynamics of interpersonal histories.

Prevailing interpretations of family relationships in old age reflect both the general weighting of gerontological studies in the direction of material needs of the elderly and reliance on quantitative research methods. The 'disquieting issues of *meaning*' (Rosow, 1967: 2) which attach to these relationships may be acknowledged in passing or assumed in interpretation, but they have rarely been directly confronted. Case studies of elderly Baysiders show that structural arrangements alone are not adequate indicators of integration. Living with kin does not necessarily mean that an old person is integrated into the familial network, nor does complete isolation from primary group contacts always detract from an older person's satisfaction with life. What *is* important is the subjective experience of the situation.

The relationships which aged Baysiders maintain with their families illustrate a number of issues which I raised in Chapter 2. First, they show that the ways in which elderly people perceive their own situation is a critical independent variable in their integration, and one which is not always predictable from quantifiable data. Second, they highlight the considerable problems that exist with blanket categorisations of the family as the 'natural' and ideal support group for a frail elder. There are socio-emotional consequences inovlved in unilateral dependence on kin which cast serious doubt on the desirability of policies and services which are directed towards the aged as family dependents rather than as individual citizens. Dependence takes on special meaning in the context of age stigma.

The Integrative Function Reconsidered

There is substantial documentation, in Australia as elsewhere, of kinship units in which extra-residential ties are maintained for the purpose of informal social interaction and aid (Basham, 1978: 131). Studies show that declining formal and informal participation with greater age is not accompanied by a corresponding decrease in rates of family interaction (Cumming & Henry, 1961).

The vast majority of older people have regular contact with non-resident family members, and important kinds of material assistance are exchanged throughout these networks (Shanas *et al.*, 1968; Riley & Foner, 1968). Moreover, for certain kinds of help, notably in emergencies such as illness, financial crisis, and bereavement, family members are the predominant sources (Moore, 1966; Rosow, 1967). These family ties are assumed to have emotional as well as instrumental support functions in the lives of elderly people. However, few studies have focused directly on the subjective aspect (Bengtson *et al.*, 1976), and some researchers (Rosenmayr, 1972; Rosow, 1967; Blau, 1973) have queried whether surveys that report old people's frequent contacts with adult children really convey anything about the actual nature of the relationships involved. Beyond establishing the existence of extra-residential kinship ties, 'questions still remain regarding the quality of the relationship between older persons and their adult children, and the meaning of the relationship to the older person' (Wood and Robertson, 1976: 303).

There is in fact little empirical support for the assumption that contact with children is positively associated with life satisfaction. Satisfaction and morale are functions not of the *frequency* of contact with children, but 'of the consistency between performance and expectation in the interaction among the aged and their adult offspring' (Smith, 1965: 153). High morale is associated not with actual contact with one's family but with *satisfaction* with that contact, whatever the frequency (Medley, 1976).

Activity in the grandparental role is similarly unrelated to life satisfaction. A review of research on grandparenthood (Wood & Robertson, 1976) indicates that the grandparental role has only limited significance for old people. The period that grandparents find most satisfying appears to be when the grandchildren are small; as they grow up, they grow away.

Blau (1973) in fact argues from her data that children cannot be counted on for continued emotional commitment to their aged parents because of the inherently a-symmetrical nature of inter-generational relations. Kerckhoff (1966: 182-3) has also shown that among retired married couples high morale is associated with *low* frequencies of seeing adult children:

> The highest average morale scores of any behavioural family type are found in that category of couples who have relatively distant children *and* who have a relatively limited mutual support relationship with these children. Similarly, the highest morale scores of any normative family type are found for couples who expect neither propinquity nor much mutual aid and affection in relation to their adult children. High morale is thus associated with both actual and expected independence between the generations.

Similarly, Helen Lopata (1973) found that widows prefer to live alone, rather than with children, although they are often lonely. Those widows in her study who were able to support themselves in their own homes reported greater peace, quiet, and independence than those living with kin.

The conventional viewpoint has it that, in old age, the family assumes greater and greater importance as a focus of affectional life. Rosow (1967: 197) tested a corollary of this proposition; namely, that the family's significance as an affective group should increase old people's emotional dependence on their children as their other activities decline. But he could find no correlation between emotional dependence on children and any age-related deprivation.

Contrary to what might be expected, he found that people living alone were actually slightly *less* emotionally dependent on children than others and that comprehensive role losses had no cumulative effect on emotional dependence. Rosow concluded that:

> Older people's emotional dependence on children is not a systematic function of *structural* determinates, demographic factors, or age-related changes in life. The prevailing assumptions and conventional ideas about emotional dependence in old age are simply unwarranted. Emotional dependence on children is not a function of disengagement, role loss and reduced participation, widowhood, objective dependence and declining competence, women's affective interests, chronic frustration because of children's absence, or the atrophy of outside functions. Emotional dependence remains impervious to many basic life changes which have profound effects on other attitudes. Thus, our conceptions require fundamental revision. Emotional dependence on children is *not* a sociological phenomenon, but a stable *psychological* relationship. (1967: 213-4, original emphasis)

Institutionalised Aspects of the Extended Family

The conceptions which family members have of their roles are central to the existence of the family as a social institution. The sociological significance of this has been most perceptively argued by Ernest Burgess (1973: 85):

> The family is more than an interaction of personalities. In this interaction, the family develops a conception of itself. When this conception of familial relations is recognised by the community, the family acquires an institutional character. This is what is meant by the family as a social institution. A family that had no conception of its role in the community, or of the responsibilities of its individual members would not be an institution, perhaps not even a family.

My own and other data suggest that only limited functions of extended family networks are institutionalised in this sense. A variety of social, economic, and political factors constrain the interaction between aged persons and other family members. The conceptions which family members hold of their role in relation to aged relatives differ not only from what governments would wish to establish, but also in some ways from what the elderly themselves expect.

In the first place, it is important to note that many Australians express the belief that care of the aged should be *primarily* a public and not a familial responsibility. The desire of families to ease the problems of aged members, Hutchinson (1954: 36) suggests from his survey: 'does not seem to be coupled with a sense that the aged person should in any case remain within the care of the kinship group. If the suffering can be as effectively reduced by some other agency relatives tend to feel that it, rather than they should do so.' This attitude is undoubtedly bound up with the absence of any historical tradition of family care, but it also reflects the socio-cultural conditions of contemporary life.

One important factor to be noted in the study of aged families is the optional nature of many kinship activities in modern society. Few obligations to kin other than members of the nuclear family constitute 'an obligation normatively defined and enforced by sanctions' (Nye, 1974: 244). Emotional significance is assigned to the conjugal nuclear unit, while the formation of close extra-nuclear kinship ties is given 'some of the voluntary character of friendships' (Basham, 1978: 131).

Within such a system, the emotional ties which bind parents to children are invariably stronger than those which they have with their own parents (Riley & Foner, 1968: 554). As in cognatic kinship systems generally, any non-reciprocated choice of kin role may lead to conflicting pressures (Barnes, 1972: 21).

As a result, the normative definition of roles of adult family members towards aged parents is not clearly delineated. They tend to be subject to confusion and conflicting expectations between responsibility and a strongly held norm of autonomy for both generations. As Hawkinson (1965: 182) has remarked, 'The adult child is not only subject to pity if he sacrifices for his aged parents, but also open to criticism if he neglects them'.

Not surprisingly then, some of the expectations which older people hold for their own roles and those of other family members, vis-a-vis the expectations held by these others, are only partially congruent. Researchers have based their interpretation of the family's integrative function on factors which have very low cognitive salience to the elderly themselves. Old people apparently receive from their adult children what they value least, and fail to receive what they desire most.

The aged do receive a good deal of material assistance from their families — more, in fact, than they expect (Riley & Foner, 1968: 554). Kin are the principal source of help in emergencies, and (residential proximity permitting) sometimes provide other services such as shopping, household repairs, and the like. But the majority of aged give as much as — and often more than — they receive; in particular, the flow of financial assistance tends to be from the older generation to the younger, at least in middle-class families (Bell, 1968).

However, affectional support is much more highly valued by the aged themselves than is material and economic assistance (Smith, 1965). The most widely held expectation *among older people* is that children should, even when they have families of their own, maintain 'close contact' with their parents. Face-to-face contact, as in visiting, is more highly valued in this regard than are various forms of help, such as care in illness and financial assistance. But actual behaviour falls short of expectations as far as amount of contact is concerned (Hansen *et al.*, 1965); it meets or exceeds them only in terms of material help given (Riley & Foner,1968: 547). In this respect, working-class aged apparently fare better than their counterparts in areas such as Bayside Heights (Martin, 1967; 1970).

What many researchers fail to recognize is that the meaning of 'help' to an older person is double-edged. As Rosenmayr (1972) contends, help may not exclude, and may even invite conflict. In the context of old age stigma and its implicit assumptions of dependence and decline, questions of power and autonomy in the provision of help to aged persons by their adult children assume a critical significance. This point has been elaborated by Hawkinson in a study of the beliefs of aged Americans concerning filial responsibility. He points out that aged parents desire 'continuity of the intimate personal ties generated during the period of child dependency' (1965: 185-6).

Yet becoming an adult calls for asserting independence from parental control and thereby severing or at least weakening the once intimate bonds. The desire to maintain independence and autonomy is a prime concern of the elderly (Clark, 1972). Yet society has not made it possible for most aged parents adequately to fulfil this independent role:

> As a result of this difference between expected behaviour and the actual resolution of the situation, the aged parent is often faced with a common dilemma. *The older person's definition of the consequences inherent in the situation is crucial for his behaviour and adjustment.* He is forced eventually to recognize that relinquishment of the parental authoritative role carries with it a possible reversion to a dependency role. (Hawkinson, 1965: 183, emphasis added).

Thus, in accepting material help from children, the aged individual is reduced to a situation of dependence, a situation in which his or her ability to define and hence control the interaction is severely curtailed.

As a result, the aged appear to fear dependence on their children even more deeply than dependence on other, less personal sources of support. The vast majority of old people in Hawkinson's study strongly emphasised independence in decision making and in financial matters, preferring that any necessary support should come from government or some other impersonal agency rather than from one's own children.

In Australia, Hutchinson reports in similar terms that 'one of the most powerful values influencing the conduct of older people and the aged is the desire for independence, especially independence of relatives' (1954: 24). Financial assistance may be accepted from relatives if it is absolutely necessary, but 'many will go to almost any lengths to avoid it' (1954: 35).

The most thorough empirical account of older people in a family context, Peter Townsend's *The Family Life of Old People* (1963), is often cited as evidence of the widespread function of extended families as support for frail aged members. In fact Townsend stresses the centrality of exchange in extended family networks. In Bethnal Green, old people with relatives close by received regular help with whatever tasks they found difficult — shopping, cleaning, help in illness and so on. However, 'what seems to be an essential principal of the daily renewal of an intimate bond between adult relatives is the reciprocation of services between them' (1963: 62). Care of grandchildren was one of the most important tasks performed by the aged; preparation of meals for those at work was another. Some old people could no longer reciprocate the services performed for them and this seemed to make them less willing to accept help and their relatives sometimes less willing to give it.

It is also clear that the family patterns of Bethnal Green, a cohesive, locality-based working-class community, are not typical of contemporary Australian suburbia. As Moore (1966) suggests, modern family systems are characterised less by balanced exchange between the generations than by a kind of 'serial service' or unilateral flow of goods and services from the older to be the younger generation, the obligation of the initial beneficiaries lying in 'passing it on' rather than 'passing it back'. Although the socialization experience ensures some kind of enduring link between the generations, the progressive reversion with aging to a position of dependence sets up intrinsic strains within such a system.

Families in Bayside Heights

The following case studies illustrate somthing of the complex links between the personal experience of an aging family member and the wider cultural processes of age stigma. Universal among my subjects was the desire to avoid becoming, as so many of them expressed it, 'a burden' on their relatives. Essentially, being a burden meant being dependent — financially, physically, and/or emotionally — on one's kin.

Extended Family Networks

An essential principle of the relationships between aged parents and their children in Bayside Heights was the ability of the old person(s) to contribute something. Those who were still able to command resources valued by the younger generation avoided to some extent being classified with the stigma of dependence and thus continued to exercise a measure of control over the definition of their situations. Wealth, not surprisingly, conferred a critical measure of autonomy and control, though it did not — again unsurprisingly — ensure emotional gratification from relationships.

An important resource in Bayside Heights, particularly among those with geographically mobile children, was house room. Many sacrificed their own perceived interests to keep up a home that was too big for their needs in order to ensure that they had something of value to offer in return for the occasional companionship of their families.

Case Study — Mrs Streetfield Mrs Emily Streetfield, 75, lives with her husband John, a prominent barrister, and their 40-year-old mentally handicapped daughter in a huge two-storey house set in spacious grounds. Their two sons live nearby. One, a medical specialist, is married with four children, all currently attending private schools; the other, a business executive whom she describes as 'a crusty old bachelor', lives alone and visits them every weekend 'for a hot meal'.

Mrs Streetfield's girlhood was dominated by the mores of her socially prominent parents. Her early ambition to attend university was thwarted by her father, who insisted that his daughter's only task in life was to be 'a stunning social success'. This she dutifully became, following a vice-regal coming out. She married well, 'with rosy visions' which the advent of children promptly converted into feelings of being 'trapped'.

During the War she seized the opportunity to realise her old ambition. With her husband away, the boys at boarding school, and a housekeeper and car to ease the way, she graduated in social work. Until about five years ago she remained actively involved in charitable committee work. She misses this outlet, both because through it she felt 'useful' and because it gave her an independent status. Now her daughter and housekeeping take up most of her time. She used to have a woman come in two days a week, but now she only employs someone once a week to do the floors: 'It gives me something to do, though I'm getting a bit beyond it'. She acknowledges that the house is far too big for their needs, but says John wouldn't hear of them moving to a smaller house. 'Anyway', she said, 'we need the space for the children'. The idea of *living* with any of her children is anathema to her: 'I suppose it would work for a family which was very united — not that we're not united, but we are rather cool towards each other'. Her bachelor son in particular, she feels, has 'grown right away from' them.

Mrs Streetfield feels 'the odd one out' in her ultra-conservative family. Politically she is even at odds with her husband, a staunch Liberal Party supporter and establishment figure. She herself espouses socialist views which she thinks were formed by her university experience: 'I'd never had a rational discussion in my life before then'. Only one of her friends, Mrs Chevalier, shares her views. With anyone else Mrs Streetfield feels compelled not to voice her ideas.

Her married children play a relatively insignificant role in her life: 'As you grow older you need your friends more [than your children]. You choose your friends; you're just sort of dumped with your family'. However, she had always cherished the hope that she could have been of special help to her grandchildren, that they would feel freer to come to her with their problems than they would to their parents. But this has not eventuated. 'I suppose they just see me as an old fuddy duddy.'

The Streetfields frequently accommodate their grandchildren, as their children travel a great deal for business and on holidays. At these times, however, relations between grandmother and grandchildren are considerably strained. Mrs Streetfield feels that they are over-indulged by their parents and attempts to exercise a surveillance over their activities which is resented and fought by the young people. She is at loss to know how to handle the situation, realising that her definition and theirs do not coincide and being aware that there is no basis in *their* social contruction of reality for her to play an authoritative role. Even a nurturant role is denied her, since conflicting norms and values e a sharing of confidences. An affective relationship with her unmarried son is similarly impossible because of divergent interests and socio-political orientations: she recognises the largely instrumental basis for their minimal amount of interaction

Mrs Streetfield continues to maintain a capacity for control in the familial interaction system, though it is neither complete nor particularly emotionally satisfying for her. The social prominence and influence of her husband is less important now for her married offspring than it was earlier in their careers and family life cycles. However, the vast family home continues to be an important resource. It offers the adult children considerable freedom to travel, knowing that their own young children can be easily accommodated and cared for over quite long periods. Without it, she is aware that she would have little to offer in return for interaction.

Mrs Chevalier, whose situation was described in the previous chapter, put forward similar reasons for continuing to live in a house which is much too big and costly for her. Her living children and all her grandchildren live outside Sydney, and stay at her place when they come to town. She needs the extra space, she says, so she can put them up at these times, despite the difficulties this causes.

For the wealthy and non-wealthy alike, care of grandchildren was the most important way in which the older generation could contribute. Substantial cash sums and other expensive gifts to children and grandchildren were also not uncommon for those who could afford them. In one case, an elderly widow took two of her teenage grandchildren along on an overseas holiday.

When the aged are unable to reciprocate, one logical response is to withdraw from family interaction. The Callaghans illustrate this option.

Case Study — The Callaghans.   Ray and Rita Callaghan, both in their 80s and quite frail, recently moved to the Bayside retirement village to avoid becoming, as they put it, a 'burden' on their daughter, who lives with her family on the other side of the harbour.

Ray spent his adult years as a tea planter in Malaya. About 10 years ago he had a coronary, so they returned to Australia and bought a house near their daughter. However, Rita's mental state deteriorated rapidly. She had never had much experience with housekeeping, and her increasing confusion soon put paid to any idea of their living a self-sufficient life. They moved to a one bedroom apartment in the Village, though Ray was still uncertain as to how they would manage with meals. They knew no-one in Bayside Heights, and their new neighbours were at first 'stand-offish'. 'They didn't want to get involved with anyone who may have become a nuisance', Ray told me. 'I don't blame them. Now they can see we take care of ourselves and our relations are quite friendly.' The Senior Citizens Club, Ray remarked, 'saved us'. They attend almost every day for the hot meal, but only occasionally stay on to socialise. On other days they go to the R.S.L. and have a meal there. When they are no longer able to move around as much, they said, they would approach the Meals on Wheels service.

For this elderly couple, apparently, the stigma of welfare service is preferable to dependence on family members. They appear to be typical of those aged Australians in Hutchinson's (1954: 35) survey who preferred 'to turn to the friendship of unrelated persons as far as possible rather than show themselves dependent upon their relatives in any way' (1954: 35).

Exchange considerations thus figure prominently in the analysis of inter-generational relations. Functional incapacity of the aged person severely limits the potential for reciprocating the help a child might provide. At the same time, the belief in generational independence maximises the value of autonomy, the ability to provide for one's own needs.

Gerontologists are correct in asserting that a dispersed family network is not incompatible with the provision of material support to aged members, particularly in times of crisis. But the norms of obligation are crosscut by conflicting norms of independence and autonomy — for *both* generations. A short-term need for, say, nursing through an illness, can be reconciled with the normative structure, for the situation does not preclude the *potential* for reciprocation in the future. But the onset of a permanent need cannot be so reconciled. In other words, the provision of *emergency* help to aged relatives appears to be an institutionalised dimension of extended family networks. It is accepted by both generations. Long-term assistance is not.

Another way in which families can provide help without unduly compromising an older person's independence is through what may be termed bureaucratic mediation. According to Sussman (1976: 211); 'The extended family seems to be the mediator between the aged and formal organisations ... Many of the relationships between old people and their kin seem to be on the level of help in coping with bureaucratic structures.' A bureaucratic mediating function was almost universally characteristic of extended family ties among Meals on Wheels recipients, and more widely among frail aged in my sample. It was performed both by children who also provided personal services and by those who did not. Even where proximity would have permitted day-to-day help, a number of children largely limited their support of aged parents to formal mediation.

Case Study — The Danbys   Mr and Mrs Danby are very old and frail, mostly bedbound. A married daughter who lives less than five minutes away requested Meals on Wheels for them. They also receive regular visits from the home nursing service, once again at the daughter's request. She keeps in touch with her parents by telephone and visits weekly.

However she feels that her responsibility for them is to ensure that these and other services are provided. 'Mum and Dad wouldn't want to think that I was neglecting my own family', she remarked. 'They have each other. They just find it hard to deal with strangers. I make sure no-one takes advantage of them and they get what they need.' The old people agreed with this assessment and were grateful for their daughter's activities on their behalf: 'We don't want to be a burden on her', they explained.

Staff and volunteers of the Meals on Wheels service not infrequently expressed resentment at what they defined as the 'interference' of relatives. 'It's always the family who rings up to complain that the meals are not suitable or arrive too late, never the oldies themselves', the supervisor remarked. Thus it seems appropriate to classify bureaucratic mediation as another institutionalised dimension of extended family ties. Through it, the norm of autonomy is not seriously violated, and the aged person is not seen to be *directly* dependent on family members.

The Marriage Relationship

In constrast to emergency help and bureaucratic mediation, the provision of ongoing companionship and emotional gratification is firmly institutionalised only within the nuclear family unit. Several case studies illustrate the centrality of marriage in the construction of reality and the strength of its integrative role in later life.

In fact, the evidence for preventive effects of 'family' relationships refers in large part to *marital* rather than to extended family ties. The distinction is sometimes not stressed in interpretations. Townsend's (1963: 256–7) analysis of institutional admission rates, for example, quotes a UK National Health Services finding to the effect that 'the existence or otherwise of surviving husbands, wives, and children is perhaps the most important single social factor governing the amount and distribution by age and sex of demand for hospital care — particularly for the older age groups in the population'.

A Canberra study of those seeking assistance from voluntary organisations (Ford, 1972) showed that the widowed, single and divorced constituted a high proportion of the sample of clients, whereas married people were markedly under-represented compared with their numbers in the population as a whole. Other Australian studies reviewed by Howe (1979: 17) lead her to conclude 'that marriage has a very protective effect and that those without a spouse present have a much greater rate of institutionalisation'. Parenthood on the other hand does not appear to offer a similarly high degree of protection (Markson, 1976).

Beyond suggesting the 'preventive effects' of marriage on rates of institutionalisation and use of care services, the case studies I collected illustrate the critical subjective role of marital ties in old age. The married couples in my sample were situationally diverse, though clearly not representative of the entire aged cohort. In some, one or both partners were infirm; some had children living nearby, others at a greater distance, and a few were childless; about half received community services of some kind. In only one case (John and Emily Streetfield) was the husband still working; this couple was also the only one to have a child living with them.

In the symbolic interactionist view, marriage constitutes a fundamental nomos-building 'subworld', a world which defines and sustains both a shared social reality and the identity of the partners. 'In each partner's psychological economy of significant others, the marriage partner becomes the other *par excellence*, the nearest and most decisive co-inhabitant of the world' (Berger & Kellner, 1964: 11).

In Simmel's terms, monogamous marriage is the most significant of all social dyads. According to Simmel (1950: 123), dyadic interaction differs from interaction in larger groups because of:

> the fact that the dyad has a different relation to each of its two elements than have larger groups to *their* members. Although for the outsider, the group consisting of two may function as an autonomous, super-individual unit, it usually does not do so for its participants. Rather, each of the two feels himself confronted only

by the other, not by a collectivity above him. The social structure here rests immediately on the one and on the other of the two, and the secession of either would destroy the whole. The dyad, therefore, does not attain that super-personal life which the individual feels to be independent of himself.

This phenomenon has as one important consequence the fact that it 'causes the thought of its existence to be accompanied by the thought of its termination much more closely and impressively than in any other group . . .'

To my knowledge, this perspective has not been applied to the study of later life, though it has been suggested (c.f. Rosenmayr, 1972: 169) that the effect of the marriage relation on inter-generational ties is an area which should be explored. In fact this constitutes only one of several aspects of the role of marriage in old age. The marital relationship itself also needs to be analysed as a source of integration, along with the effects of disruption of the bond through widowhood.

Case Study — The Davenports   Dick and Bessie Davenport are in their late 60s. He was a bank manager until he retired some four years ago. Both are in good health, though Bessie (according to Dick) is 'getting a bit vague'. She repeats herself all the time, he says, without realising it. 'It's a bit frightening', Dick confided to me. 'I suppose it means we're getting old.'

Since they are living on superannuation and still have some savings, money is not an immediate problem. They went on a package tour of Europe last year, and are planning to visit their married daughter in another state in the near future. They are going to combine this visit with a leisurely motor tour of the country. However, they are somewhat anxious about their future economic position, when the savings are gone.

They had thought about 'retiring to the seaside' as one couple with whom they were friendly has done. But they decided against it, 'at least as long as the children are small'. By 'the children' they are referring to their two grandchildren. Their son Bob lives in a neighbouring municipality, and Bessie and Dick babysit at his home or theirs. Bob's wife Maureen went back to work part-time when the older child reached school age. She leaves the toddler with his grandparents while she is away.

Apart from this family contact, the Davenports keep in touch with married couples of their own age, including an old school friend of Bessie's and several former workmates of Dick's. None of them lives in the area, but they exchange visits regularly about once a month with each couple. They attend theatre parties, concerts, and the like.

Recently one of these male friends suffered a heart attact. 'I suppose we'll all start dropping off soon', Dick commented with an unconvincing laugh.

This couple exemplify a number of significant patterns. First, their lifestyle is fairly typical of the 'young-aged', middle-class couples in my sample. Their mobility is as yet unimpeded by health or financial problems. They feel there are a lot of things they want to do with their retirement leisure, and plan to experience them all as a couple. They are dimly aware of possible future restrictions, and there is an element of 'let's do as much as possible while we still can' in their attitude. Both potential reductions in money and health figure here, though the latter appears more prominent in their thinking. Second, they place considerable importance on their ability to 'help out' as far as their family is concerned. They seem to feel that their usefulness in this respect is at its height now and will be much more limited in future. Third, their attitudes towards aging and death appear to be in a state of flux. Bessie's 'vagueness' has come as something of a shock to Dick: it is the first sign of aging he has recognised. His own retirement apparently did not have the same effect, or at least not to the same extent. In addition, the ill health of an age peer has begun to make his own mortality more of a conscious reality.

For Bessie and Dick, the subjective experience of aging is only beginning. They are still a couple, and are planning the rest of their lives in these terms. However the experience of a similarly situated couple, the Knights, suggests that certain conditions and consequences may be associated with anticipatory socialisation into the world of the non-couple. Their case history also highlights a more complex facet of marital relations in later life.

Case Study — The Knights   Ken Knight, 69, is a retired middle-level public servant. His wife Meg is 66. They have four grown children. Two live interstate and are seen infrequently. Of the others, a married son lives on the other side of the city and visits once a week, and an unmarried daughter, Tina, shares a house with friends in a nearby suburb. She comes for dinner at least weekly and helps out in various ways: occasional shopping, paying bills in the city, and so on.

Ken's health has deteriorated over the past few years. He has suffered two mild heart attacks though he continues, against his doctor's orders, to drink and socialise regularly at his club. Meg is in good health and plays golf three times a week with a group of same-age female friends. However she has become increasingly depressed and anxious since Ken's first heart attack. Terrified of being 'left alone', she has developed chronic insomnia and is self-admittedly addicted to sleeping pills.

She and Ken never really shared a social or emotional life. He had his workmates and club, she her house, children, and female friends and relatives. As a young woman, her only ambition was to be a wife and mother. She had shown a flair for painting at school, but hasn't touched a brush since she was married. Apart from the thrice-weekly golf ritual, she just 'potters around the house and garden'. She confesses that the reality of married life did not match the 'rosy visions' of it she had before marriage.

Ken is a rather overbearing, demanding, self-opinionated fellow. He lived for his work and his sex-segregated peer group. The family ran a poor third. His children describe him as 'selfish', 'quarrelsome', and 'pretty senile'. They feel their mother has 'sacrificed herself' to him and 'wasted her life'. Neither the local son nor the daughter expressed much grief over the prospect of his probable early demise, though they are greatly concerned about their mother — a concern which seems to be almost as much for themselves as for her. 'She already depends on me a lot', Tina said. 'I hate to think what will happen when she's alone. I feel terribly sorry for her, and guilty because I don't want to do any more than I'm doing now, but I do have my own life, don't I?'

The son, a college lecturer, maintains that he will 'never see Mum want for anything'. He has offered to pay for a part-time housekeeper, and would like his mother to put herself on the waiting list for a unit at Bayside Village. But he is adamant that he could never bring her into his house; she is equally adamant that she would never want to live with any of her children. 'I love her, of course', he remarked, 'but we have nothing in common. She drives me mad sometimes with her ideas about things: she doesn't think — never reads a newspaper — "Menzies was the best thing that ever happened to this country" — that sort of thing. Golf and the old biddies she gets around with, that's all she ever talks about. Of course she never had much of a life, but that's not my fault, is it?'

Both children made comments to me along the lines of, 'I don't know why she stays with him. He makes her life a misery. She'd be better off on her own or living with Aunty Claire [Meg's widowed sister]'. Since his retirement and illness, Ken has become even more demanding of her and resents her going out, even to play golf.

The Knights are at much the same life cycle stage as the Davenports and have similar financial resources. The major objective differences are that they have no local grandchildren and that Ken is in poor health. The style of their married life shows even greater contrasts and presents something of a paradox, expecially as far as Meg's attitude is concerned.

To outsiders, including their own children, the marital relationship is not an emotionally satisfying one, and never has been. Yet Meg continues to structure her life around Ken and shows signs of severe emotional disturbance at the prospect of his absence. Until Ken's illness and its effects on her, the children had always seen Meg as 'the strong one', in the relationship. Why does she cling so strongly to a relationship which has by her own account provided her with so little direct gratification?

The answer, I belive, lies in the fact that Meg is anticipating the disruption to her 'construction of reality', but has nothing to put in its place. Her perception of the world and of her place in it is based on the marital relationship, however intrinsically unsatisfying it may be. She lacks a sense of herself as an individual and any meaingful pattern of activity in which she is so defined. Her adult years have been spent in a limited social world; they have not provided her with the 'breadth of perspective' which permits initiating activity, rather than passive response, to be seen as a viable modality. Her reaction to the anticipated reality of widowhood illustrates the extent to which she sees her husband's death as, in effect, her social death. In the months following Ken's illness, she had her own will drawn up. When the children visit she keeps asking them if they have any favourite items among her household and personal effects.

The vast majority of marriages however were companionate and emotionally supportive. For most couples, the spouse was the single most important 'other' with whom a life meaning, as well as any social activities, was shared. The most tightly closed and intensely interdependent marital subworld was that of George and Edna Cartwright.

Case Study — The Cartwrights Both in their mid 80s the Cartwrights have lived in their rambling, out-of-repair cottage for more than 50 years. They have no living children. Between them they had 11 siblings, but all are now dead.

Edna is almost blind, George has a bad heart and a chronic respiratory condition which, especially in cold weather, often leaves him bedridden. They receive Meals on Wheels and are visited by a home nursing sister. These services are their only external contacts.

My first interview with them was hampered by their suspicion that I was, despite my disclaimers, somehow connected with the home nursing sister. The latter had apparently been attempting to persuade them to go into a nursing home, a prospect which filled them with terror. They were adamant that they wanted to remain 'independent' and 'to die in our own home', despite the obvious difficulties they had with basic day-to-day functioning. By the third visit, however, they seemed convinced that I was not part of any 'plot' along these lines, though they still saw me as allied to the service in some way. On my last visit George saw me to the door and entreated me to 'tell them not to put Edna in a home' if he should die first.

This was just one example of the extent to which each of these old people identified with the interests of the other, even beyond death. 'We're in bed today', Edna reported while greeting me on one occasion, when only George was in fact laid up. The life of each revolved totally around the other. He would get the afternoon newspaper and read it aloud to her; when he was ill, her conversation was almost totally devoted to the subject.

Clearly for this elderly couple the meaning of their lives was coterminous with their relationship. Each defined self only in terms of the other: independence and interdependence were one and the same thing. To a lesser degree, this was true of most of the other couples.

For a few, though, the marital relationship did not provide enough, or even any, emotional gratification. Mrs Streetfield felt dissatisfied in this respect. One other couple were seriously estranged, and in another case there was a divergence of interests and habits.

Case Study — The Bellinis   Maria Bellini was born in Italy but has lived in Australia for 40 years. Her husband Carlo is an Australian-born Italian. Their marriage was arranged. Maria is only in her 60s, but recently she suffered a stroke and began attending the Bayside Hospital day care centre for rehabilitation. Their two daughters both married Italian men and have moved to the outer suburbs. Mr and Mrs Bellini drive out there every Sunday, but the daughters are too restricted by the demands of their own young families to reciprocate these visits. Carlo is a gregarious and active man who used to own a fleet of taxis. He spends a lot of time away from home, at clubs, soccer matches and the like with his brother and male friends. Maria never really learned English, so when her daughters moved from the area she lost her major source of companionship. Carlo pays for a housekeeper to come in three days a week, and drives Maria to the day care centre on Tuesday and Thursday. This provides her with 'a bit of company', but cannot really fill the emotional gap in her life.

Case Study — The Hills   Betty Hill, 74, and her husband Frank, 78, are permanently estranged though they share the same house. He has 'his half', and she has hers. She cooks and washes for him, but they do not eat together. Their married daughter and a brother of Betty's live in the city, but both are some distance away from Bayside Heights. Her brother visits once a week, but she finds the journey by public transport too taxing and rarely goes to see him. The daughter keeps in touch by phone and visits once or twice a month. She works in her husband's business and has her own daughter and baby grandson nearby.

Most of Betty's weekdays are spent at the Senior Citizens Club where she has been president for the past two years. The other members know of the unhappy marital situation and, according to them, voted her into office out of sympathy, to give her something to do. She has only one close friend, a widow and fellow club member. They go out together to a concert or film every weekend. Her evenings are devoted to television; she seemed rather ashamed of this.

She suffers from arthritis which restricts her mobility somewhat. She is rather fearful of further deterioration in her health, for it would necessitate, she feels, a nursing home: 'Frank wouldn't look after me. I wouldn't want him to anyway.' She insists she would not expect nor accept care from her daughter either. The prospect of losing the ability to 'do for' herself is anathema, as is the idea of an instituion.

With these exceptions, couples tended not to find loneliness a problem. Each spouse may maintain some separate interests, but companionship is always available. Decision making is based on the fact that they are a couple. Children and grandchildren, if there are any, are a source of pride and interest, and they value the contact they have with them. But they are not a central component of life meaning, nor are they dependent on them in any way. If anything, many of these couples have given far more to their offspring than they have received, a fact which is not resented.

Widowhood

The children of those aged couples who obtained emotional support and day-to-day companionship and help from each other did not have to deal with the conflict of interests which confronted many of those with a widowed parent. Through short-term help and bureaucratic mediation, they could fulfil their institutionalised responsibilities and ensure the material well being of the older couple. When other needs arose in an aged relative as a consequence of bereavement and/or long-term incapacity, the optional quality of kinship activities became an important variable in analysis. In this situation, familial behaviour can only be understood as the product of situationally specific constraints. Chief among these, as I have discussed elsewhere (Swain, 1981), are geographic proximity, social distance, and interpersonal dynamics.

In all the families I interviewed, the ability of relatives to provide aged members with ongoing companionship and care varied with their proximity.

Case Study — Mr Crawford   Mr Crawford, a widower, lives alone in the family home he was raised in. His only son, who lives in another city some 200 km away, takes his father for extended visits about twice a year. For his daily needs, Mr Crawford relies on Meals on Wheels and on the companionship of the middle-aged widow who lives next door. She also does his laundry. These arrangements do not entirely satisfy Mr Crawford. He wishes he still had same-age friends in the area; most of his former mates have died or moved away.

Obviously proximity is a necessary condition for regular support. Proximity of relatives is not, however, a *sufficient* condition for the maintenance of instrumentally and/or emotionally oriented extended family ties. Other factors, alone or in combination, affect the range and depth of these relationships. One such factor was social distance between family members.

The emergence of cultural differences between the generations through social mobility has been shown by others to be a critical limiting condition in patterns of family support (Townsend, 1963; Streib and Thompson, 1960; Johnson, 1971: 79–80). The degree to which there is similarity of beliefs, values, and life circumstances between the generations, and hence a basis for sharing interests and activities will affect the range and depth of family contacts.

Case Study — Mrs Vyden   Mrs Vyden, 85, lives alone in a shabby, rambling house. Her only source of income is the pension. The house would be worth a great deal, but she refuses to contemplate the idea of moving. Both she and her late husband came from working-class backgrounds. Mrs Vyden was 'on the stage' in her youth. She was vague about the theatres she had worked in, though I received the impression that it was some kind of variety work. She was equally vague about her husband's occupation — he was 'in business'. The voluntary workers believed that he was involved in some kind of 'shady' operation, though I could not confirm this. In any case, he had apparently been successful enough to send their only daughter to a private school and purchase a house in Bayside Heights. However, he died suddenly in middle age and apparently left no other assets or source of income for his widow. The daughter married into an upper-status family who had, according to Mrs Vyden, hoped for a 'better match' for their son, and they have three children. The family lives less than 10 minutes away from Mrs Vyden. The daughter telephones regularly, but she rarely sees her or the children: 'I'm a bit of an embarrassment to Vicky', she told me, a fact which she apparently accepts, but not without hurt. Apart from getting Meals on Wheels, Mrs Vyden used to have 'very good neighbours' who mowed her lawn, brought in her newspapers and so on. But they have recently moved, and her daughter is pressing her to go into a private nursing home which she (Vicky) would pay for. Mrs Vyden is increasingly unable to get around as a result of serious respiratory problems and is very lonely.

This extreme socio-cultural diversity was unusual in my sample. A more common reason for the failure of families to exercise their option of emotional support lay in interpersonal dynamics.

All the case histories I collected showed the importance of the psychological qualities that an elderly person brings to all aspects of his or her life, including interaction with family members. Some families simply chose to interact as little as possible with a querulous or depressing parent, though they continue to ensure that basic material needs were met. This option resolves normative ambiguity in favour of the younger generation.

Case Study — Mrs Charlesworth   An 89-year-old widow, Mrs Charlesworth, received Meals on Wheels for several years, despite the fact that two of her married sons lived in the same street. Apparently she had long ago alienated her daughters-in-law by her domineering manner.

An extremely wealthy woman from a socially prominent family, she had raised her sons to jump to her commands. When they married, she had insisted that they live nearby and expected their continued loyalty and submission. Over the years, she became increasingly frail, and also (according to one daughter-in-law) developed imaginary complaints which manifested themselves when she could not get her way. The wives' resentment prevailed over their husbands' misgivings. After a fall which left her bedridden, she was placed in a nursing home.

In two other cases, a problematic situation was resolved by relatives exercising their option for benign neglect.

Case Study — Mrs O'Donnell and Miss Parkinson   Pearl O'Donnell, an 89-year-old widow, shares an old neglected cottage with her 85-year-old unmarried sister, Lily Parkinson. Pearl is confined to bed or to a wheelchair: her unaided mobility is restricted to swinging herself from one to the other. Lily, a former nurse, is remarkably active for her age. She can get about to shop, travels on public transport and so on.

The two sisters receive Meals on Wheels, and both used to attend a day care centre twice a week. Now only Pearl goes. Lily takes the opportunity to visit the only surviving friend from her nursing days. For many years a neighbour had performed various small services for them — shopping, telephoning and so on — but she has now moved away and they know no-one else in the area.

Pearl has three sons. The eldest is married but has no children. He lives on the other side of the city and visits every Sunday. He used to take them for a drive at these times, but has not done so since they started going to the day care centre. He feels they get out enough now and that it is too much trouble to get Pearl about. Another lives with his family in the outer suburbs but never visits: he says he does not want to bring his children into the house in its rundown, unpleasant condition. The third son is also married and lives in another state; he came for a short visit at Christmas but had not been seen for three years prior to that. Pearl is bitter and hurt at what she calls her family's neglect; she says they are only interested in getting their share of the valuable piece of real estate the house stands on.

About six months ago Pearl had a heart attack and was placed in a nearby nursing home. She soon discovered her family had booked her in permanently, and not temporarily as she had thought. When she learned of this she left and lives in terror of being sent back. Her vestiges of independence constitute the only source of control she has in defining her life situation. Though she is nearly blind she continues to do handicraft work. Lily clings equally tenaciously to her independence. Staff at the day care centre report that when she used to attend their biggest problem was getting her to admit that there were some things she could not do. She would pitch in enthusiastically to any activity, which frequently meant that staff had to do the job all over again when she had left.

Case Study — Mrs Kraus Mrs Kraus, 65, occupies a spacious, elegant apartment with panoramic views of Sydney Harbour. She owns the unit, which has a conservative market value of about $75 000 though she complains that maintenance costs and rates constitute a real financial burden. Since her husband died suddenly some five years ago, she has taken in a series of boarders, ostensibly for economic reasons. She is adamant that she would never accept financial assistance from her family, though they have offered it: 'I've always been independent'. However, in interviews with other family members I learned that her son-in-law in fact now 'rents' her spare bedroom as a tax arrangement. She was never happy with boarders, regarding them as intruders in what had been her family home. All had moved out after a few months residence following clashes over domestic arrangements and/or 'personality'.

Mrs Kraus was born in Austria, where she grew up on a large rural property. Her father was a successful businessman, and both sets of grandparents were wealthy landowners. Her three brothers died during World War II, as did her brother-in-law. Her only sister died shortly after emigrating to South America, where a now middle-aged niece of Mrs Kraus lives with her husband and son. The only contact she has with this group of kin are letters exchanged three or four times a year. Her son-in-law plans a visit there shortly on business, and they are urging her to accompany him and stay for a while but she refuses, maintaining that she doesn't want to be 'a burden' on him during the trip.

Mrs Kraus was educated in a Catholic convent. At 23 she married a prominent Vienna lawyer, and their only daughter was born in Austria. The family came to Sydney 'in luxury' in 1940, where they were joined by her husband's two brothers and brother-in-law, all of them architects. Between them they established a successful real estate building enterprise in Bayside Heights. One of their earliest constructions was the apartment block she now lives in. Her two sisters-in-law and a nephew also occupy units in the building. Her daughter married a doctor and they now live with their three daughters in a neighbouring suburb. Her other sister-in-law also lives nearby, though she does not see her often: 'she [the sister-in-law] has a good friend, also a widow', Mrs Kraus explained. The implication (I gathered) was that Mrs Kraus's companionship was not needed. Apart from the nephew who lives next door (and whom she only sees in passing — 'he's camp, not my type of person'), she has little contact with these affinal relations. Two other nephews are in Sydney. She does not even know where one of them lives; the other she sees perhaps three or four times a year, 'when he has time'.

When Mr Kraus and his brothers were alive, they and their families formed an intimate solidary group. They detested the lack of sophistication in Australian culture, and relied on each other to preserve a semblance of the European lifestyle they had enjoyed.

Since her husband died, her daughter and grandchildren are, she maintains, 'all I've got'. They have a family dinner at the daughter's house every Sunday, and she has the grandchildren over to dinner occasionally. Otherwise, she told me, her daughter phones her almost every day, although there are apparently periods when she neglects to do this. At these times Mrs Kraus is reluctant to initiate contact: 'I don't like to disturb them'. Occasionally her daughter picks her up and takes her home for an afternoon. Mrs Kraus does not feel close to her daughter, and has strained relations with her son-in-law. They in turn express the situation more cogently: she 'drives them mad'. The weekly dinner is apparently a war of nerves, with Mrs Kraus unable to relax and always trying to 'do something to help'. To them it is simply annoying and disruptive. The family recognise her loneliness and feel guilty about not being able — or willing — to help. If she were to come and live with them, one granddaughter told me, 'it would break up my parents' marriage'. As for Mrs Kraus, she says she couldn't bear to impose herself. 'They have me on special occasions and once a week and that's all I want'. Clearly, she actually desires much more.

Far more than for her daughter, Mrs Kraus 'lives for' her grand-daughters, especially the eldest, Jane, with whose upbringing she was most closely involved. When the children were small, Mrs Kraus's son-in-law had a practice in an outer Sydney suburb, and Mrs Kraus was a frequent babysitter, despite the fact that she could not drive and had a travel long distances by public transport. She could have afforded a car, but Mr Kraus objected to women driving.

Jane in particular was also often sent to stay with her for reasons which, in Mrs Kraus's view, showed her daughter as 'not an especially good mother'. Now that the girls are approaching adulthood she sees them far less often than she desires and feels that they are growing further away. Sometimes, she complains, they are even 'too busy' to show up for Sunday dinner, which is her only regular contact with them. Her fondest hope is that one of them would move into her apartment, a hope that will according to them, never be realised. At the time of my last interview with her she was desolate over the fact that Jane had gone to America for an indefinite stay. She prayed that at least Jane would take up her father's offer to pay for a short visit home so they could see her graduate. I asked her why she didn't go to America to visit herself, and she said she felt she would be unwelcome, that her presence would get in the way of young people's activities.

The girls' reaction to their grandmother's obsessive concern for them parallels that of their parents: they feel she 'smothers' them. Their concern for her appears to stop at feelings of guilt and obligation. Jane, 'feels terrible' when she misses Sunday dinner and Mrs Kraus 'gets all upset' at her absence. The youngest girl visits her occasionally but would move out of home if Mrs Kraus came to live with them. Apparently relations with their late paternal grandmother, Mrs Larkins, were quite different. Jane commented guiltily: 'I was sorry it was Grandma Larkins who died and not Grandma Kraus'.

Mrs Kraus has one obsessive concern in her life, a concern that arouses even greater passion than her living family: the late Mr Kraus. My first interview with her had not lasted 10 minutes before her memories of him had evoked a flood of tears — a scene I was to see on several occasions. Her bereavement five years previously was relived in minute detail for me. Each week on the day and hour of his death she ritually lights his bedside lamp. His personal effects are exactly as he had left them. Although she now suffers from the loneliness of a large empty flat, she would never dream of moving because of the memories of 'all the happy times' she had there with him. Her whole life, she told me, had been built around her husband. She never did anything without him, and his wish was her command: 'Whatever he wanted or didn't want, that was what I did or didn't do'. For example, she has never learned to drive because she promised her husband that she wouldn't. Her family interprets her former marital situation as one in which she was 'totally dominated'. Apparently when he died she had no idea of how much money they had, how bills should be paid, and so on. She did not even know that she had been on the pension for some years. Grandfather Kraus was not a welcome visitor in the daughter's home, and while he was alive the two families saw even less of each other than they do now. To Mrs Kraus, his death means: 'I have nothing to live for any more.'

When she is not talking about her own personal tragedy, Mrs Kraus is often talking about someone else's: the deaths of her brothers-in-law, fatal accidents involving former neighbours and acquaintances, her only close friend's terminal illness, and so on. My interview reports invariably begin with 'more tales of death and tragedy today ...' or words to that effect.

Most of her days are spent watching television, listening to classical music on the radio, and cleaning up the flat. She makes a point of walking to the shopping centre every day, and has dinner regularly at 6.00 p.m. She has never belonged to any clubs, does not play bridge or golf — she 'would find that kind of life empty'. The family often suggest she get out and do things, but she dismisses them with, 'What would I do?' She expresses the view that she would be better off now if she had never experienced the happy times of her life: 'Not having them any more makes it so much worse'.

The central meaning of Mrs Kraus's life — the means by which she integrates her different situations and biographical episodes and from which she derives her situationally specific goals and definitions — is clearly her now defunct status of wife to a particular kind of man in a particular lifestyle. 'I devoted my life to him'; and she is now left with only minimal resources with which to develop a different overall life meaning.

The loss is felt so keenly that she would prefer never to have experienced it in the first place. Her identity was as his wife, her duties and rights clearcut, requiring no decision making on her part. Together, in the midst of the Australian 'cultural vacuum' she so abhores, they could perpetuate to an extent the elite European lifestyle with which both so strongly identified. In this, her husband and his brothers constituted the core reference group.

Her daughter, however, internalised an upper middle-class Australian lifestyle. Rather than sharing her mother's world view, she was alienated by Mr Kraus's demeanour as the overbearing European patriarch, and could not sympathise with her mother's passivity and dependence.

Now within a few short years all those with whom she shared this meaning are dead. The role of family matriarch is beyond her capabilities: her efforts at 'helping' at the family dinner are culturally inappropriate and merely annoy. Apart from occasional money gifts (she gave her daugher $1 000 for her last birthday), she has nothing of value to exchange for companionship now that the grandchildren are grown and independent.

So she clings to memories of her husband as the only way to retain a sense of meaning in her life. By memorialising him she keeps intact, symbolically at least, a lifestyle integrated around the only values she has ever cherished. This process is in turn validated in the way she selects certain life situations as somehow epitomising 'the way things are'. She interprets her life as a tragedy, but if she can find tragedy everywhere her own position becomes somehow more tenable. Thus her conversation constantly turns to the deaths of others, the suffering of those left behind, and so on.

Clearly for Mrs Kraus the death of her husband amounted to a particularly sudden and violent break with her past. With him, and to a lesser but nonetheless significant extent with her brothers-in-law, there vanished a part of her youth that they alone remembered. As well, the plans for a future, the life project, became meaningless and represented only a bitter failure. Memories alone maintain the relationships she had. Her family — the only living contacts with a meaningful life now vanished — see her only as a burden.

Extended Family Households

In some cases, bereavement has a different outcome — the formation of an extended family household. I observed two cases of two-generation households, in which the carer appeared to be as psychologically dependent on the relationship as the 'cared-for' was physically reliant. Two other households contained three generations.

Case Study — Mrs Bridges   Mrs Bridges, a wealthy widow in her late 70s, has come in recent years to manifest increasingly problematic behaviour, such as getting 'high' on sedatives and wandering around the house, injuring herself in a fall on one occasion and almost gassing herself on another. She has been widowed for more than 30 years and her only child, an unmarried son in his late 50s has always lived with her. A professional man, and wealthy in his own right, he retired when his mother began to exhibit this behaviour and to insist that she could not bear to be alone while he was at work. She was briefly induced by her doctor to attend a local day care centre twice a week. During this time the son was at least able to get out and play golf, a sport to which he has always been passionately devoted. But after a short time she refused to go any more and demands Mr Bridges' constant presence. Mr Bridges concedes that the situation leaves him 'desperate', but sees no other solution than to accede to his mother's demands.

Mrs Bridges' control of the situation is clearly facilitated by the paucity of significant social relationships which her son maintains with others. The fact that he has never married may well reflect a life-long personality characteristic. At the same time, Mrs Bridges displays no desire for autonomy from him, in contradistinction to the values expressed by her age peers. Rather it is control she values: she actively manipulates the relationship to maximise their mutual interdependence and isolation from outside contact.

The only other two-generation household in my sample was also a case in which the arrangement antedated the older person's frailty and fulfilled needs for the younger.

Case Study — Mrs Day   Now 88, Catherine Day grew up as the second youngest of a large and extremely poor family. Her mother survived to a great age, and during her final years was cared for by Catherine. Her two daughters were in their teens when Mr Day died and Mrs Day has since been in receipt of the pension. One daughter died some years ago, having moved interstate after her marriage. Her children have had little contact with Mrs Day. The other daughter, Molly, never married and has always lived at home. Molly worked in a clerical job which she disliked and Mrs Day acted as sole housekeeper. Molly retired at 55 and received a pension.

As Mrs Day's physical capacity has declined over the years, her daughter has gradually assumed more and more of the housekeeping functions. Though still relatively mobile, Mrs Day is now heavily dependent on her daughter. Mrs Day keeps in touch, mainly by phone, with her only surviving brother. She exchanges very occasional visits (via her daughter's car) with one long-standing same-age female friend. Apart from visits to the doctor she seldom goes out. She has never belonged to any clubs or pursued any hobbies apart from knitting and reading. She laments the dearth of people her age in the area, but refuses to join a Senior Citizens Club. An intensely private person, she has friendly but superficial contact with neighbours.

Mrs Day is now almost totally dependent on Molly for her day-to-day needs. Yet Molly in turn has structured her own life around this dyadic relationship. She is a friendly outgoing woman and has a number of same-age friends, mainly former workmates, but she spends most of her time with her mother. They go for drives, and watch television 'constantly'.

Three-generation Households

Two families had formed a three-generation household following the bereavement of an aged member. This type of support mechanism is decidedly not a normatively sanctioned option. The incorporation of an aging relative into a three-generation household is in fact negatively evaluated by old and young alike.

Hutchinson's (1954) survey found that aged Australians share with the younger generation a strongly expressed aversion to the idea of joint living arrangements. This attitude is underscored by a belief system which stresses the importance of generational independence.

Researchers have been unable to establish independent sociological variables involved in decisions to establish a three-generation household. Robins (1962) found that the three-generation pattern is adopted in response to situational pressures, typically involving a need on the part of the old member, and would in all likelihood not have been initiated in the absence of those pressures. There was no conclusive indication from his data as to why this particular response was adopted by these families when it is not by others. Robins also notes that the mutually supportive aspects of the families he studied were not readily apparent beyond housekeeping assistance rendered by the old member and the occasional household in which a second generation female was freed for employment.

My data support these generalisations and offer some further insight into the role of personality characteristics in family interaction patterns.

Case Study — Mrs Brady   Tess Brady, an active 75 year old, lives in a self-contained flatette attached to her daughter's house. This arrangement was worked out when she was widowed some six years ago. She sold the family home and paid for the building costs involved in converting a rear section of her daughter's home into a bed-sitting room with small bathroom and kitchen. She is completely independent of her family, financially and physically, and insists she would have it no other way. She does all her own housekeeping, as well as some of her daughter's. When the grandchildren were younger (they are now 12, 15 and 19) she frequently took care of them too. Tess is equally emotionally independent of her family. She spends little time with them, and they all eat together only once a week (a meal which Tess cooks). She does not expect more than this: 'They have their own lives and interests'. The important thing for her is 'just knowing someone is there if I need them'. She attends church regularly and helps out at the Women's Auxiliary.

Case Study — Mrs Parker Julia Parker, a 76-year-old widow, lives with her son, daughter-in-law and two grandchildren. She had the large two-storey house converted into a duplex after her husband died 10 years ago. She occupies the top half, and her son's family live downstairs. She is financially independent and does all her own housekeeping. However she has no outside interests, and is constantly bemoaning the emptiness of her life since her husband died. Her morose attitude and unwillingness to find anything positive about her situation makes interaction with her an unpleasant experience. She used to enjoy gardening, but now rarely ventures downstairs as, she says, she is worried about 'disturbing' her son's family. She spends most of her time upstairs alone, a fact which she blames on her family's 'neglect', though she has not initiated any extra-domestic activity herself. At the same time, the son's attitude was decidedly unhelpful. Julia has no phone in her part of the house, but her son will not always take calls for her.

In structural terms, the family and material situations of both women are similar. The contrasts, however, are striking. Both shop two or three times a week, for example, but for Mrs Brady it is a 'necessary nuisance' that she gets over and done with as soon as possible, whereas for Mrs Parker it is a way of 'getting away from the house'; she likes to 'window shop' and is always buying gifts (sometimes quite expensive ones) for her grandchildren. Mrs Parker watches television 'a lot', Mrs Brady 'never has time'. Mrs Parker knows 'no-one' in the area; Mrs Brady knows 'a lot to say hullo' and 'quite a few very well'. For Mrs Parker, widowhood meant she had 'nothing to live for any more' — it's like a living death to be alone'; for Mrs Brady her husband's death was 'a terribly difficult thing to face, of course, but you have to keep going and I keep busy'.

Clearly the two women have brought vastly different attitudes and psychological resources to their respective situations. The mere fact of shared accommodation does not ensure integration.

In summary, then, it is the marital rather than the parental relationship which discussions of the 'preventive effects' of family life are largely tapping. As the previous discussion has shown, the distinction between aged persons with and without a 'family' is over-simple. It obscures the fact that many older Australians who *do* have relatives, including children, also use care services, are admitted to institutions, and feel lonely.

The 'preventive effects' approach tends to ignore or, at best, to over-simplify the *multiple* facets of family relationships and the dynamics of their interrelationships. The family consists, structurally, of a set of bonds — between spouses, with individual children, between spouse and child(ren), as well as with in-laws, siblings, and more distant kin (Nimkoff, 1962). How these disparate yet interlocking ties may affect the total set *and each other* needs far more serious examination.

The Single Old

One final case history will be presented to illustrate the fact that, for some individuals, a familial network of any kind is not essential for the fulfilment of an individual life meaning. Non-participation is a viable old age option for these people, who thereby exercise decisive control over their situation.

The limited research which has been conducted on single older people suggests that they tend to be life-long social isolates (Townsend, 1963; Tunstall, 1966; Gubrium, 1976). Qualitative data show that single old people, 'have a rather special attitude to old age ... Their circumstances coalesce to give them the status of being a long-term single person. These circumstances involve personal independence, long-term continuity in life events, and relatively minimal social involvements' (Gubrium, 1976: 194).

Miss Schmidt fits this description well. From her life history presented below, it is clear that self-validation has never rested on interpersonal relations. Her life meaning is defined in terms of creative self-expression, and its achievement does not depend on participation in any social network. Physical infirmity constitutes the only potential disruption to control over her life situation.

Case Study — Miss Schmidt Eva Schmidt, now 81, came to Australia from her native Vienna in 1937. A Jewess, she lost all her family during the War except for a nephew who now lives in America. Shunning what she saw as the 'crass materialism' and status-seeking of Jewish emigre society in Sydney, she has always lived alone (now in a small rented bed-sit apartment) and maintains a strict guard on her independence and privacy. Far from being anti-social, however, she is a charming, cultured and intelligent woman whose days are filled with activity, though only occasionally in the company of others. One long-standing female friend lives nearby and sometimes accompanies her to concerts; she occasionally chats with neighbours, of whom I was one, and occasionally goes to the Senior Citizens Club for the craft and a meal. She has developed a deeply personal philosophy of life in which the arts and creativity figure prominently. An accomplished seamstress, she took up painting last year and produces more than creditable work. She listens to classical music on the radio and attends as many concerts as she can afford. The old-age pension and a small annuity from the German government are her only source of income.

The extent of her social isolation was dramatically illustrated during the period of fieldwork. As her neighbour of some months, I was used to running into her on the stairs, hearing her radio, and seeing her occasionally at the Senior Citizens Club. One day she simply disappeared. At first I assumed she must have been staying with friends or family (I did not know much about her situation at this time). No-one at the Club knew where she was, and after a week had passed I enquired of our landlady if she knew anything of what had happened. She did not, and informed me that as far as she knew there was no-one with whom she could be staying. I contacted the police, and she was eventually located in a public hospital where she had been taken after injuring herself in a fall on the street. She had told the staff that there was no-one to be contacted.

Miss Schmidt's attitude toward old age is vividly portrayed in a little essay she presented to me after learning of my research interest. It is reproduced below:

'How to prepare for — and live happily with — old age. While you are still in the midst of a busy life — with an aborbing job perhaps — you must find time to look for a hobby that you keep up into ripe old age. Read all the available books about — while your eyesight allows you to do so, but select something that should not be looked at as escape, but should become an interesting part of your life, then, when retirement comes you won't sink into second childhood but take up your hobby earnestly and joyfully start on your second youth.

Start now doing regular daily exercise, particularly breathing exercises — nothing strenuous or jerky.

In middle age stick to a sensible diet. Keep drinking, smoking and social activities under control. Avoid fatigue and tension at all costs.

Miss Schmidt's life has never been defined around others. Rather she has continuously defined herself — in a conscious, philosophical sense — as a unique being, taking satisfaction in solitary creative expression, whether active (craft, painting) or passive (music). Rejecting any mystification (especially religious) of life and hence of death, she finds the physical handicaps that come with age a burden, but the metaphysical aspects have not brought a loss of desire to experience the present. For her, in fact, the break between past and present is barely perceptible in terms of a life meaning.

The source of values out of which Miss Schmidt constructs her life meaning is not a network of people with whom she is in direct association. Her reference group is tied neither to time nor place, but consists of an intellectual and cultural symbolic category. Her self-image does not depend on the vagaries of personal situations, but has a continuity and permanence through time. Her own praxis, moreover, is congruent with these values.

For most older people, by contrast, self-validation has been fostered and maintained through interaction in various personal networks. With any disruption to these networks, 'self-validation loses its routine proving-ground' (Gubrium, 1976: 180). A life meaning which has been socially sustained must now be sustained alone, or through some other means. One alternative is to reintegrate one's life around other networks. Some older people in my sample had taken this option, others reacted to age-related deprivations by becoming 'disengaged', (see p. 198).

Summary and Discussion

Qualitative data derived from a diversity of family situations have highlighed the problems involved in generalising about the 'integrative' effects of family ties. Most studies have taken quantifiable patterns of contact as the basis for statements about the integrative role of family relationships in later life. But, for a number of reasons, evidence for the supportive functions of dispersed kinship networks cannot be derived solely from statistical correlations.

As numerous writers have pointed out, the *quality* of family relationship cannot be gleaned from rates of behaviour. Frequency of contact tells us little about the nature of that contact, its meaning for the interactants, or its affective value. Whether, for example, the contact is maintained through genuine affection or out of a sense of grudging obligation will have a critical bearing on its integrative value for the old person. Conventional measures of help are also complicated in old age by the imbalance in resources between the generations which may lead to dependence. Family relations are not immune to the pervasive influence of age stigma.

Anderson (1971: 8–9) has emphasized that family relationships are so highly charged with emotional and moral overtones that it is difficult, for both researcher and respondent, to approach them in an objective, value free way. Further, the family is not a fixed and unchanging structure but a dynamic process: it lacks clearly identifiable boundaries and its relationships are as much a response to the interplay of personalities as to the shaping influence of social forces (Burgess, 1973: 81–94).

Statistical data necessarily emphasise social structure rather than the dynamics and cognitive or affective context of behaviour (Basham, 1978: 318). As a result of stressing the structural features of family life, Rosenmayr (1972: 194) suggests, sociologists may well have produced 'a picture that *looks* more harmonious and integrated than it really is'. In other words, frequency of contact with relatives is not a valid index of integration or segregation (whatever else it may be), for it fails to tap the crucial dimension of the functional and affective quality of family relationships. Measures of exchange supposedly come closer to this task, but even here we cannot assume the meaning of interaction. Rosenmayr (1972: 194) contends: 'Although help certainly is a very important criterion it may not and cannot generally exclude conflict. Even the attitudes that accompany help may be of a kind to invite conflict, and help may cause conflict.' Gross measurements can tell us that certain patterns exist, they cannot tell us what they mean. They can tell us *how many* kinds, but not *what* kinds of relationships an elderly person maintains.

The institutionalisation of extended family responsibilities is limited to emergency help and bureaucratic mediation. Affective integration is institutionalised only within the conjugal, nuclear unit. Beyond these dimensions, familial behaviour is situationally specific and subject to a complex interplay of constraints. One of these is the distance — geographic and social between members.

At the same time, culturally-prescribed attitudes and norms affect the interaction of family members in a variety of ways. The norm of inter-generational autonomy, the belief in public responsibility, and the importance of reciprocity, can limit the nature and the level of support which families are willing to provide or which the elderly themselves are willing to accept. In addition, whether an older person will be offered minimum, perhaps grudging assistance, or whether he or she will be treated with genuine affection will always reflect to large degree the quality of his or her makeup and attitudes.

An idealising tendency is reflected in the failure of gerontological research to recognize that the family is, among other things, a power structure (c.f. Collins, 1975). While anthropologists (e.g., Simmons, 1945), have stressed this feature and its importance in defining the nature of inter-generational relationships in pre-literate societies, few sociologists have systematically explored its ramifications for the position of the modern aged.

The framework I have adopted allows us to consider particular case histories from the point of view that family members have different resources and, hence, differential access to control in the family interaction system. Further, it allows us to take into account individual variation. There is an understandable tendency among sociologists to search for the structural determinants of behaviour at the expense of more nebulous and intangible characteristics such as personality. Yet there is evidence that such characteristics help to shape behavioural outcomes in old age.

Clearly, in order to supply a comprehensive explanatory framework, we need information of a very different kind from that which most of the available literature provides. The statistical patterns of behaviour in later life are adequately documented, at least to the point where truly relevant questions have been exposed. What is needed now is some insight into the systems of perception and meaning of which those statistical patterns are partly the results.

In Chapter 8 I analyse different patterns of participation and their relationship to subjectively experienced life satisfaction. Systematic correlations emerge. Using my model of integration, I show that the key explanatory variables here are autonomy and control.

8 Stigma, Self and Others

Behavioural patterns in old age are far from uniform. Some older people do not seem to have greatly altered the amount or nature of their involvement with the social environment. Some have substituted new forms of interaction for old. Others interact less often in certain networks, or cease participation altogether.

There appears to be no systematic relationship between the extent of network activity, or social involvement, and life satisfaction or morale. Neither activity nor disengagement theories of 'successful' aging are therefore empirically adequate. Existence of this variety does not, however, mean that research on aging must inevitably proceed to some kind of psychological reductionism whereby 'personality' becomes the only salient dimension in analysing life responses.

I have argued that behavioural outcomes in later life need to be examined in subjective as well as objective terms; in particular, through the meanings which individuals attach to behaviour and the extent to which they control these definitions. The parameters within which a person defines his or her life situation and imposes a greater or lesser degree of control are his or her unique biography and present social and material situation within a particular cultural context.

In the preceding chapters I have taken as the focus of analysis three major types of networks in which elderly people participate: formal organisations, friends, and family. I showed how the effects of age stigma helped to shape patterns of interaction within each of these networks, and how older people employed a variety of strategies to cope with these effects. In this chapter, I focus on the subjective and objective relatedness of individual old people to all of their relevant networks, in particular on patterns of stability or change in network involvement. I outline a framework which shows the relationship between the social-cultural context of stigma on the one hand, and participation in networks on the other. This framework helps to explain the lack of correlation between network activity and life satisfaction demonstrated elsewhere in the gerontological literature. Life satisfaction, I argue, is largely a product of the extent to which an older person is in control of his or her definition of self.

A Taxonomy of Participation Patterns

Videbeck and Knox (1965) have proposed a non-normative, descriptive framework for analysing participation patterns which allows us to systematise the factors of stability and change in later life. Their framework replaces the adjustment concept with a taxonomy of alternative responses to aging in which the mutually exclusive categories are based on plausibility and probability but do not presuppose that any particular response is 'normal' and/or 'desirable'. Using a slightly modified version of this taxonomy I have categorised the participation patterns of non-institutionalised elderly Baysiders as shown in Figure 1.

Figure 1 *Participation Patterns and Life Satisfaction**

		Earlier Pattern of Participation		
		Active	**Inactive**	
Present Pattern	**Active**	Ia: *Satisfied* The Davenports Mr Bellini Mr Hill Mrs Brady Mr Knight Ia: *Dissatisfied* Miss Jones Mrs Knight	Ib: *Satisfied* Miss Martin Mr Fletcher MrsBuchanan Mrs Chevalier Ib: *Dissatisfied* Mrs Hill	II
	Inactive	III: *Satisfied* The Callaghans The Danbys III: *Dissatisfied* Mrs Bellini Mrs Kraus Mrs Day Miss Lewis Mrs Brown Mrs Walton (?) Mr Crawford	Mrs Hughes Miss Coleman Miss Parkinson Mrs Streetfield Mrs Parker Mrs O'Donnell Mrs Williams Mrs Vyden	IV: *Satisfied* Miss Schmidt The Cartwrights IV: *Dissatisfied* Mrs Bridges

Ia. Continuance of earlier type and relatively great amount of participation.
Ib. Maintenance of relative amount of participation but change in type.
II. 'Late blooming' participation where present level is higher than earlier pattern.
III. 'Disengagement' where present level of participation is lower than earlier pattern.
IV. Continuance of earlier tendency toward inactivity.
(Adapted from Videbeck and Knox, 1965: 39).
*Totally institutionalised subjects excluded.

Through comparative analysis of life histories, I will illustrate how selective participation in, or withdrawal from, different networks reflects the interaction between biography and present resources (c.f. Streib & Schneider, 1971: 4-5), and how principles of interpersonal costs and rewards underlie alternative participatory responses (c.f. Rodriguez, 1975; Hess, 1976a: 32-3).

Where previous chapters have analysed repsonses to cost/reward considerations within particular networks, the present discussion focuses on the interrelations between networks, or the individual's life space. The life space is not conceptualised in terms of a combination of social roles, but as the totality of an individual's system of values, meanings, and intentions (Riegel, 1959: 808) — his life meaning.

For heuristic purposes, participation is conceptualised as non-instrumental activity in the following domains: immediate family within the household; extended family relations; neighbourly contact; friendships; and voluntary associations. Exclusive participation in two or fewer domains is rated low. Interaction of a primarily non-expressive variety (if, for example, a visit to the Senior Citizens Club is solely for the purpose of having a meal, or — as in the case of Mrs Hill — if interaction with a household member is limited to the performance of instrumental activity) is not classified as participation.

The amount and kind of activity in which an elderly person engages is not controlled by any single factor. It is not simply the result of a particular 'personality type', nor is it adequate to cite the operation of impersonal 'social forces'. Rather, it is the outcome of interaction between individual biography, present resources, and situational factors.

Stable Forms of Participation

Certain situational factors, of course, are prerequisite for certain kinds of participation. Stable high participation demands at minimum that the social environment itself has remained relatively stable. Similarly, stable participation (high or low) suggests that individual needs and resources have remained relatively unchanged.

The stable high participators (Type la) in my sample shared the following characteristics:

Their health was relatively unimpaired; that is, participation in earlier types of networks had not been precluded by physical incapacity.

Their financial status had remained relatively unchanged; the actual amount of income appears to be less important than its stability.

Previous networks are still intact, and the subject's relative status in them is unchanged.

On the other hand, there is no commonality among these subjects in terms of life satisfaction. Two of them (Miss Jones and Mrs Knight) expressed strong feelings of dissatisfaction with their lives. In both cases, dissatisfaction antedated the onset of old age. Neither woman has ever found meaning in solitary activity, but their need for expressive involvement with others has not found any truly fulfilling outlet. They have many social contacts, but these contacts are not meaningful. Clearly the compilation of currently occupied social roles is of itself a research task with fairly limited analytical value.

The other form of stable participation (Type IV) represents the continuity of a low need for extensive social involvements. Stable low participators are characterised by a life history of minimal involvement in social networks. This category includes a life long isolate (Miss Schmidt), a highly companionate couple (the Cartwrights), and a possessive widowed mother (Mrs Bridges). Both Miss Schmidt and the Cartwrights express satisfaction with life, despite their objectively deprived material and social circumstances. Mrs Bridges' case is somewhat equivocal in view of her history of psychological problems.

Thus the least 'problematic' old people in my sample are those whose favourable definitions of self continue to be sustained in a relatively unchanged environment. This includes people with both high and low amounts of social involvement. For Type Ia participators, self-validation has always been fostered and maintained through interaction in various personal networks, and these networks are still intact. There has not been any disruption to their social environment which would cause self-validation to lose its 'routine proving ground' (Gubrium, 1976: 180).

For Type IV participators, the routine proving ground of the self may well be, as for the Cartwrights, a single dyadic relationship. For Miss Schmidt, self-validation has never rested primarily on intense or extensive personal interaction with others. It has been sustained alone.

If, however, the social environment remains unchanged but has never previously sustained a favourable identity, stability alone will not provide satisfaction in later life. Miss Jones illustrates this possibility. Miss Jones' personal experience is limited to the world of a leisured elite in which 'success', for a woman, was traditionally measured in terms of 'making a good match', leading a social life and, of course, having children. Though many of her age peers are now widowed, they at least have achieved these symbols of success. In terms of this set of values, Miss Jones' life has been a failure. Nor can she call upon compensatory achievements to show that she has made something of her existence in the universal terms that have come to symbolise success for some women in modern culture. Lacking any firsthand experience of the modern world, its alternative lifestyles are as remote from her ability to realise as her ability to marry and reproduce.

Miss Jones is not at all the 'particular type of social personality' claimed by Gubrium (1976) for the single elder. Her participation in interpersonal networks has not been minimal. On the contrary, her world has consisted of extensive, though relatively superficial, face-to-face interaction. Unlike Miss Schmidt, Miss Jones is dissatisfied with her life. Both women have contact primarily with others of their own age. However, whereas Miss Schmidt's participation is highly selective and reinforces rather than detracts from her feeling of control over her self and her destiny, Miss Jones' extensive social participation is in reality conditioned by the lack of alternative means of filling her days. For her, solitary behaviour is not meaningful. Miss Schmidt compares herself favourably to other old people, both the particular individuals she meets at the Senior Citizens Club and the abstract category of 'other people my age', while Miss Jones compares herself and her cohort unfavourably with 'the women of today'.

Unstable Forms of Participation

For most of the old people in my sample, as Figure 1 demonstrates, self-validation has lost at least part of its routine proving ground. Ill health, bereavement, separation, and/or retirement have removed social contexts in which a life meaning had previously been sustained.

Participation patterns may change in three ways. A high original amount of interaction may continue, but in different contexts (Type Ib). An earlier low rate of involvement may increase (Type II). Or activity may decline (Type III). Only the first and third of these logical patterns occur in my data.

Like stable high participators, Type Ib subjects have not suffered any major restrictions in their mobility. They are healthy enough to maintain a relatively high amount of outside activity. Unlike stable participators, though, they are deprived in various ways relative to their earlier years, and these deprivations have made previous participation contexts unavailable or inappropriate.

Several women are relatively deprived financially in comparison with their middle years. All Type Ib subjects have lost one or more significant others through death, estrangement, or geographic separation. Their response to this disruption of earlier networks has been to continue a pattern of fairly extensive social activity but in different contexts.

By contrast, the majority of people with age-related deprivations did not 're-engage' in this way. The characteristics of this last group (Type III) are diverse. Many are frail; many live alone. Some are still married. A few subsist on the pension, but most have adequate means and several are quite wealthy. This category includes some of those most dissatisfied with life (Mrs Kraus, Mrs Day, Mrs Bellini, Mrs Parker), but others express contentment despite, in some cases, severe objective difficulties.

Once again we are confronted with the impossibility of explaining subjective assessments in terms of objective measures. How, for example, are we to account not only for alternative participation patterns but also for varying psychological responses within the same pattern? The model I propose offers a partial answer to these questions.

Activity, Meaning and Control

Patterns of action and interaction in old age need to be analysed within a framework of meaning and control. A major component of meaning for the elderly is the definition of old age itself. Role theorists have stressed that age identification is a crucial intervening variable in the study of age-related changes. In social-cultural terms, old age is negatively evaluated and loaded with undesirable stereotypes, central to which is the attribution to the elderly of a dependent, childlike status.

My own data and that of other researchers (Hutchinson, 1954; Fontana, 1977; Hawkinson, 1965; Stephens, 1975) documents the importance which elderly people attach to independence and the correlative dread of becoming dependent, a 'burden', on others. Independence is a cultural modality in Western society; self-reliance is imbued with moral and ethical value. Yet prevailing cultural patterns serve to define the aged in our society as dependent. Avoiding dependence, then, is crucial to escaping the stigma of old age. Only in these terms is it possible to appreciate the significance of psychological evidence as to the particularly high salience of a need for autonomy in the motivation of older people (Kuhlen, 1959: 859; Clark, 1972).

Old people may be defined by the social context as useless, decrepit and dependent, but the experience of one's own identity is more likely to be of one's self in the fullness of acceptable adult being. Time and again my informants reacted quite spontaneously to questions about age identification by remarking that subjectively they were still the same individual they had been in their young adulthood. According to Mead (1934), individuals not only orient themselves to the expectations of others, but habitually engage in an internal conversation. Mead refers to this phenomenon as the characteristic of the self as an object to itself. We organise our memories, Mead suggests, upon the string of ourselves, and in this activity of imagination the self is quite distinguishable from the organism which interacts with the environment, including its own body.

It is in this context that the concept of the former self as a referent other (Townsend, 1968; Lowenthal & Robinson, 1968; Blau, 1973: 144) assumes its full significance. In the act of recollection the individual can control a favourable definition of self. The problem in old age lies in maximising congruence between subjective identity and objective assessments of one's self. I have termed these efforts to control positive definitions of self in the face of age stigma, 'coping strategies'. My data suggest the existence of a variety of coping strategies. Some are behavioural, others symbolic. Satisfaction with life is, in these terms, an index of the extent to which an individual old person is in control of his or her definition of self.

The case studies demonstrate that stability of the social environment, though a necessary precondition for continuity in behavioural patterns, is not a sufficient condition for a positive self-conception. Nor is disruption of the social environment necessarily associated with a negative self-conception. The key to analysing the meaning of stability and change in interaction patterns lies, first, in understanding how the older individual interprets the social environment, and second, in locating the source of control in the interaction setting. In other words, availability of social networks and the characteristics of those networks set limits to patterns of action and interaction, but do not determine them.

Interpretation of Stability and Change

Maintenance of a positive self-conception in later life is facilitated by a continuation of the environment in which the individual has habitually interacted. Such continuity reflects both relatively unchanged personal resources of health and income, and the persistence of the environment itself: 'Stabilities in the organisation of behaviour and of self-regard are inextricably dependent upon stabilities of social structures' (Becker & Strauss, 1956: 263).

One response to disruption of the social environment is represented by Type Ib participators. In this response, a favourable self-image has been sustained through reintegration of available networks. Both a behavioural and a symbolic shift are involved here. When networks are disrupted, some old people begin to participate in new networks. If such a shift in contexts of participation is to maintain congruence between subjective and objective assessments of self, it needs to be accompanied by a shift in one's points of reference and comparison.

Jim Fletcher, for example, experienced an involuntary withdrawal from work, but still continued to think of himself for a time as 'one of the boys', (see p. 127). When this image could no longer be sustained, the actual work network became an invidious source of comparison. Through his activities in the Senior Citizens Club Jim could begin to compare himself with people who were 'really' old, and hence main tain distance from the category himself.

'Poor dear' hierarchies are the strongest expression of this phenomenon. Mrs Buchanan lost successively the social supports of her spouse, her daughter, and her same-age companion. However, she was able to continue her commitment to interpersonal relations by joining the Senior Citizens Club and taking on a care taking role within it. Thus she obtained a face-to-face network in which she could continue to define herself as useful and worthy of admiration.

As the old person moves objectively down the scale and becomes a 'poor dear' to successive others, there may continue to be an even lower category with whom her own situation still compares favourably. Miss Lewis' relegation to the institution may have placed her at the bottom of an outsider's hierarchy, but she in turn looked upon her fellow residents — 'they're a bit mental' — as 'poor dears'.

Type III participators, on the other hand, have not substituted new forms of activity for those they have lost. This response has proved perfectly satisfying for some. Not surprisingly, the satisfied 'disengaged' include those married couples who, despite physical frailty, have retained their most significant other. The Callaghans and the Danbys have been able to 'bow out gracefully' as age-related impairments restricted their mobility and capacity for reciprocal social involvement. By voluntarily withdrawing from close involvement with their families, they have avoided the potential for dependence and maintained a form of control over their definitions of the situation.

Mrs Bellini, by contrast, cannot now reintegrate her life around the marital relationship. Marriage with Carlo was an arranged, largely instrumental affair. Her identity has primarily been as a mother, rather than as a wife, and this identity is now denied her. Even if she desired to participate in new social contexts, her own ill health and lack of English would preclude it. She no longer has much capacity for control over her situation.

In many ways Mrs Bellini's situation more closely resembles that of the dissatisfied widows than of the satisfied wives, once again highlighting the inadequacy of role occupancy *per se* as an index of integration. As Lopata has pointed out:

> Widowhood creates a problem of personal adjustment for women when it calls for behaviours not incorporated into the personality during marriage...Maturity, as the ability to make rational choices based on a 'breadth of perspective' containing frames of reference of many different groups and creativity, as the capacity to perceive and build new actions, may be required in situations lacking automatic adjustment systems. (1972: 302)

The operative variable here, 'breadth of perspective', has been conceptualised by Warshay (1962: 151):

> Perspective is a capacity or potential of the actor that he brings to a situation and which determines the kind of meaningful responses possible in that situation. Breadth of perspective refers to the broadness of scope of perspective, to the range of meanings and ideas that make it up.

The sources of values selected by individuals for the guidance of their behaviour are probably not easily changed in old age. A group in which one participates or which serves as a point of comparison may be quite different from a group whose values and beliefs constitute one's point of view, and thus provide the normative foundation for one's life meaning. Since individuals in old age are, to themselves, 'the same' as they have always been, it is likely that earlier value systems also continue to operate. Unless a major change in life meaning occurs, as is possible with breadth of perspective, it is likely that in old age reference groups change not quantitatively but qualitatively. Participation in an actual network may cease, but the values which these represented may continue to serve as meaningful though perhaps inappropriate frames of reference. Reference groups become, in a sense, symbolic (Lowenthal & Robinson, 1976: 451).

Mrs Kraus, for example, no longer has the explicit guidance of her husband, but his values continue to shape her behaviour: 'He made me promise never to drive a car, so of course I don't.' Mrs Kraus is therefore incapable of reintegrating around new networks, nor can she reintegrate around her living family, where her capacity for control is severely limited. It is not *her* situational definition — 'You are all I've got, I have suffered a terrible tragedy, therefore you should show you care more about me than you do' — which dominates family interaction. Other family members act on the basis of a different definition: 'We're all you've got because you're never done anything for yourself; it's unfair to blame us because you're lonely. If you were a different sort of person you would't have these problems. You only make us feel guilty.' Given the situation, no alternative course of action to the weekly obligatory dinner and the ritual phone calls seems possible. No family member sees any advantage in giving her the increased contact she craves. And, given her own expressed acknowledgement of the in-utility to them of what she has to offer, the initiative for contact rests firmly with them. The only resource Mrs Kraus can lay claim to is the normatively sanctioned expectation that elderly parents should not be abandoned or neglected completely. Beyond this, the family's defini-tion of neglect becomes subject to calculative control mechanisms designed to minimize inconvenience and guilt.

Involvement in Social Networks

The behavioural and symbolic strategies which people adopt to cope with subjective and objective problems associated with aging emerge through analysis of their involvement in social networks. Of necessity, this discussion has presented a somewhat sharp and static picture of individual patterns. Through time, the lines must blur and shift. Com-panionate couplehood will be lost through the death of one partner; a satisfying independent lifestyle will be jeopardised by failing health; the grief of bereavement may subside and new interests be found. My research has captured the situations of elderly Baysiders at a particular point in time, though life history materials have provided some dynamic insights.

What I have sought to stress, in non-evaluative terms, is the rich variety of pathways in old age and the sociological naivete of assum-ing that the 'meaning' of life in later years can be derived from a com-pilation of currently occupied social roles. The existence of this in-dividual variety does not, however, mean that sociological generalisa-tion is impossible. On the contrary, the parameters of investigation lie in the interaction between individual biography and the social en-vironment: 'Earlier choice and present chance step in to give each old age its particular aspect' (de Beauvoir, 1970: 561).

I have operationalised the social environment through analysis of the networks in which elderly people participate. Symbolic interac-tionism is much concerned with the consequences for both the interac-tive relationship and for the self of the character and nature of the 'other'. The process of selection of others is an important theme in the literature:

Some people find, in this welter of 'others' some complex balance or compromise among several. Others let one or another tyrannise them. The nature of the combinations and balances is part of the organisation of society itself. Judging the relative influence of various 'others' upon individuals is indeed one of the problems with which social surveys are most concerned. (Hughes, 1962: 123)

However, actual quantifiable participation in networks is only part of the story. Equally, if not more important, are the cognitive and expressive motivations for participation — the meanings attached to it — and the degree of control the individual maintains over his or her membership of the network.

The social networks I have discussed range from the interpersonal (family and friends) to a combination of the interpersonal and formal (voluntary associations) and the essentially impersonal (community services). Clearly different kinds of networks include or exclude possibilities for elderly interactants to sustain a favourable self-conception and to control the interaction.

Certain generalisations regarding the limiting characteristics of different kinds of networks emerge from my data. In view of the small sample they must remain tentative until tested on a larger scale. However the strength of their representation in this sample and their corroboration in other studies leads me to believe that they will be found to have a broader applicability.

In the first place, I propose that self-validation through interaction in a family network is inherently problematic in a Western sociocultural context. Only through the marital tie can a conception of one's self as an unstigmatised and valued person typically be sustained. In a multi-generational structure such as the family, the individual elder is always, in comparison with other members, defined as 'old'. Many older people affirmed that objective age differences are reinforced within the family context by the attitudes of younger members towards them. They are treated, they told me, as relatively incompetent and as people to be 'humoured', rather than respected. Australian survey data (Hutchinson, 1954) support the suggestion that this feeling is widespread among the older generation, while American data (Blau, 1973) replicate the finding that children cannot provide the kind of emotional support old people need.

With advancing age, the locus of control in family interaction shifts progressively to the younger members. Old age so often involves the gradual loss of resources through which a balanced exchange process can be maintained. When resources become imbalanced, old people frequently choose to withdraw from interaction rather than accept services they cannot reciprocate. For some, the stigma of welfare services is preferable to dependence on children. Fear and avoidance of such dependence has been more extensively documented in Australia and overseas (Hutchinson, 1954; Hawkinson, 1965).

Further, there appears to be no systematic relationship between extent of family involvement and participation in other kinds of networks. Emotional dependence on children is not a product of 'loss of roles' in other areas, but rather a stable psychological characteristic. Rosow's (1967) data add weight to this generalisation.

A different set of constraints affects the integration of older people into age-homogeneous networks, though socio-psychological principles of exchange continue to operate. I identified two principal subtypes of friendship: intimate and associate. Intimate friends, like spouses, typically share a conception of each other which antedates the ravages of old age. With a friend of long standing, the individual's former unstigmatised self is likely to be presented and accepted as the 'real' person. Thus this type of friendship offers positive integrative value (Blau, 1973). Many friends in old age are, however, associates rather than intimates. This appears to be particularly true for the age segregated. In the context of age stigma, lack of a shared history seems often to preclude genuine intimacy.

Associate networks were further classified into reciprocal and hierarchical types. In the former, control is diffused throughout the network and self-validation may be bolstered by the feeling that one 'belongs' yet is at the same time autonomous. Within an hierarchical network, on the other hand, a self-validating position can only be maintained by some of the participants. The caretakers, whose participation is voluntary and active, are effectively in control of the interaction and can maintain a positive self-image. Those at the bottom of a 'poor dear' hierarchy must either find someone even worse off than themselves to pity or else accept a deferent and submissive role.

Welfare networks set the most stringent constraints on integration. Here the stigma attaching to old age is compounded by the stigma of welfare itself. The best an individual welfare recipient can do is to redefine the situation in less unfavourable but still unsatisfactory terms. Members of the Senior Citizens Club, for example, define it not as a welfare facility for *old* people, but as a venue for *lonely* people. While some stigma attaches to a public acknowledgement that one is lonely, it is apparently preferable to an ackwoledgement that one is old.

Implications for Theories in Social Gerontology

With the exception of the age stratification model (Riley, Johnson & Foner, 1972), theory development within social gerontology has tended to focus not on the totality of social aging but on a single aspect of it; namely, the process of adjustment to old age. There is growing consensus that the various theories which have emerged, despite the claims of their originators, are not really mutually exclusive or contradictory but represent instead complementary approaches to essentially the same set of problems (c.f. Fontana,1977; Hendricks & Hendricks, 1977).

The aim of this study was not to present a unified theory of aging and the aged which subsumes these varying perspectives. The scope of the empirical data I have discussed is clearly inadequate to such a task. In any case, the wisdom behind or the need for a theory applicable only to the later years is open to question (Hendricks & Hendricks, 1977: 105). However, the requirement for expositional neatness demands some attention to the implications of my data for prevailing gerontological frameworks. This discussion can be made to serve a double purpose by restating and highlighting, within a broader theoretical context, the key explanatory factors in my model of integration.

Disengagement and Activity Theory

My data are not alone in suggesting the inadequacy of either of these views to account for the observed variety of old age behaviour patterns. Fundamental to the criticisms which have been levelled against disengagement theory is the charge that it fails to take into account the existence of individual variation. A principal finding of my research was the centrality of individual biographies to the coping styles which old people developed in the face of age-related stigma and deprivations. Two major obstacles to the generalisability of activity theory emerged. First, not all types of activities have the same value for preserving a positive self-image in old age. Participation in age-graded organisations, for example, is not in itself a culturally meaningful activity, though some elderly members may find sustenance for a non-stigmatised self-conception through patterns of secondary adjustment. In other words, the meaning of a role is not, as activity theory implies, necessarily a 'given' of the normative content of that role. Second, activity theory fails to recognise the importance for adjustment outcomes of the degree of control which an elderly participant can exercise within his or her personal networks. I have shown that the composition of an individual's social networks will reflect his or her capacity to define the situation in favourable terms. Non-voluntary activity will have a negative effect on subjective feelings of life satisfaction, however extensive that activity may be.

The Aged as a Subculture

Rose's (1965) notion that age segregation is instrumental in the formation of an aging group consciousness and solidarity, that is, in the development of an aged subculture, has received less empirical testing than the previous theories. Disagreement has been largely based on demonstrating that the characteristics of the aged do not fulfil traditional definitions of minority groups (Streib, 1968). Yet there is empirical support for some of the elements of Rose's framework. Among some categories of elderly, associational patterns based on age segregation appear to foster an awareness of belonging to a particular group (Rosow, 1967), while the postulation of a partially distinctive status system among the age segregated has been confirmed in my data and that of others (Hochschild, 1973).

The crucial flaw in Rose's argument lies in the fact that old age is a social stigma. Objective indicators of belonging to a stigmatised category have the opposite effect to that posited by Rose. Rather than enhancing the affinity which older people feel for each other, the operation of agism, as of any other stigma, produces at best an ambivalent attachment to the stigmatised category. Rather than representing the development of an aging subculture, the existence of a differential status hierarchy among the aged reflects attempts by individual old people to *distance* themselves from the category. The potential for growth of aging group consciousness is weakest among the middle stratum elderly who participate in voluntary organisations for the aged. Persons of middle-class status have, subjectively, the most to lose by accepting the aged label. The Bayside Heights data suggest that upper middle-class Australian aged people participate involuntarily in age-graded organisations.

Senior Citizens Clubs are a last resort for those who have suffered substantial relative deprivation in economic or social terms, and generally in both. They simply have no alternative resources with which to satisfy basic instrumental and/or affective needs and, in participating, they further redefine the experience in ways which deny that old age *per se* has anything to do with it.

Personality Theories

There is considerable evidence, which my own data support, that aged personalities are very often the extensions of earlier coping styles into later life (Neugarten *et al.*, 1968). Operationalising personality in non-clinical and non-evaluative terms, I have shown that individuals organise their past and present experiences around a central life meaning which, in the majority of cases, is continuous over the life span. There is some suggestion in my data, however, and from others (Fontana, 1977) that major discontinuities in central life meaning and in other aspects of personality do occur. Moreover, personality theory or, rather, the developmental model of personality employed by Neugarten and her associates, does not offer any analytic tools for examining situational variations in the *expression* of continuity or change in life meaning. My data show that, in order to maintain a pre-existing coping style, many old people transfer their participation from one network to another, change the group to which they compare themselves, and/or experience a real or symbolic shift in the sources of values which guide their behaviour. The motivation for these changes, I suggested, is the search for continued control over one's life definitions.

Class and the Aged

Major economic divisions exist within the aged category and constrain the life options of individuals in significant ways. At the same time, however, the experience of aging is influenced by a factor common to all, namely, the negative evaluation of old age *per se*.

A unidimensional class analysis both obscures this cultural constant and assumes, incorrectly, that subjective understandings necessarily correlate with material circumstances. Case studies clearly demonstrate the fallacy of this view.

Marxist analysis further assumes 'that old age presents very similar problems for both sexes — it is the class differences that are dominant' (Ward, 1978: 50). But the situation of many elderly widows in my sample casts doubt on this assertion. Downward mobility following bereavement, for example, is not a problem for men. Futher, elderly males typically have more options for reorganisation and redefinition following loss and change. Not least of their potential resources is the experience of work, which men like Jim Fletcher have put to new, image strengthening directions. Other possibilities such as remarriage or simply companionship with the opposite sex are maximised for older men, given the numerical over-representation of older women.

Aging as Social Exchange

This approach to adjustment in old age takes account of the fact that there is a reciprocal relationship between aging individuals and their social environments. The exchange perspective subsumes, implicitly at least, the existence of individual variation in personal needs and desires but postulates that the actual outcome of age related changes will reflect the interplay between life history and the resources available in the social environment. The range and nature of alternative resources will affect the pattern of integration ultimately adopted.

In these terms, decrements or shifts in network involvement reflect the operation of a cost benefit analysis, in which a principal motivation is the desire to maintain control over life definitions, and thus retain a non-stigmatized identity. As the influence which old people are able to exercise over their social environment declines, they will (as far as possible and necessary for their particular life orientation) realign the personal relationships in their social world to maxmise a favourable self-image and a capacity for control. The decrements of age may progressively reduce the bargaining power of the aged individual, until the only resource he or she has to exchange is esteem and compliant passivity.

Participation and Life Satisfaction

It is interesting to speculate on how my elderly subjects would be classified using a role/adjustment approach to integration. Miss Jones, with her extensive social activity, and Mrs Kraus, with her regular family contact, would doubtless be 'integrated'. Miss Schmidt, on the other hand, would be 'unintegrated' and socially poorly adjusted. But the relationship between social participation and morale is neither so simple nor so direct.

The majority of elderly people in my sample had suffered 'loss of roles' and decreased amounts of social interaction. But they did not all respond to this situation with feelings of dissatisfaction, anomie, lowered self-esteem, or whatever. Similarly, those with no or minimal 'role loss' did not invariably hold positive images of themselves and express satisfaction with their lives.

It is widely held that extended family roles are especially 'integrative' for the elderly. My data do not support this assertion. However strongly institutionalised the extended family may be around certain instrumental activities, it is decidedly not an all-purpose support system for its aged members. With the partial exception of the conjugal bond (and even in this small sample three wives were dissatisfied), occupancy of familial roles does not — and in most cases cannot — automatically ensure emotional satisfaction.

Idealisation of family roles and relationships has for so long coloured sociological analyses of this institution that researchers often tend to speak as if all the principles governing familial interaction are of a totally different order to those governing other forms of social involvement. Yet playing familial roles entails costs and benefits and involves problems of definition and control.

From my research in Bayside Heights, it appears that older people bring at least one common set of needs, desires and motivations to all their interaction settings: they wish to avoid identifying themselves as 'old' *in the terms by which that status is socially defined*. Western cultural patterns stigmatize the aged, and the core element of age stigma is the attribution of dependence.

This phenomenon constitutes an independent variable in the explanation and interpretation of participation patterns in old age. It is equally as significant in the interaction between older people and their families as it is in their relationships with each other and with the non-aged. Those older people who can control favourable definitions in these terms have greater life satisfaction and higher self-esteem than those who cannot.

On occasion, the ability to maintain control may necessitate withdrawal from, or reduced activity in, certain networks, including familial networks, and/or the transference of participation to other networks. This socio-psychological mechanism has been confused with inevitable and functional characteristics associated with 'disengagement', or with universal needs for certain levels of social activity. It has also been claimed to show the existence of various personality types, some of whom are better 'adjusted' than others, or to suggest that the aged are begining to develop group consciousness and solidarity.

There are elements of descriptive value in all these formulations. But as explanations of cause and effect they are one-sided, 'outsider' views of aging. As de Beauvoir (1970: 16)put it: 'Every human situation can be viewed from without — seen from the point of view of an outsider — or from within, in so far as the subject assumes and at the same time transcends it'.

Only by approaching the elderly as subjects rather than objects of research can we expect to extend our understanding of the 'problems' of aging — and their solutions. Many old people *do* transcend their situations, though perhaps not in the ways non-aged propose they can or should. If we took our cues less from 'objective' research and more from the aged themselves we may well find some new answers to old questions.

It is, of course, equally clear that understanding the situations of today's elderly involves recognition of much broader sociological factors. The various coping strategies aged persons adopt are a response to socially constructed definitions and socially imposed restrictions and deprivations. Although my research has focused on the experience of aging from the perspective of the individual social actor, it has done so against a theoretical background which stresses the shaping and limiting conditions of economic, political and cultural structures. I have merely sought to describe and explain some of the variability which characterises individual action in the face of these constraints.

9 Conclusion

Social gerontology is not a unitary formal domain of scientific enquiry. Its substantive focus — the category of old people — can be analysed from a variety of biological, medical, sociological and psychological perspectives. The *raison d'etre* of social gerontology as a separate field of enquiry rests ultimately on the application of research to the social problems of old age.

The notion of integration has supplied the conceptual bridge whereby definitions of these social problems have been translated into programmes of scientific enquiry. However conventional measures of integration, based on readily quantifiable factors, have failed to provide the necessary kinds of data. Most research continues to be overly concerned with 'objective' dimensions of interaction and has either ignored the subjective aspect or taken the meaning of interaction as a given of role content.

The data I have discussed, by their very nature, focus attention on the experiences and behaviour of individual aged persons. Generalisations which emerge directly from these kinds of observations tend to remain at the level of personal action and interpersonal relations. The analytical framework of symbolic interactionism sheds considerable light on these issues.

I believe that this is a vitally important corrective to dominant research strategies in the field of social gerontology. At the same time, such an approach is ill suited to the task of guiding public policy or broad welfare strategies. It can however fulfil an important sensitising function for those engaged in such tasks.

The most important implication of this study for policy makers and suppliers of welfare is simple. If public measures are truly to benefit the aged, and not just to construct an elaborate aging enterprise, they cannot afford to rely on structurally derived assumptions about the meaning of behaviour in old age. Meaning is situationally specific, and what is 'objectively' good or bad for an older person may not subjectively be so defined.

There is, however, an important constant in the experience of aging which needs always to be borne in mind. In our social structure, the aged are offered a devalued place. Unlike some other stigmatised categories, all old people have experienced life as a non-stigmatised, young individual. Abominations of the body which progressively objectify a new status can accordingly be perceived as not defining the 'true' self which one has constructed throughout a lifetime of meaningful activity. This definition, if nothing else, can be sustained to the end.

The strategies which old people in Bayside Heights have employed to cope with threats to their identity are part of a wider social story. Rates and frequencies of participation in different kinds of social networks undoubtedly vary according to socio-economic status, geographical setting, and other variables. The statistical patterns are a problem for other kinds of research than that on which this study is based.

I believe that the management of identities spoiled by age will show underlying commonalities, wherever it is encountered. The need to maintain psychological integrity in the face of a fall from youthful grace is a constant, although there are as many paths to its fulfilment or failure as there are individual biographies and unique social situations.

Participation patterns in old age reveal the ongoing attempts of older people to maintain a positive image of self, an image of a person to whom the age stigma designation cannot justifiably be applied. The ways in which older people define themselves and their situations need to be taken into account. One of the strongest needs is to feel in control of these definitions.

Current thinking on old age welfare in Australia fails to accord due weight to this dimension. As a result, specific welfare programmes may become two-edged swords for their clients, and obscure the complexity of the problem they are supposedly addressing. The plea for an expansion of domiciliary services is a case in point.

The issue of home care has become a focal point of gerontological discussions, and is even tending to be promoted as something of a panacea for a wide range of old age problems. It is described, for example, as an alternative to institutionalisation which is both cheap and desirable, in that it supposedly ensures continued integration of the elderly through participation in family life.

In comparison with other countries, Australia has a relatively high level of institutionalisation of its aged (Rowland, 1980). This is hardly a situation to be applauded. Providing old people with meals, nurses, and chiropodists in their own homes is clearly a more pleasant prospect. But is this a genuine alternative?

In the first place, some old people do not have a home, or one in which they are happy and secure. Second, although there appears to be an unacceptably high level of inappropriate placement (Doobov, 1980), home care services and total institutions are not ultimately 'in competition' for the same aged population. They are points along a continuum of advancing degrees of frailty (Brody, 1976).

A common proposition of home care exponents is that frail elders, left in their own home but with domiciliary support for their material needs, are not really alone: they have their families. Welfare agencies, the argument continues, merely lighten the instrumental burden on children. Leaving aside the problem of those who have no children or none within reach, we must still question the assumption that the modified extended family is, or can be, an institution of ongoing support for aged members in either objective or (especially) in subjective terms.

It has indeed been well documented that those old people without family (but especially marital) ties are over-represented among the institutionalised aged population. This has been used as evidence for the 'preventive effects' of family relationships in old age, a formulation which contains an empirically unjustified inference about the family relationships of the *non*-institutionalised.

Demonstration that older people who lack family ties are more likely to rely on non-familial sources of support than are those who possess such ties is important. But it obscures two other important facts. First, many older Australians who do have a family are also admitted to institutions; conversely, many without relatives are not. Second, lack or loss of family (notably spouse) is only one of a cluster of characteristics shared by the institutionalised elderly. They are also characterised, as a population, by advanced old age (half are over 80), poverty, impaired mental and physical functioning, multiple chronic disabilities, and by having experienced a series of severe personal and social stresses (Brody, 1976: 265). It is methodologically inappropriate to single out any one item as *the* explanatory variable in institutionalisation. Even less justified is the inference that the non-institutionalised are 'protected' from this dependency by family support.

In any case, the question of whether family dependence is 'good' for old people involves other, more qualitative considerations. As this and other discussions have shown, family dependence is precisely what the majority of aged wish to avoid. Where inter-generational interaction is characterised by an unequal distribution of economic and social resources, the older person is hard pressed to meet a need for personal service with dignity and autonomy. Even the stigma of welfare services appears, for many, to be preferable to becoming a family 'burden'.

The expansion from the 1960s of domiciliary services, designed to keep aged persons in their own homes, was pragmatically motivated by the escalating costs of institutionalisation (Jones, 1979: 42) rather than by social philosophy. Allusions to 'family support', however, have an important smokescreen effect. They help to obscure the fundamental economic and political processes which create aged dependency.[1] By reinforcing an image of the aged as inherently and inevitably dependent on someone, they also perpetuate invidious stereotypes which justify and promote the expansion of an aging enterprise run by middle-class professionals, and further suppress the capacity of elderly people to 'do for' themselves.

The domiciliary care versus institutionalisation propostion has also diverted attention from the question of what is actually entailed in the provision of home-based services. The problems of institutions have been well documented (Henry, 1963; Fontana, 1977; Swain & Harrison, 1979), but, as this study has demonstrated, in-kind welfare services are not without their invidious characteristics. From the perspective of their aged clients, they are high on stigma.

In-kind services also may not be inexpensive, at least not if they offer good quality care. From an investigation of the costs of domiciliary care for a group of elderly sick patients under the care of the British home nursing service, Opit (1978) concludes that there may be little economic advantage in home care as compared with residential or hospital custodial care for seriously disabled elderly patients. He notes further that the level of care provided in the home is often inadequate or inappropriate, and that even with a much larger investment in home support services, 'the quality of life for some of these patients or their families may be far from compatible with any civilised humanitarian standards' (Opit, 1978: 158).

Dilemmas such as these will not be resolved by simplistic either/or formulations. We do not yet have answers to the problems of old age, in large part because we have not been asking all the relevant questions. Even so, we cannot expect to research our way into an old age utopia, certainly as far as identity needs rather than material well being are concerned. As Rosow (1976a) has pointed out, we already know the solution to material needs in old age: money. But genuine integration, as the autonomous expression of a valued identity, is another story. Goffman (1963: 150) remarks in the general context of spoiled identities that a person with stigmatised attributes is simultaneously like and not like everyone else:

This contradiction, this joke is his fate and his destiny. It constantly challenges those who represent the stigmatised, urging these professionals to present a coherent politics of identity, allowing them to be quick to see the 'inauthentic' aspects of other recommended programmes but slow indeed to see that there may be no 'authentic' solution at all.

The aged themselves perceive that the dilemma of aging is at heart an existential dilemma, a problem of meaning. And they approach its solution in existential terms, by attempting to impose upon it new definitions of meaning. Clearly, the 'problem' of old age cannot satisfactorily be resolved unless the structural and cultural arrangements of this society are transformed. For the immediate future, this is undoubtedly more pious hope than probability. It will not be hastened by research and policies which offer more of the same, within the prevailing social construction of reality.

Notes

1. As Collins and Boughton (1977: 28) remark in the context of the Henderson Report, 'the cost of bringing *individuals* (as opposed to 'income units') out of poverty is too high...for private capital'. Among other things, reliance on family care for the aged involves a tacit acceptance of the exploitation of unpaid female labour in the household, since the care of frail, aged family members is overwhelmingly a female responsibility (NSW Council on the Aging, 1975).

Bibliography

Abbott, C., Brown, C. & Crosble, P., (1973). 'Exchange as symbolic interaction: For what?' *Amer. Sociol. Rev.*, 38, pp. 504–6.

Albrecht, R., (1951a): 'The social roles of old people', *J. Geront.*, 6, pp. 138–45.

_____(1951b): 'Social roles in the prevention of senility', *J. Geront.*, 6, pp. 380–86.

Altman, D., (1979): '*Rehearsals for Change*', Fontana, Melbourne.

Anderson, M. (ed.), (1971): *Sociology of the Family*, Penguin, Harmondsworth.

Anderson, N.N., (1965): 'Institutionalisation, interaction, and self-conception in aging,' In, A.M. Rose and W.A. Peterson (eds.), *Older People and Their Social World*, F.A. Davis Company, Philadelphia, pp. 245–57.

Arth, J., (1962): 'American culture and the phenomenon of friendship in the aged,' In, C. Tibbitts and W. Donahue (eds.), *Social and Psychological Aspects of Aging*. Columbia University Press, New York pp. 529–34.

Australian Council of Social Services, (1974): *Statement to the Committee of Enquiry into Aged Persons Housing*, Australian Council of Social Service, Sydney.

Australian Department of Social Security, (1974): *Housing the Aged*, AGPS, Canberra.

Australian Institute of Urban Studies, Task Force on Housing For Australia, (1975): *Report: Housing for Australia: Philosophy and Policies*, Australian Institute of Urban Studies, Canberra.

Babchuk, N. and Booth, A., (1969): 'Voluntary association membership: a longitudinal analysis,' *Amer. Sociol. Review*, 34.

Back, K.W., (1976): 'Personal characteristics and social behavior: theory and method,' In, R.H. Binstock & E. Shanas (eds.), *Handbook of Aging and the Social Sciences*, Van Nostrand Reinhold, New York pp. 403–31.

Barker, G., (1971): 'Our infirm aged', Part 1: 'Old people stripped of dignity', Part 2: 'Victoria — no place for growing old', *Age*, 10 March, p. 8; 11 March p. 8.

Barnes, J.A., (1972): *Social Networks*. Addison-Wesley Module in Anthropology 26, Addison-Wesley, Reading, Mass.

Basham, R., (1978): *Urban Anthropology: The Cross-Cultural Study of Complex Societies*, Mayfield, Palo Alto.

Bateson, G., (1958): *Naven*, (2nd edn.), Stanford University Press, Stanford.

Becker, H.S. (1963): *Outsiders: Studies in the Sociology of Deviance*. The Free Press of Glencoe, Collier-Macmillan, London.

Becker, H.S. and Strauss, A., (1956): Careers, personality and adult socialisation, *Amer. J. of Sociol.*, 62, 3, pp. 253–63.

Bell, B.D., (1976): 'Role set orientations and life satisfaction: a new look at an old theory', In, J.F. Gubrium (ed.), *Time, Roles, and Self in Old Age*, Human Sciences Press, New York pp. 148–64.

Bell, C., (1968): *Middle Class Families*, Routledge & Kegan Paul, London.

Bell, C. and Newby, H., (1971): *Community Studies: An Introduction to the Sociology of the Local Community*, George Allen & Unwin, London.

Bell, I.P. (1976): 'The double standard', In, B.B. Hess (ed.), *Growing Old in America*, Transaction Books, New Brunswick, N.J.: pp. 150–62.

Bengtson, V.L., Olander, E.B. & Haddad, A.A., (1976): 'The "generation gap" and aging family members: toward a conceptual model', In, J.F. Gubrium (ed.) *Time, Roles, and Self in Old Age*, Human Sciences Press, New York pp. 237–63.

Bennett, K.C. & Ahammer, I.M., (1977): 'Toward a social deficit model of aging', *Aust. J. of Social Issues*, 12, 1(Feb.) pp. 3–18.

Berger, P.L., (1963): *'Invitation to Sociology: A Humanistic Perspective'*, Penguin, Harmondsworth.

Berger, P.L. and Berger, B., (1976): *Sociology: A Biographical Approach*, Penguin, Harmondsworth.

Berger, P. and Kellner, H., (1964): 'Marriage and the construction of reality', *Diogenes*. 46, Summer, pp. 1–23.

Berger, P.L. and Luckmann, T., (1967): *The Social Construction of Reality: A treatise in the Sociology of Knowledge*, Doubleday, New York.

Berger, P.L. and Pullberg, S., (1966): 'Reification and the sociological critique of consciousness', *New Left Review*, 35, 1, pp. 56–71.

Biddle, B.J. and Thomas, E.J., (1966): *Role Theory: Concepts and Research*, Wiley, New York.

Binstock, R.H. and Shanas E. (eds.), (1976): *Handbook of Aging and the Social Sciences*, Van Nostrand Reinhold, New York.

Binstock, R.H. (1976): 'Interest — group liberalism and the politics of aging', In, R.C. Atchley and M.M. Seltzer (eds.), *The Sociology of Aging: Selected Readings*, Belmont, Calif,: Wadsworth pp. 206–32.

Blau, P. M., (1964): *Exchange and Power in Social Life*, Wiley, New York.

Blau, Z. S., (1956): 'Changes in status and age identification', *Amer. Sociol. Review* 21, pp. 198–203.

_____(1973): *Old Age in a Changing Society*, New Viewpoints, Franklin Watts, New York.

Blumer, H., (1962): 'Society as symbolic interaction', In, A.M. Rose (ed.), *Human Behavior and Social Processes: An Interactionist Approach*, Routledge & Kegan Paul, London pp. 179–92.

Bolder, J., (1971): 'Researching the old and poor', *Sunday Review*, 25 April, 831.

Borrie, W.D., (1975): *Population and Australia: A Demographic Analysis and Projection*, First report of the National Population Enquiry, 1, AGPS, Canberra.

————(1977): 'Some social aspects of aging', *Proceedings* of the 13th Annual Conference of the Australian Association of Gerontology, Adelaide, 28 Sept. — 1 Oct., pp. 12-20

————(Chairman), (1978): *Population and Australia: Recent Demographic Trends and their Implications*, Supplementary Report of the National Population Enquiry, AGPS, Canberra.

Bott, E., (1971): *Family and Social Network*, (2nd Edn.), Free Press, New York.

Bourdieu, P. (ed.), (1965): *Un Art Moyen*, Les Editions de Minuit, Paris. Transl. T. Schofield (unpubl.).

Bowen, C., (1959): 'Old people's clubs', *Bulletin*, Post-Graduate Committee in Medicine, University of Sydney, April, pp. 63-9.

Bower, H.M., (1974): 'Aged families and their problems', In, J. Krupinski and A. Stoller (eds.), *The Family in Australia: Social, Demographic and Psychological Aspects*. Pergamon Press, Sydney pp. 118-36.

Breen, L.Z., (1960): 'The aging individual', In, C. Tibbitts (ed.), *Handbook of Social Gerontology: Societal Aspects of Aging*. Uni. of Chicago Press, Chicago. pp. 145-62.

Brockington, F. and Lempert, S.M., (1966): *The Social Needs of the Over-80s: The Stockport Survey*, Manchester University Press, Manchester.

Brody, E.M., (1976): 'A Million Procrustean beds', In, B.B. Hess (ed.), *Growing Old in America*, Transaction Books, New Brunswick, N.J. pp. 259-72.

Bromley, D.B., (1974): *The Psychology of Human Aging*, (2nd edn.) Penguin, Harmondsworth.

Brotherhood of St Laurence, (1957): *The Carrum Downs Story: An Account of the Brotherhood of St Laurence Village Settlement for Elderly People at Carrum Downs, Victoria*, Brotherhood of St Laurence, Fitzroy, Vic.

Brubaker, T.H. and Powers, E.A., (1976): 'The stereotype of "old": a review and alternative approach', *J. Geront.*, 31, 4, July, pp. 441-47.

Bryson, L. and Thompson, F., (1972): *An Australian Newtown: Life and Leadership in a New Housing Suburb*, Penguin, Harmondsworth.

Bull, C.N. and Aucoin, J.B., (1975): 'Voluntary association participation and life satisfaction: a replication note', *J. Geront.*, 30, 1, Jan., pp. 73-76.

Bultena, G. and Powers, E., (1976): 'Effects of age-grade comparisons on adjustment in later life', In, J.F. Gubrium (ed.), *Time Roles, and Self in Old Age*, Human Sciences Press, New York. pp. 165-78.

Burgess, E.W., (1960): 'Family structures and relationships', In E.W. Burgess (ed.), *Aging in Western Societies*, Univ. of Chicago Press, Chicago.

————(1973): *On Community, Family, and Delinquency*, Selected writings edited by L.S. Cottrell, Jr., A. Hunter and J.F. Short, Jr. Univ. of Chicago Press, Chicago.

Butterworth, M., (1973): 'A look at patients in private nursing homes', *Australian Social Welfare*, 3, Sept., pp. 16-19.

Carter, L., (1971): 'Housing the aged by local government', *Local Government Administration*, 16, Feb., pp. 25-26, 28-29.

Carver, V. and Liddiard, P. (eds.), (1978): *An Aging Population: A Reader and Sourcebook*, Hodder and Stoughton in association with The

Open University Press, London.

Cavan, R.S., (1962): 'Self and role in adjustment during old age', In, A.M. Rose (ed.), *Human Behavior and Social Processes*, Routledge & Kegan Paul, London, pp. 526–36.

Cavan, R.S., Burgess, E.W., Havighurst, R.J. & Goldhamer, H., (1949): *Personal Adjustment in Old Age*, Science Research Associates, Chicago.

Clark, M., (1968): 'The Anthropology of aging: a new area for studies of culture and personality', In, B.L. Neugarten (ed.), *Middle Age and Aging*, Univ. of Chicago Press, Chicago, pp. 33–43.

_____(1972): 'Cultural values and dependency in later life', In, D.O. Cowgill and L.D. Holmes (eds.), *Aging and Modernisation*, Appleton-Century-Crofts, New York, pp. 263–74.

Coe, R.M., (1965): 'Self-conception and institutionalisation', In, A.M. Rose and W.A. Peterson (eds.), *Older People and their Social World*, F.A. Davis, Philadelphia: pp. 225–43.

Collins, J. and Boughton, B., (1977): 'Capitalism and poverty: a critique of the Henderson Report', *Intervention*, pp. 3–33.

Collins, R., (1975): *Conflict Sociology*, Academic Press, New York.

Comfort, A., (1977): *A Good Age*, Macmillan, Melbourne.

Congalton, A.A., (1961): *Status Ranking of Sydney Suburbs*, Univ. of NSW Kensington.

Connell, R.W., (1978): 'Social class and personal socialisation', In, F.J. Hunt (ed.), *Socialisation in Australia*, Australia International Press and Publications, Melbourne pp. 170–201.

Cove, V., (1973): 'A need to care for the aging mind,' *Mercury* (Hobart), 18 July, p. 24.

Cumming, E., (1963): Further thoughts on the theory of disengagement, *International Social Science Journal*, 15, pp. 377–93.

Cumming, E. and Henry, W.E., (1961): *Growing Old: The Process of Disengagement*, Basic Books. New York.

Cutler, S.J., (1976): 'Age profiles of membership in sixteen types of voluntary associations', *J. Geront.*, 31, 4, July, pp. 462–70.

_____(1977): 'Aging and voluntary association participation', *J. Geront.*, 32, 4, July pp. 470–79.

Dargaville, R., (1974):... *Just the Beginning: the origins and development of accommodation for elderly people provided by the Brotherhood of St Laurence*, Brotherhood of St Laurence, Fitzroy, Vic.

Dawe, A., (1971): 'The two sociologies', In, K. Thompson and J. Tunstall (eds.), *Sociological Perspectives: Selected Readings*, Penguin, Harmondsworth pp. 524–54.

De Beauvoir, S., (1970): *Old Age*, Trans. P. O'Brian, Penguin Harmondsworth

De Brito, G., (1971): 'The plight of the pensioner', *Daily Mirror*, 20 September; p. 14; 21 September, p. 34.

Department of Social Security, (1978): *Annual Report 1977–78, AGPS*, Canberra.

De Vos, G. & Wagatsuma, H., (1966): *Japan's Invisible Race*, Univ. of California Press, Berkeley.

Dewdney, M. and Collings, J.S., (1965): *Living on the Old Age Pension: A Study of Problems, Attitudes and Prospects in Richmond, Victoria,* Hospitals and Charities Commissions, Victoria.

Dixon, J., (1977): *Australia's Policy Towards the Aged: 1890-1972,* Canberra College of Advanced Education, Canberra Series in Administrative Studies 3.

Donovan, F., (1960): Municipal activities for the aging: clubs, Meals on Wheels, home-help services, In, A. Stoller (ed.), *Growing Old: Problems of Old Age in the Australian Community,* F.W. Cheshire, Melbourne, pp. 30-39.

Doobov, A., (1980): *Relative Costs of Home Care and Nursing Home and Hospital Care in Australia,* Commonwealth Department of Health Monograph Series No. 10, AGPS, Canberra.

Douglas, V., (1977): 'A study of health and welfare services in Melbourne', Research Report, In, Commission of Enquiry into Poverty, Social/Medical Aspects of Poverty Series, *Community Health Services.* AGPS, Canberra.

Dowd, J.J., (1975): 'Aging as exchange: a preface to theory', *J. Geront.,* 30, 5, Sept, pp. 584-94.

Duigan, M.G., (1975): *A Study of the Hindmarsh (South Australia) Community,* Research Report for the Commission of Enquiry into Poverty, AGPS, Canberra.

Ellis, I., (1981): 'Pensioner organisations and action,' In, A.L. Howe (ed.), *Towards An Older Australia,* Univ. of Queensland Press, St. Lucia.

Emerson, R., (1962): 'Power-dependence relations', *Amer. Sociol. Review,* 22, Feb., pp. 31-41.

_____(1972): 'Exchange theory', In, J. Berger, M. Zelditch, & B. Anderson (eds.), *Sociological Theories in Progress,* Vol. 2, Houghton-Mifflin, Boston.

Encel, S., (1970): 'The family', In, A.F. Davies and S. Encel (eds.), *Australian Society: A Sociological Introduction,* Cheshire, Melbourne. pp. 273-91.

Estes, C.L., (1974): 'Community planning for the elderly: a study of goal displacement', *J. Geront.* 29, 6, Nov, pp. 684-91.

Estes, C.L., (1979): *The Aging Enterprise,* Jossey-Bass, San Francisco.

Fallding, H.J. (1957): 'Inside the Australian family', In, A.P. Elkin (ed.), *Marriage and the Family in Australia,* Angus & Robertson, Sydney.

Fink, A., (1973): 'Senior Citizens' clubs', In, F. Ehrlich (ed.), *New Thinking on Housing for the Aging,* NSW Council on the Aging, Sydney pp. 54-61.

Fischer, D.H., (1978): *Growing Old in America,* Oxford University Press, Oxford.

Fontana, A., (1977): *The Last Frontier: The Social Meaning of Growing Old.* Sage Publications, Beverly Hills.

Forbes, C., (1973): 'Can we grow old gracefully?' In 3 parts: Part 1, 'The old rebel against death', Part 2, 'Anger in their twilight', Part 3, 'Death — the worry of their lives', *Age,* 29 October, p. 9; 30 October, p. 9; 31 October, p. 9.

Ford, B., (1972): 'The community — who are the aged?', *Proc. Aust. Assoc. of Gerontology,* 1, 4, pp. 203-10.

_____(1979): *The Elderly Australian*, Penguin, Harmondsworth.

Foster, A.J., (1970): 'Housing and welfare of the aged,' In, S. Sax, (ed.), *The Aged in Australian Society*, Angus and Robertson Sydney, pp. 88–100.

Frenkel-Brunswick, E., (1968): 'Adjustments and reorientation in the course of the life span', In, B.L. Neugarten (ed.), *Middle Age and Aging*, Univ. of Chicago Press, Chicago pp. 77–84.

Frizell, H., (1969): 'What shall we do about grandma?', *Sydney Morning Herald*, 28 Oct., p. 8; 29 Oct., p. 14; 30 Oct., p. 8; 31 Oct., p. 12.

_____(1971): 'Alone and afraid', *Sydney Morning Herald*, 6 March, p. 6.

Gates, J., (1968): 'Building for the aged — the architect's role,' 12th Geriatric Conference *Proceedings*, Hospitals and Charities Commission, Victoria, pp. 58–64.

Gibson, R.M., (1970): 'Social aspects of aging, with particular reference to the Hunter Valley Region', In, S. Sax (ed.), *The Aged in Australian Society*, Angus and Robertson Sydney, pp. 116–24.

Glaser, G. and Strauss, A.L., (1967): *The Discovery of Grounded Theory: Strategies for Qualitative Research*, Weidenfeld & Nicolson, London.

Goffman, E., (1959): *The Presentation of Self in Everyday Life*, Penguin, Harmondsworth.

Goffman, E., (1961): *Asylums*, Penguin, Harmondsworth.

_____(1962): 'On cooling the mark out: Some aspects of adaptation to failure', In, A.M. Rose (ed.), *Human Behaviour and Social Processes*, Routledge & Kegan Paul, London, pp. 482–505.

_____(1963): *Stigma: Notes on the Management of Spoiled Identity*, Penguin, Harmondsworth.

_____(1967): *Interaction Ritual: Essays on Face-to-Face Behaviour*, Penguin, Harmondsworth.

Gouldner, A.W., (1968): 'The sociologist as partisan: sociology and the welfare state', *American Sociologist*, 3 May, pp. 103–16.

Green, J.R.B., (1971): 'Planning and design for housing for the aged', *Social Service*, 22, May–June, pp. 13–19.

Gubrium, J.F., (1973): *The Myth of the Golden Years: A Socio-Environmental Theory of Aging*, Charles C. Thomas, Springfield, Ill.

_____(1976): 'Being single in old age', In, J.F. Gubrium (ed.), *Time, Roles, and Self in Old Age*, Human Sciences Press, New York, pp. 179–95.

Gutmann, D., (1968): 'Aging among the Highland Maya: a comparative study, In, B.L. Neugarten (ed.), *Middle Age and Aging*, Univ. of Chicago Press, Chicago, pp. 444–52.

_____(1976): 'The hunger of old men', In, B.B. Hess (ed.), *Growing Old in America*, Transaction Books, New Brunswick, N.J., pp. 55–80.

Hailstone, B. and Guerin, B., (1973): 'Hospitals and the health plan', In 3 parts. Part 1, 'Prognosis by guess-work,' Part 2, 'Hospital care cost growing', Part 3, 'Passing of the pensioner service', *Advertiser*. (Adelaide), 18 August, p. 23; 20 August, p. 4; 22 August, p. 4.

Hamilton-Smith, J., (1973): *A Study of Volunteers in Social Welfare Agencies in Victoria*, A report produced for the Victorian Council of Social Services, Institute of Applied Economic and Social Research, (Technical Paper No.

Hammerman, J., (1978): 'Health services: their success and failure in reaching older adults,' In, H.D. Schwartz and C.S. Kart (eds.), *Dominant Issues in Medical Sociology*. Addison-Wesley, Reading, Mass., pp. 464–69.
6), (vi, 104p.), Univ. of Melbourne, Melbourne.

Hansen, G.D., Yoshioka, S., Taves, M.J. & Caro, F., (1965): 'Older people in the Midwest: conditions and attitudes', In, A.M. Rose and W.A. Peterson (eds.), *Older People and their Social World*. F.A. Davis Company, Philadelphia, pp. 311–22.

Harper, A.C. and Morey, S., (1977): 'Glebe: Community need and service organisation', Research Report, In Commission of Enquiry into Poverty, *Community Health Services*, AGPS, Canberra.

Havighurst, R.J., (1952): 'Roles and status of older people', In, A.I. Lansing (ed.), *Cowdry's Problems of Aging*. Williams & Wilkins, Baltimore, pp. 1019–31.

Havighurst, R.J. and Albrecht, R., (1953): *Older People*, Longmans, Green, New York.

Havighurst, R.J., (1963): 'Successful aging,' In, R. Williams, C. Tibbitts, and W. Donahue (eds.), *Processes of Aging*, Atherton, New York.

Havighurst, R.J., Neugarten, B.L. and Tobin, S.S. (1968): 'Disengagement and patterns of aging', In, B.L. Neugarten (ed.), *Middle Age and Aging*. Univ. of Chicago Press, Chicago. pp. 161–72.

Hawkinson, W.P., (1965): 'Wish, expectancy, and practice in the interaction of generations,' In, A.M. Rose and W.A. Peterson (eds.), *Older People and their Social World*. F.A. Davis, Philadelphia, pp. 181–90.

Health Commission of NSW (1979): *Psychosocial Problems of Sydney Adults*, Health Commission of NSW Division of Health Services Research.

Heath, T., Murcutt, G. and Davis, B., (1965): 'St John's Village, Glebe, NSW. — An appraisal', *Architecture in Australia*, 54, Sept., pp. 107–14.

Henderson. R.F., (1975): *First Main Report of the Australian Government Commission of Inquiry into Poverty, Vol. 1*, AGPS, Canberra.

Henderson, R.F., (1977): 'Criteria for welfare: needs or earnings?', *Aust. J. of Social Issues*, 12, 2, May, pp. 100–109.

Hendricks, C.D. and Hendricks, J., (1976): 'Concepts of time and temporal construction among the aged, with implications for research,' In, J.F. Gubrium (ed.), *Time, Roles, and Self in Old Age*, Human Sciences Press, New York, pp. 13–49.

Hendricks, J. and Hendricks, C.D., (1977): *Aging in Mass Society: Myths and Realities*, Winthrop, Cambridge, Mass.

Henry, J., (1963): *Culture Against Man*, Random House New York.

Hess, B.B. (1972): Friendship. In M.W. Riley, M. Johnson, and A. Foner (eds.), *Aging and Society*. New York: Russell Sage Foundation, 357–393.

_____(1976a): 'America's aged: who, what, when, and where?', In, B.B. Hess (ed.), *Growing Old in America*, Transaction Books, New Brunswick, N.J., pp. 17–33.

_____(1976b): Stereotypes of the aged, In, B.B. Hess (ed.), *Growing Old in America*, Transaction Books, New Brunswick, N.J., pp. 449–61.

_____(1976c). 'Self — help among the aged' In, F. Riessman (ed.), *Older*

Persons: Unused Resources for Unmet Needs, Sage Publications, Beverly Hills: pp. 88-99.

Hochschild, A.R., (1973): *The Unexpected Community*, Prentice-Hall, Englewood Cliffs, New Jersey.

_____(1976a): 'Communal life — styles for the old'', In, B.B. Hess (ed.), *Growing Old in America*, Transaction Books, New Brunswick, N.J. pp. 320-36.

_____(1976b): 'Disengagement theory: a logical, empirical, and phenomenological critique', In, J.F. Gubrium (ed.), *Time, Roles, and Self in Old Age*, Human Sciences Press, New York, pp. 53-87.

Hodges, J., (1977): 'The involvement of local government in the planning of aged persons accommodation', Paper presented at the 12th Annual Conference of the Australian Association of Gerontology, September, Adelaide.

Hoekstra, M.M., (1976) *The Aged and Housing in Perspective*, Ian Buchan Fell Research Project on Housing, Faculty of Architecture, University of Sydney, Vol. 1, Publication 17, Sydney.

Holmes, A.S. (Chairman), (1977): *Report of the Committee on Care of the Aged and the Infirm*, AGPS Canberra.

Homans, G.C., (1961): *Social Behavior: Its Elementary Forms*, Harcourt, Brace, and World, New York.

Horin, A., (1975): 'Scandal blows up over U.S. nursing homes', *National Times*, 10-15 February; p. 11.

Horowitz, L., (1975): *A Study of Community Aid Centres in New South Wales*, Research Report for the Commission of Enquiry into Poverty, AGPS, Canberra.

Housing Commission of Victoria, (1966): *The Problem of Housing Victoria's Elderly Persons*, Housing Commission of Victoria, Melbourne.

Howe, A.L. (1977): 'The changing distribution of Melbourne's aged population: patterns and implications', Paper presented at the 13th Annual Conference of the Australian Association of Gerontology, Adelaide.

_____(1979): 'Family support of the aged: some evidence and interpretation', *Aust. J. of Social Issues*, 14, 4, Nov., pp. 259-73.

Hudson, R.B. and Binstock, R.H., (1976): 'Political systems and aging', In, R.H. Binstock and E. Shanas (eds.), *Handbook of Aging and the Social Sciences*, Van Nostrand Reinhold, New York, pp. 369-400.

Hughes, E.C., (1962): 'What other?', In, A.M. Rose (ed.), *Human Behavior and Social Processes*, Routledge & Kegan Paul, London, pp. 119-27.

Hutchinson, B., (1954): *Old People in a Modern Australian Community*, Melbourne University Press, Melbourne.

James, B., (1960): 'Clubs for older people in an English community', In, E. W. Burgess (ed.), *Aging in Western Societies*, Univ. of Chicago Press, Chicago, pp. 443-45.

Johnson, M., (1978): 'That was your life: a biographical approach to later life', In, V. Carver and P. Liddiard (eds.), *An Aging Population: A Reader and Sourcebook*, Hodder and Stoughton in association with The Open University Press, pp. 99-113.

Johnson, S.K., (1971): *Idle Haven: Community Building Among the*

Working-Class Retired, University of California Press, Berkeley.

Johnson, W.J., (1969): 'Housing for elderly people', *Hospital Administration* 17, Feb., pp. 16-18.

Jones, M.A., (1977): 'Social policy', In, A.F. Davies, S. Encel and M.J. Berry (eds.), *Australian Society: A Sociological Introduction*, Longman Cheshire, Melbourne, pp. 73-94.

_____(1979): *The Australian Welfare State*, George Allen & Unwin, Sydney.

Kalish, R.A., (1977): 'Attitudes and aging: myths and realities', In, R.A. Kalish (ed.), *The Later Years: Social Applications of Gerontology*. Brooks/Cole Publishing Company, Monterey, Calif. pp. 57-62.

Kane, R.L. & Kane, R.A., (1978): 'Care of the Aged: Old Problems in Need of New Solutions', *Science*, vol. 200, 26 May, pp. 913-19.

Kastenbaum, R. & Durkee, N., (1964a): 'Young people view old age', In, R. Kastenbaum (ed.), *New Thoughts on Old Age*, Springer, New York, pp. 237-49.

_____(1964b): 'Elderly people view old age', In, R. Kastenbaum (ed.), *New Thoughts on Old Age*, Springer, New York pp. 237-49.

Kemeny, J., (1977): 'A political economy of home ownership in Australia', *Aust. and N. Z. of Sociology*, 13, 1, Feb., pp. 47-52.

Kerckhoff, A.C., (1966): 'Family patterns and morale in retirement', In, I.H. Simpson and J.C. McKinney (eds.), *Social Aspects of Aging*, Carolina, Duke University Press, Durham, North Carolina pp. 173-92.

Kewley, T., (1965): *Social Security in Australia*, Sydney University Press, Sydney.

Komarovsky, M., (1940): *The Unemployed Man and His Family*, Dryden, New York.

_____(1973): 'Some problems in role analysis', *Amer. Sociol. Review*, 38, Dec., pp. 649-62.

Kuhlen, R.G., (1959) 'Aging and life-adjustment', In, J.E. Birren (ed.), *Handbook of Aging and the Individual*, Univ. of Chicago Press, Chicago, pp. 852-97.

Lamb, J., (1971): *Accommodation of the Aged in Victoria*, University of Melbourne School of Architecture and Building.

Laslett, P., (1976): 'Societal development and aging', In, R.H. Binstock & E. Shanas (eds.), *Handbook of Aging and the Social Sciences*, Van Nostrand Reinhold, New York, pp. 87-116.

Leanse, J., (1977): 'The senior center, individuals, and the community', In, R. A. Kalish (ed.), *The Later Years: Social Applications of Gerontology*, Brooks/Cole Publishing Company, Monterey, Calif., pp. 322-27.

Lefroy, R.B., (1977): 'The elderly person and family life', *Aust. J. of Social Issues*, 12, 1, Feb., pp. 33-42.

Liebow, E., (1967): *Tally's Corner: A Study of Negro Streetcorner Men*, Little, Brown, Boston.

Lopata, H.Z., (1972): 'Role changes in widowhood: A world perspective', In, D.O. Cowgill and L.D. Holmes (eds.), *Aging and Modernisation*, Appleton-Century-Crofts, New York, pp. 275-303.

_____(1973): *Widowhood in an American City*, Schenkman, Cambridge, Mass.

Lowenthal, M.F. and Haven, C., (1968): 'Interaction and adaptation: intimacy as a critical variable', In, B.L. Neugarten (ed.), *Middle Age and Aging*, Univ. of Chicago Press, Chicago, pp. 390–400.

Lowenthal, M.F. and Robinson, B., (1976): 'Social networks and isolation', In, R.H. Binstock & E. Shanas (eds.), *Handbook of Aging and the Social Sciences*, Van Nostrand Reinhold, New York, pp. 432–56

Lozier, J. and Althouse, R., (1976): 'Social enforcement of behaviour toward elders in an Appalachian mountain settlement', In, B.B. Hess(ed.), *Growing Old in America*, Transaction Books, New Brunswick, N.J., pp. 358–89.

McIlwraith, S., (1972): 'Hospitals help aged — at home', *Sydney Morning Herald*: 18 January, p. 7.

Maddox, G.L. and Wiley, J., (1976): 'Scope, concepts and methods in the study of aging', In, R.H. Binstock & E. Shanas (eds.), *Handbook of Aging and the Social Sciences*, Van Nostrand Reinhold, New York, pp. 3–34.

Mannes, M., (1954): Coming of Age: report on the Hodson Center', *Reporter*, 11, pp. 32–35.

Markson, E., (1976): 'A hiding place to die', In, B.B. Hess (ed.), *Growing Old in America*, Transaction Books, New Brunswick, N.J. pp. 285–97.

Martel, M.U. (1968): 'Age-sex roles in American magazine fiction (1890-1955)', In, B.L. Neugarten (ed.), *Middle Age and Aging*, Univ. of Chicago Press, Chicago, pp. 47–57

Martin, C., (1971): 'The twilight years in a C-class hospital', *West Australian*, 9 March, p. 8.

Martin , J.I., (1957): 'Marriage, the family and class', In, A. Elkin (ed.), *Marriage and Family in Australia*, Angus & Robertson, Sydney.

_____(1967): 'Extended kinship ties, an Adelaide study', *Aust. and N. Z.J. Sociol.*, 3, pp. 44–63.

_____(1970): 'Suburbia: Community and network', In, A.F. Davies and S. Encel (eds.), *Australian Society: A Sociological Introduction*, Cheshire, Melbourne pp. 301–39.

Mauss, M., (1954): *The Gift*. Free Press, New York.

Mead, G.H., (1934): *Mind, Self and Society*, Univ. of Chicago Press, Chicago.

Medley, M.L., (1976): 'Satisfaction with life among persons 65 years and older: a causal model', *J. Geront*. 31, 4, July, pp. 448–55.

Meltzer, B.N., Petras, J.W.. and Reynolds, L.T., (1975): *Symbolic Interactionism: Genesis, Varieties and Criticism*, Routledge & Kegan Paul, London.

Merton, R.K., (1968): *Social Theory and Social Structure*, Free Press, New York.

Mills, C.W., (1959): *The Sociological Imagination*, Penguin, Harmondsworth.

Moffitt, I., (1970): 'On the pension; Pensioner power and how they hope to get it', 'By bus to have a bath', 'Waiting for a letter that might come tomorrow', *Australian*. 2 November, p. 9; 3 November, p. 11 4 November, p. 13.

Moore, W.E., (1966): 'Aging and the social system', In, J.C. McKinney and F.T. de Vyver (eds.), *Aging and Social Policy*, Appleton-Century-Crofts, New York pp. 23-41.

Municipality of Willoughby Retirement Community Committee, (1971): *Willioughby Retirement Community: A Report to the Mayor for Presentation at a Public Meeting*. NSW: Municipal Council, Willoughby.

NSW Council On The Aging, (1975): *Dedication: A Report of a Survey on Caring for the Aged at Home carried out in NSW — Australia — June-Dec. 1975*, NSW Council on the Aging, Sydney.

Neugarten, B.L., (1968): 'Adult personality: toward a psychology of the life cycle', In, B.L. Neugarten (ed.), *Middle Age and Aging*, Univ. of Chicago Press, Chicago, pp. 137-47.

_____(1976): 'Middle age and aging', In, B.B. Hess (ed.), *Growing Old in America*, Transaction Books, New Brunswick, N.J., pp. 180-97.

Neugarten, B.L. and Hagestad, G.O., (1976): 'Age and the life course', In, R.H. Binstock & E. Shanas (eds.), *Handbook of Aging and the Social Sciences*, Van Nostrand Reinhold, New York, pp. 35-55.

Neugarten, B.L., Havighurst, R.J. and Tobin, S.S. (1968): 'Personality and patterns of aging', In, B.L. Neugarten (ed.), *Middle Age and Aging*, Univ. of Chicago Press, Chicago pp. 173-77.

Nimkoff, M.F., (1962): 'Changing family relationships of older people in the United States during the last 50 years', In, C. Tibbitts and W. Donahue (eds), *Social and Psychological Aspects of Aging*, Columbia Univ. Press, New York, pp. 405-14.

Oeser, O.A. and Emery, F.E., (1954): *Social Structure and Personality in a Rural Community*. Routledge & Kegan Paul, London.

Oeser, O.A. and Hammond, S.B., (1954): *Social Structure and Personality in a City*, Routledge & Kegan Paul, London.

Opit, L.J., (1978): 'Domiciliary care for the elderly: economy or neglect?', In, V. Carver and P. Liddiard (eds.), *An Aging Population: A Reader and Sourcebook*, Hodder and Stoughton in association with the Open University Press, pp. 148-59.

Palmore, E. and Whittington, F., (1971): 'Trends in the relative status of the aged', *Social Forces*, 50, pp. 84-91.

Pearson, G., (1975): *The Deviant Imagination: Psychiatry, Social Work and Social Change*. Macmillan, London.

Pegrum, R., (1975): *The Architecture of Old Age: A Study of the Relationship of Older People with the Built Environment*. Royal Australian Institute of Architects, Canberra.

Pihlblad, C.T. and McNamara, R.L., (1965): 'Social adjustment of elderly people in three small towns', In, A.M. Rose and W.A. Peterson (eds.), *Older People and their Social World*, F.A. Davis, Philadelphia, pp. 49-73.

Plath, D.W., (1972): 'Japan: the after years', In, D.O. Cowgill and L.D. Holmes (eds.), *Aging and Modernisation*, Appleton-Century-Crofts, New York, pp. 133-50.

Platten, N., (1970): 'Housing for the aged', *Architecture in Australia*, 59, Oct., pp. 741–766.

Pollak, O., (1948): *Social Adjustment in Old Age: A Research Planning Report*. Bulletin 59, Social Science Research Council, New York.

Pollard, H.M., (1970): 'Demographic aspects of aging', In, S. Sax (ed.), *The Aged in Australian Society*, Angus and Robertson, Sydney, pp. 32–57.

Pound, K.J., (1975): *Terrace Apartment Houses: A Review of the First Two and a Half Years of Operation, 30/11/72 to 19/8/75*, Brotherhood of St Laurence, Project Report, Fitzroy, Vic.

Prinsley, D.M. and Cameron, K.P., (1979): 'Old people living alone — is organised observation necessary?', *Aust. J. of Social Issues*, 14, 4, Nov., pp. 297–300.

Pudney, C.W., (1973): *Factors to be Considered in Designing and Providing Accommodation for Aged People*, South Australian Council on the Aging, Adelaide.

Radford, A.J. and Peever, M.V., (1976): *The Elderly in the Mount Gambier Area*, Report of a Study on Accommodation and Services Needs of the Elderly in the Mount Gambier Area. Unit of Primary Care and Community Medicine, Flinders University of South Australia.

Richards, L., (1978): *Having Families: Marriage, Parenthood and Social Pressure in Australia*, Penguin, Harmondsworth.

Richardson, M., (1971): '1971: a doubly bad year for pensioners', *Age*, 1 September, p. 8.

Riegel, K.F., (1959): 'Personality theory and aging', In, J.E. Birren (ed.), *Handbook of Aging and the Individual*, the Univ. of Chicago Press Chicago, pp.797–851.

Riley, M.W. and Foner, A. (eds.), (1968): *Aging and Society. Volume One: An Inventory of Research Findings*, Russell Sage Foundation, New York.

Riley, M.W., Johnson, M. and Foner, A. (eds.), (1972): *Aging and Society. Vol. 3: A Sociology of Age Stratification* Russell Sage Foundation, New York.

Robb, W.L. and Rivett, K., (1964): *Needs Among the Old : A Survey in Marrickville, NSW*, Municipality of Marrickville.

Robins A.J., (1962): 'Family relations of the aging in three-generation households', In, C. Tibbitts and W. Donahue (eds.), *Social and Psychological Aspects of Aging*, Columbia Univ. Press, New York, pp. 464–74.

Robjohns, H.C., (1972): 'The Retirement Village — a 10 year survey of residents of independent flats in the protective environment of Aldersgate Village', Australian Association of Gerontology, 8th Annual Conference *Proceedings* 1, 4, pp. 211–13.

Rodriguez, C., (1975): 'A cost-benefit analysis of subjective factors affecting assimilation: Puerto Ricans', *Ethnicity*, Vol. 2, pp. 66–80.

Rogers, L., (1975): 'Biology and human behaviour', In, J. Mercer (ed.), *The Other Half*, Penguin, Harmondsworth.

Rooney, J.F. (1976): 'Friendship and disaffiliation among the skid row population', *J.Geront.* 31, 1, Jan., pp.82–88

Rose, A.M., (1960): 'The impact of aging on voluntary associations', In, C. Tibbitts (ed.), *Handbook of Social Gerontology: Societal Aspects of*

Aging, Univ. of Chicago Press, Chicago, pp. 666–97.

――――(1965a): 'A current theoretical issue in social gerontology', In, A.M. Rose and W.A. Peterson, (eds.), *Older People and their Social World*, F.A. Davis, Philadelphia, pp. 359–66.

――――(1965b): 'The subculture of the aging: a framework for research in social gerontology', In, A.M. Rose & W.A. Peterson (eds.), *Older People and Their Social World*, F.A. Davis, Philadelphia, pp. 3–16.

Rosenmayr, L., (1972): 'The elderly in Austrian society', In, D.O. Cowgill and L.D. Holmes (eds.), *Aging and Modernisation*, Appleton-Century-Crofts, New York, pp. 183–96.

Rosow, I., (1962): 'Retirement housing and social integration', In, C. Tibbitts & W. Donahue (eds.), *Social and Psychological Aspects of Aging*, Columbia Univ. New York, Press, pp. 327–40.

――――(1967): *Social Integration of the Aged*, Free Press, New York.

――――(1968): 'Housing and local ties of the aged', In, B.L. Neugarten (ed.), *Middle Age and Aging*, Univ. of Chicago Press, Chicago, pp. 382–89.

――――(1976a): 'And then we were old', In, B.B. Hess (ed.), *Growing Old in America*, Transaction Books, New Brunswick, N.J., pp. 41–54.

――――(1976b): 'Status and role change through the life span', In, R.H. Binstock & E. Shanas (eds.), *Handbook of Aging and the Social Sciences*, Van Nostrand Reinhold, New York, pp. 457–82.

Ross, J.K., (1977): *Old People, New Lives: Community Creation in a Retrement Residence*, The Univ. of Chicago Press, Chicago.

Rothchild, S., (1954): 'Sixty-five and over', *Commentary*, 18, pp. 549–56.

Rowland, D.T., (1980): 'Living arrangements and the later family life cycle in Australia', Paper presented at the Regional Congress of the International Association of Gerontology, Melbourne.

Runciman W.G., (1971): 'Relative deprivation and the concept of reference group', In, K. Thompson and J. Tunstall (eds.), *Sociological Perspectives*. Penguin, Harmondsworth, pp. 299–315.

Ryan, J.G.P., (1979): 'The general practitioner and community health', In, R. Walpole (ed.), *Community Health in Australia*, Penguin, Harmondsworth.

Sach, S., (1975): 'Accommodation for the aged in Melbourne', Research Report, In, Commission of Enquiry into Poverty, *The Aged,* AGPS Canberra.

Samuel, P., (1974): 'Pensioners falling way behind', *Bulletin*, 2 February, p. 16.

Sarbin, T.R. and Allen, V.L., (1968): 'Role theory', In, G. Lindzey & E. Aronson (eds.), *The Handbook of Social Psychology*, Vol. 1 (2nd edn), Addison-Wesley, Reading, Mass., pp. 488–567.

Sartre, J.P., (1956): *Being and Nothingness*, Philosophical Library, New York.

Schutz, A., (1974): 'Subjective and objective meaning', In, A. Giddens (ed.), *Positivism and Sociology*, Heinemann, London pp. 33–52.

Seeley, J.P.; Sim, R.A.; and Loosley, E.W., (1956): *Crestwood Heights*, Constable, London.

Shanas, E., (1970): 'What's new in old age?', In, E. Shanas (ed.), *Aging in Contemporary Society*, Sage Publications, Beverley Hills, pp. 5-11.

Shanas, E., Townsend, P., Wedderburn, D., Friis, H., Milhoj, P., and Stehouwer, J. (1968): *Old People in Three Industrial Societies*, Routledge & Kegan Paul, London.

Sheingold, C.A., (1973): 'Social networks and voting: the resurrection of a research agenda', *Amer. Sociol. Review*, 38, pp. 712-20.

Sherman, S.R., (1975a): 'Patterns of contact for residents of age-segregated and age-integrated housing', *J. Geront.*, 30, 1, Jan., pp. 103-7.

_____(1975b): 'Mutual assistance and support in retirement housing', *J. Geront.*, 30, 4, July, pp. 479-83.

Silcock, B., (1971): Part 1, 'Our chances of living longer', Part 2, 'Cells provide a clue to aging', Part 3, 'Contrasting theories', Part 4, 'Possibilities in the battle to slow aging', *Sydney Morning Herald*, 23 March, p. 7; 24 March, p. 7; 25 March, p. 7; 26 March, p. 7.

Silverman, D., (1971): 'The action frame of reference', In, K. Thompson & J. Tunstall (eds.), *Sociological Perspectives: Selected Readings*, Penguin, Harmondsworth, pp. 562-79.

Simmel, G., (1950): *Sociologie: Untersuchungen uber die Formen der Vergesellschaftung* 1908, Reprinted in K.H. Wolff (ed. and trans.). *The Sociology of Georg Simmel*, Free Press, New York.

Simmons, L., (1945): *The Role of the Aged in Primitive Society*, Yale Univ. Press, New Haven.

Singelmann, P., (1972): 'Exchange as symbolic interaction: Convergences between two theoretical perspectives', *Amer. Sociol. Rev.*, 37, pp. 414-24.

Smith, H.E., (1965): 'Family interaction patterns of the aged: a review', In, A.M. Rose and W.A. Peterson (eds.), *Older People and their Social World*, F.A. Davis, Philadelphia, pp. 143-61.

Smith, M. (1975): 'Millions wasted on geriatrics: survey; Health services are badly located: report', *Age*, 3 December, p. 15.

Smith, V., (1971): 'Day centres, home care for the aged', *National Times*, 18-23 October, 1, p. 10.

Sorrell, D., (1972): *Accommodation and Care for the Aged: A Call for Community Action*. New South Wales Council on the Aging, Sydney.

Starr, B.C., (1972) 'The community', In, M.W. Riley, M, Johnson, & A. Foner (eds.), *Aging and Society: A Sociology of Age Stratification*, Russell Sage Foundation, New York, pp. 198-235.

Stephens, J., (1975): 'Society of the alone: freedom, privacy, and utilitarianism as dominant norms in the SRO', *J. Geront.*, 30, 2, Mar., pp. 230-35.

_____(1976): 'Romance in the SRO: Relationships of elderly men and women in a slum hotel', In, B.B. Hess (ed.), *Growing Old in America*, Transaction Books, New Brunswick, N.J., pp. 250-57.

Stephenson, M.O., (1971): 'A personal enquiry into the poverty of the older single woman', *J. of the Aust. Public Health Assoc. (W.A. Branch), Health in the West*, Supplement No. 1.

Stone, L., (1977a): *The Family, Sex and Marriage in England 1500-1800*, Weidenfeld & Nicolson, London.

———————(1977b): 'Walking over grandma', *New York Review of Books*, May 12.

Streib, G.F., (1968): 'Are the aged a minority group?' In, B.L. Neugarten (ed.), *Middle Age and Aging*, Univ. of Chicago Press, Chicago pp. 35–46.

Streib, G.F. & Schneider, C.J., (1971): *Retirement in American Society*, Cornell Univ. Press, Ithaca, New York.

Streib G.F. & Thompson, W.E., (1960): 'The older person in a family context', In, C. Tibbitts (ed.), *Handbook of Social Gerontology: Societal Aspects of Aging*, Univ. of Chicago Press, pp. 447–88.

Sudnow, D., (1971): 'Dead on arrival', *Transaction/Society*, 9, Nov. — Dec., pp. 36–43.

Summers, A., (1975): *Damned Whores and God's Police: The Colonisation of Women in Australia*, Penguin, Harmondsworth.

———————(1976): Part 1, 'A tragic and costly mess', Part 2, 'The nursing home mess', *National Times*, 13–18 Sept., pp. 4–5; 20–25 Sept., p. 7.

Sussman, M.B., (1976): 'The Family life of old people', In, R. H. Binstock & E. Shanas (eds.), *Handbook of Aging and the Social Sciences*, Van Nostrand Reinhold, New York, pp. 218–43.

Swain, C., (1979): 'Images of the good old days: some notes on a gerontological myth', *Mankind*.

———————(1981), 'Family roles and support', In, A.L. Howe (ed.), *Towards an Older Australia*, Univ. of Queensland Press, St. Lucia.

Swain, C. and Harrison, J., (1979): 'The nursing home as total institution: a case study and suggestions for the aged care system', *Aust. J. of Social Issues*, 14, 4, Nov. pp. 274–84.

Taietz, P., (1976): 'Two conceptual models of the Senior Center', *J. Geront.*, 31, 2, Mar., pp 219–22.

Taylor, I., Walton, P. and Young, J., (1973): *The New Criminology: For a Social Theory of Deviance*, Routledge & Kegan Paul, London.

Taylor, R., (1979): 'Health and class in Australia', *New Doctor*, 13, pp. 22–28.

Teaff, J.D. Lawton, M.P., Nahemow, L. & Carlson, D., (1978): 'Impact of age integration on the well being of elderly tenants in public housing', *J. Geront* 33, 1 Jan., pp. 226–33.

Tibbitts, C., (1960a): 'Origin, scope, and fields of social gerontology', In, C. Tibbitts (ed.), *Handbook of Social Gerontology Societal Aspects of Aging*, Univ. of Chicago Press, Chicago, pp. 3–26.

———————(ed.) (1960b): *Handbook of Social Gerontology: Societal Aspects of Aging*, Univ. of Chicago Press, Chicago.

Tolhurst, S., (n.d.): *Games and Activities for Senior Citizen Centres*, NSW Council on the Aging, Sydney.

Toon, J., (1975): 'The town planning implications of aging populations', In, *Elderly Avalanche? Local Government and Patterns of Retirement, Proceedings*, Seminar conducted by the NSW Council on the Aging, NSW Council on the Aging, Sydney, pp. 42–51.

Townsend, P., (1963): *The Family Life of Old People: An Enquiry in East London*, Penguin, Harmondsworth.

_____(1968): 'Isolation, desolation, and loneliness', In, E. Shanas *et al.* (eds.), *Old People in Three Industrial Societies*, Routledge & Kegan Paul, London, pp. 258–87.

Treanton, J.R., (1962): 'Some sociological considerations on the problem of adjustment in older people', In, C. Tibbitts & W. Donahue (eds.), *Social and Psychological Aspects of Aging*, Columbia Univ. Press, New York, pp. 665.

Trela, J.E., (1971): 'Some political consequences of senior center and other old age group memberships', *Gerontologist*, 2, pp. 118–123.

_____(1976): 'Social class and association membership: an analysis of age-graded and non-age-graded voluntary participation', *J. Geront.*, 31, 2, Mar., pp. 198–203.

Trollope, A., (1967) (1873) *Australia*, P. D. Edwards and R. B. Joyce, (eds.), Univ. of Queensland Press, St Lucia.

Tuckman, J. and Lorge, I., (1954): 'Classification of the self as young, middle aged or old', *Geriatrics*, 9, pp. 534–36.

Tunstall J., (1966): *Old and Alone*, Routledge & Kegan Paul, London.

Turner, R.H., (1962): 'Role-taking: process versus conformity', In, A.M. Rose (ed.), *Human Behavior and Social Processes*, Routledge & Kegan Paul, London, pp. 20–40.

Twibill, G., (1970): 'The retirement village — a new social phenomenon', Australian Association of Gerontology, 6th Annual Conference, *Proceedings*, 1, 2, pp. 77–79.

Videbeck, R. and Knox, A.B., (1965): 'Alternative participatory responses to aging', In, A.M. Rose and W.A. Peterson (eds.), *Older People and their Social World*. F.A. Davis, Philadelphia, pp. 37–48.

Von Mering, O. & Weniger, F.L., (1959): 'Social-cultural background of the aging individual', In, J.E. Birren (ed.), *Handbook of Aging and the Individual*, Univ. of Chicago Press, Chicago, pp. 279–335.

Wallace, A.F.C., (1961): *Culture and Personality*, Random House, New York.

Ward, J., (1978): 'Class and the aged', In, *Aging in Australia, Australian Association of Gerontology*, pp. 49–52.

Ward, R.A., (1977): 'The impact of subjective age and stigma on older persons', *J. Geront.* 32, 2, Mar., pp. 227–32.

Warshay, L.H., (1962): 'Breadth of perspective', In, A.M. Rose (ed.), *Human Behavior and Social Processes*, Routledge & Kegan Paul, London pp. 148–76.

Weber, M., (1947): *The Theory of Social and Economic Organisation*, Free Press, New York.

Weinholt, L.J., (1973): 'Housing for the aged', *Architecture in Australia* 62, June, pp. 58–59.

Weir, M.B., (1966): 'Aged cottage homes', *Building and Architecture* 5, April, pp. 45–50.

Weyland, M., (1975): 'An intergenerational housing project', In, Australian Frontier Consultation Report., *An Inter-generational Housing Project and the Development of New Housing Patterns in Australia*, Australian Frontier, Melbourne.

Whyte, W.F., (1955): *Street Corner Society*, Univ. of Chicago Press, Chicago, (2nd edn.).

Wild, R.A., (1974): *Bradstow: A Study of Status, Class and Power in a Small Australian Town*, Angus & Robertson, Sydney.

————(1977): 'Social stratification and old age', *Aust. J. of Social Issues*, 12, 1, Feb., pp. 19-32.

————(1978): *Social Stratification in Australia*, George Allen & Unwin, Sydney.

Williams, M.L., (1976): 'One of the best retirement centers', In, B.B. Hess (ed.), *Growing Old in America*, Transaction Books, New Brunswick, N.J., pp. 311-19.

Williams, R.H., (1960): 'Changing status, roles and relationships', In, C. Tibbitts (ed.), *Handbook of Social Gerontology: Societal Aspects of Aging*, Univ. of Chicago Press, Chicago, pp. 261-97.

Williams, R.H. & Loeb, M.B., (1968): 'The adult's social life space and successful aging: some suggestions for a conceptual framework', In, B.L. Neugarten (ed.), *Middle Age and Aging*, Univ. of Chicago Press, Chicago, pp. 379-81.

Williams, R.H. and Wirths, C.G., (1965): *Lives Through the Years*, Atherton Press, New York.

Wilson, D., (1975): 'Accommodation for the aged', *Growing Older*, 6, Dec., pp. 11.

Wirth, L., (1938): 'Urbanism as a way of life', *Amer. J. Sociol.* 44, pp. 1-24.

Wolf, E.R., (1966): 'Kinship, friendship, and parton-client relations in complex societies', In, M. Banton (ed.), *The Social Anthropology of Complex Societies*, Tavistock, London, pp. 1-22.

Wood, V. and Robertson, J.F., (1976): 'The significance of grandparenthood', In, J.F. Gubrium (ed.), *Time, Roles, and Self in Old Age*, Human Sciences Press, New York, pp. 278-304.

Woodrow, J., (1975): 'Aged persons housing under investigation', *Shelter* 16. Feb., p. 12.

Wrong, D.H., (1961): 'The oversocialised conception of man in modern sociology', *American Sociological Review*, 26, 2, April, pp. 183-93.

Wydell, R., (1975): 'A statistical profile on the aged in NSW, In, *Elderly Avalanche? Local Government and Patterns of Retirement, Proceedings*, Seminar conducted by the NSW Council on the Aging, NSW Council on the Aging, Sydney, pp. 3-29.

Yeomans, J., (1976): 'Keep granny happy in a high-rise', *Advertiser*, 7 August, p. 24.

Zimmerman, M., (1976): 'Old-age poverty in preindustrial New York City', In, B.B. Hess (ed.), *Growing Old in America*, Transaction Books, New Brunswick, N.J., pp. 81-104.

Index